ISBN 978-1-331-52702-2
PIBN 10180644

English
Français
Deutsche
Italiano
Español
Português

www.forgottenbooks.com

Mythology Photography **Fiction**
Fishing Christianity **Art** Cooking
Essays Buddhism Freemasonry
Medicine **Biology** Music **Ancient**
Egypt Evolution Carpentry Physics
Dance Geology **Mathematics** Fitness
Shakespeare **Folklore** Yoga Marketing
Confidence Immortality Biographies
Poetry **Psychology** Witchcraft
Electronics Chemistry History **Law**
Accounting **Philosophy** Anthropology
Alchemy Drama Quantum Mechanics
Atheism Sexual Health **Ancient History**
Entrepreneurship Languages Sport
Paleontology Needlework Islam
Metaphysics Investment Archaeology
Parenting Statistics Criminology
Motivational

THE RIGHT HONOURABLE

WILLIAM HENRY SMITH, M.P.

Yours very truly
W H Smith

Yours very truly
W H Smith

LIFE AND TIMES

OF

THE RIGHT HONOURABLE

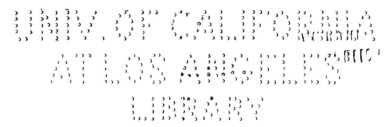

BY

SIR HERBERT MAXWELL, Bart., M.P.

WITH

PORTRAITS AND OTHER ILLUSTRATIONS

Civis talis, qualis et prudentissimus
et fortunâ optimâ esse debet.—CICERO.

IN TWO VOLUMES

VOL. I.

PREFACE.

IN preparing these Memoirs, there has been present to me the difficulty besetting every one who attempts to deal with political events during the lifetime of many who have borne a part in them. There is much that cannot be alluded to without reviving slumbering controversy, or reflecting on the actions of public men, until the charitable finger of Time shall have touched the harshness out of recent events, and brought them into right perspective with the history of the country.

Yet I am not without the courage to hope that in recording the chief incidents in the career of one with whom it was my privilege to be associated, and to follow as leader during some anxious and eventful years, I may have succeeded in avoiding obvious errors, and giving a true account of a life nobly led and purely ended. In whatever measure that hope may be realised, it is owing to the abundance of material placed at my disposal by the family and friends of Mr Smith, and to the assistance willingly given by many who had been associated with him in commercial, philanthropic, and political affairs. It is possible that in the attempt to give a true impression of the course steered by Mr Smith in politics, I have found it necessary to refer to the actions of those opposed to him in terms which their friends may consider unfavourable. They will, however, be slow to suspect me of any intention of serving the ends of party, or indeed of any motive other than that of giving a faithful narrative.

In requesting me to undertake the compilation of these volumes, Lady Hambleden has reposed a degree of confidence in me which I am not likely to undervalue. She has put at my disposal the private papers and correspondence of her husband, and her daughters have greatly lightened my labours by arranging these, and copying some which were least easy to decipher.

Among others who have given me valuable information have been the Duke of Rutland, the Marquis of Salisbury, the Earl of Harrowby, the Earl of Iddesleigh, Lord Rowton, Lord Ashcombe, the Right Hon. Edward Stanhope, M.P., the Rev. Sir Emilius Laurie, Sir Edward Lawson, Sir Henry Acland, Mr Penrose Fitzgerald, M.P., the Rev. Canon Jacob, the Rev. Canon Ince, the Rev. Canon Pinder, the Rev. M. A. Nisbet, Mr W. Lethbridge, Captain Blow of the Pandora, Mr White and Mr Monger of 186 Strand. To all these, as well as to others too numerous to mention, my hearty thanks are due.

HERBERT MAXWELL.

Monreith, *October* 1893.

CONTENTS OF THE FIRST VOLUME.

CHAPTER I.

1784–1846.

PAGE

Introductory—The brothers Smith—Their parentage—The house in Duke Street—They set up a branch office in the Strand—The junior partner buys out his brother—Letter from Leigh Hunt—Birth of a son, William Henry—His boyhood—Goes to Tavistock grammar-school—His aversion to Methodism—Desires to enter Holy Orders—Defers to his father's wishes and enters the business—His indifference to games and his love of music—Correspondence with William Ince, ... 1

CHAPTER II.

1846–1854.

Disappointment in choice of a profession—Residence at Kilburn House—Young Smith enters the business, and on coming of age becomes his father's partner—His influence in the office — Beginning of the bookstall business — Acquires monopoly of the North-Western Railway stations —His dealings with *employés*—Expansion of the business —Work on the Committee of King's College Hospital, . 42

CHAPTER III.

1854–1893.

Effect of the repeal of the newspaper stamp-duty—Growth of
the business—Smith & Son become sole agents for the
' Times'—Failing health of the senior partner—Increasing
work—Its effect upon young Smith—The firm become contractors for railway advertising—Extracts from letters and
journal—The principles of private life carried into business
affairs—The lending library set on foot—Publication of
cheap novels—Its success and abandonment—Present aspect
of the Strand office—Early morning work—Despatch of
newspapers, ... 65

CHAPTER IV.

1855–1865.

Smith is elected to Metropolitan Board of Works—His marriage in 1858 to Mrs Leach—Old Mr Smith retires from
business—Philanthropic work—The Bishop of London's
fund—Friendship with Lord Sandon—Smith contemplates
standing as a Liberal for Boston—And for Exeter—Is blackballed for Reform Club—Becomes Conservative candidate
for Westminster—His address to the electors—The election
—And its result, ... 99

CHAPTER V.

1865–1868.

Death of Lord Palmerston—And of the elder Smith—Earl Russell's Reform Bill—And Mr Disraeli's—Dissolution of Parliament—Smith is elected for Westminster—The Revivalist
movement, ... 128

CHAPTER VI.

1868–1869.

Petition against Mr Smith's return—The trial and verdict—
Smith's maiden speech—Debate on pauperism—Smith's
mistrust of charitable donations—Anecdotes illustrating his
principles of giving—The Telegraph Bill—Debates on disestablishment of the Irish Church, ... 145

CHAPTER VII.

1870-1871.

Visit to Paris—State of parties in Parliament—The smoking-room of the House of Commons—Irish Land Bill—Elementary Education Bill—Smith's motion on the Thames Embankment—Defeat of the Government thereon—Letter on affairs in France — Smith elected to first London School Board—Religious difficulty arising there settled on his motion—Assists emigration to Canada—Debates on Army Bill, Budget, and Ballot Bill—Damaged position of the Government — Irish Home Rule — Mr Gladstone's speech at Aberdeen, ... 167

CHAPTER VIII.

1872.

Meeting of Parliament — Unpopularity of Ministers — The Ballot Bill—The Thames Embankment Scheme again—Smith sails for America—Journal of travel, . . . 201

CHAPTER IX.

1873-1874.

Increasing unpopularity of Ministers—Irish University Bill —Defeat and resignation of the Government—Disraeli declines to form a Cabinet—Mr Gladstone resumes office —Debate on Budget Resolutions—Dissensions in Cabinet—Dissolution of Parliament—General election—Conservative victory—The poll in Westminster—Disraeli forms a Cabinet—Mr Smith becomes Financial Secretary to the Treasury—Resigns Treasurership of S.P.C.K., . . . 236

CHAPTER X.

1874-1876.

Retirement of Mr Gladstone from lead of Liberal party—Debates on Public Worship Regulation Bill—Beginning of Smith's friendship with Northcote—He settles to work at the Treasury—Visits Bournemouth—Mr Gladstone and the Vatican Decrees—Lord Hartington chosen leader of the Liberals — The session — Official visits to Edinburgh and Dublin—The Suez Canal shares—Consolidation of the Home Rule party—The Burials Bill—Visits to the dock-yards—Work, ... 260

CHAPTER XI.

1876–1878.

Difficulties of the Government—The Bulgarian atrocities— The "Bag-and-Baggage" policy—The Journal of a Dis-contented Man—Obstruction in the House of Commons— Death of Mr Ward Hunt—Smith appointed First Lord of the Admiralty—Misgivings as to his own ability—Proposal to put the Post Office in commission — Congratulatory banquet in St James's Hall—War between Russia and Turkey—Meeting of Parliament—The Fleet sent to Galli-poli—Resignation of Lords Carnarvon and Derby—Votes of censure—The Berlin Congress—"Peace with Honour," . 286

CHAPTER XII.

1878.

Journal of a tour to Cyprus, ... 335

ILLUSTRATIONS TO THE FIRST VOLUME.

                                                                    PAGE

PORTRAIT OF THE RIGHT HON. W. H. SMITH, .   . *Frontispiece*

THE HOUSE AT KILBURN, ...   44

MESSRS W. H. SMITH AND SON'S PREMISES IN THE STRAND,   58

MESSRS W. H. SMITH AND SON'S STRAND PREMISES (IN-

    TERIOR), ...   90

KNOT USED IN TYING PARCELS OF NEWSPAPERS,   .   .   91

ANOTHER PORTRAIT OF THE RIGHT HON. W. H. SMITH,   .   128

LIFE AND TIMES

OF

THE RIGHT HON. W. H. SMITH.

CHAPTER I.

1784–1846.

INTRODUCTORY——THE BROTHERS SMITH——THEIR PARENTAGE——
THE HOUSE IN DUKE STREET——THEY SET UP A BRANCH
OFFICE IN THE STRAND——THE JUNIOR PARTNER BUYS OUT
HIS BROTHER——LETTER FROM LEIGH HUNT——BIRTH OF A
SON, WILLIAM HENRY——HIS BOYHOOD——GOES TO TAVISTOCK
GRAMMAR-SCHOOL——HIS AVERSION TO METHODISM——DESIRES
TO ENTER HOLY ORDERS——DEFERS TO HIS FATHER'S WISHES
AND ENTERS THE BUSINESS——HIS INDIFFERENCE TO GAMES
AND HIS LOVE OF MUSIC——CORRESPONDENCE WITH WILLIAM
INCE.

NOT very long before the following pages began
to be penned, Sir Charles Bowen commented with
caustic good-humour on what he termed the

growing tendency of the age to write ponderous biographies of Nobody.

It must always be a matter of opinion to what exact degree of eminence a man should rise above the mean level of character, or what store of achievement it should be possible to lay to his account, before the public are invited to the perusal of his biography.

> " Oh ! vain attempt to give a deathless lot
> To names ignoble, born to be forgot."

There is an ominous sentence in one of Horace Walpole's letters : " One can never talk very long about folks that are merely excellent—I mean, unless they do not deserve it, and then their flatterers can hold forth upon their virtues by the hour." The affection of his family — the predilection of his friends—the gratitude of those whom he may have benefited—the admiration of humbler men from among whom he may have raised himself—the success with which Fortune, so partial in her favours, so indifferent to merit, may have filled his sails,—all these have to be liberally discounted before the figure of a public man can be viewed in the just perspective essential to critical narrative.

But when such a man has brought his life out of a surrounding no more than commonplace, when he has conducted an ordinary commercial undertaking to a position beyond competition, and then, having accomplished what would satisfy most men as a life's work, has set himself to political enterprise, and, by sheer dint of the esteem awarded, not to audacity or surpassing powers of speech, but to unselfish integrity and faultless common-sense, has risen from one office of trust to another, till his party at a moment of extreme perplexity, by an involuntary and common impulse, turned towards him and laid upon him the hazardous duties of leader, —when a man has set his hand to so much and succeeded in every step of his career, in such a life there cannot fail to be much that is worthy of record, much that will be of service for the guidance and encouragement of others.

It is this feeling which has actuated the writer of the following Memoirs : there has been also the additional motive of warm personal regard towards the subject of them, and gratitude for unvarying kindness. It is difficult, in dealing with the actions and character of one lately departed, to avoid undue eulogy and to keep in right proportion incidents of private life which, however much their memory may be cherished by relatives and intimate friends, cannot be expected to occupy the interest of general readers. The object, therefore, has been ἀληθεύειν ἐν ἀγάπῃ —affectionately to tell the truth ; to state impartially the origin and incidents of a life which rose from circumstances of comparative obscurity to those of distinction and responsibility ; to show the qualities and principles which secured for William Henry Smith the unbounded confidence of those who were associated with him, and the ungrudging respect of those who, in public life, were opposed to him.

In the primitive community, while the use of metals was still limited and the craft of working them was known only to a few, he who possessed it became the most important person in the village to those whose business it was to maintain life by implements, or defend it by weapons of iron.   Hence in every such society the smith, or worker in iron, became a central figure, and hence the frequency with which, when surnames became fixed, that of Smith established itself in every part of our land where English was spoken. As society became more complex under the feudal system, the smith, or he who wrought, took a lower place in the social scale than the *hláford*— lord, or he who gave loaves : the seller, instead of being all-important to the buyer, became dependent on his favour. But inasmuch as metal work is necessary to every branch of industry, and the humblest hamlet possessed its forge, so it has come to pass that Smith is the commonest surname among our people, and to trace the lineage of one of that name, upon whose descent obscurity has fallen, is almost as hopeless a task as can be set to the genealogist.[1]

Of Henry Walton Smith, who towards the close of the eighteenth century came to London from Devonshire, it has not been possible to ascertain the parentage, although inquiries have been made and renewed by his descendants at intervals between the years 1844 and 1887. It is said that he was educated at Harrow, and it is known that by his marriage he gave deep offence to his family, who seem thereafter to have withdrawn all countenance from him.[2] His wife's name was Anna

---

[1] Various degrees of importance are attached to patronymics by different people. Sydney Smith, on being asked who was his grandfather, replied, "I know something about my father, because I remember him, but of my grandfather I know nothing, except that he disappeared about the time of York assizes." On the other hand, it is told of the late Lord Chelmsford, an exceedingly dignified individual, that while he was still Sir Frederick Thesiger, he was one day accosted in the street by somebody who mistook him for an acquaintance and addressed him as "Smith," upon which Sir Frederick drew himself up and said, with awful *hauteur*, "Sir, do I *look* like a person of the name of Smith?"

[2] The following memorandum, apparently written about the year

Eastaugh, to whom he was married at Christ Church, Middlesex, on October 27, 1784. That the bride was of humble parentage is apparent from the fact that, instead of signing the register, she appended her mark X to it. They had three children, the youngest of whom, William Henry, was born in 1792. Very shortly after the birth of this child, the father died, aged about thirty-five, and his widow would never in after-years tell her children anything about their father's family, except that, from the time of his death, she never received either help or notice from them. The only fragments of correspondence by Henry Walton Smith which remain, are portions of letters to his sweetheart, afterwards his wife

1841, is in the handwriting of his youngest son, William Henry Smith, senior :—

"My father's name was Henry Walton Smith. His father was an officer in the Navy. Henry Walton Smith died in August 1792, when I was a few days old, since which time I know nothing of his family."

This seems to have been written for the information of his son (the subject of this Memoir), who at this early age (sixteen) had already begun those endeavours to trace the origin of his family which he continued to within a few years of his death. In 1841 he received a letter from his father :—

"I do not think it worth while troubling ourselves about the old Family Arms : the Herald Office would require me to prove my right to use them, which I cannot do, through the circumstance of my Father having quitted this life while I was only a few days old. If I should ever happen to be at or near Wrington, I might make enquiries,—it is a matter of such very little consequence that I do not wish enquiries to be made."

— "dearest Anna," "my Nanny," and "my dearest Nanny"—written in most affectionate terms, but referring also to circumstances of grief and perplexity in which he found himself, the nature of which is not explained, though it was probably of a pecuniary kind. In one of these letters he desires his wife to send him another volume of 'Pamela.' Having no independent means, Henry Smith and his wife were forced to separate shortly after their marriage; he entered the service of one Mr Rogers, and she lived with a Mrs Brown at 96 Watling Street, London. From Richmond, Smith writes a desponding letter, of which the only date is "Sat. morning, 3 o'clock."

. . . Mr Rogers is in a state that would alarm a stronger mind than mine. I have been up with him ever since we have been here, and I believe his stay in this variegated life is of very short duration. The melancholy situation in which he lies makes nature shudder, and at the same time tells me the miserable state of man. . . . I cannot say I am well; if I did it would be flatt'ring myself too much, therefore if anything should happen it will only rid you of a troublesome fellow and make you once more easy; and then perhaps you may form connexions with one who will better deserve your esteem. . . . Our Lifes are in the hand of an all wise Creator, and he will dispose of them as seemeth best.

Somewhere within the first quarter of the

present century, the brothers Henry Edward and
William Henry Smith, sons of Henry Walton
Smith, set up the business of "newsmen," as it
was then termed, in an unpretending shop in
Duke Street, Grosvenor Square. Probably there
was nothing to distinguish it from dozens of
other houses doing a similar business—nothing
to mark it as the source of what has grown into
an important tributary of the Pactolus of British
trade. In those days penny and halfpenny dailies
may, indeed, have been somebody's dream, but
one not more likely to be realised than any other
dream. Besides the paper - tax, there was the
duty imposed on each copy of every newspaper :
the sheets, before going through the press, had
all to be sent to Somerset House to receive the
official stamp. There was also the advertisement-
tax, payable by the publisher.[1]

But in spite of these restrictions, the business
of Messrs Smith prospered and increased, so that
it - became desirable to secure premises near the
offices of the principal newspapers. About the
year 1820 the house 192 Strand was purchased,
and formed into a branch office, the head office
remaining in Duke Street.

---

[1] The practice of withholding information as to the price of books
under review in magazines or journals originated in the intention
of avoiding the tax on advertisements.

Now the partners in this firm were of very different degrees of capacity, and the younger brother, William, soon found that, as the scope of their transactions extended, so the necessity for organisation and punctuality increased. Henry, the elder, was old-fashioned, and, in truth, somewhat dilatory. Part of his duty was to prepare the addresses for country parcels at the Duke Street office; these were then sent off to the Strand, where William attended to their despatch by the mails. Many a time the neighbours used to see the younger brother running out in his shirt-sleeves into the Strand, watch in hand, looking impatiently for the lingering messenger, before whose arrival the day's papers could not be sent off, and exclaiming, " What *is* that lazy brother of mine about ? "

At last the situation became intolerable. Punctuality was the very soul of the business, and punctuality was just what the senior partner could not contribute; so an arrangement was made by which William Henry became sole proprietor of the concern.[1] Sole proprietor and sole manager, also, in every sense of the word. He was no believer in delegated authority or subdivision of responsibility. He worked as hard as any apprentice in the daily, manual

[1] Henry Edward Smith died in 1846.

labour, being noted as the quickest packer in
the establishment. He prided himself on this,
and it was a standing rule that any lad who
could pack up a greater number of newspapers
than his master in the morning was entitled
to a gratuity of a shilling. Indefatigable himself, he was intolerant of anything short of the
utmost exactitude in others; he was relentless
in reproof of negligence, and so stern in dealing
with any shortcoming that, as is a common experience, his presence had an effect the reverse of
inspiriting on his staff. Nevertheless, to use the
expressive phrase of one who knew him well,
and still occupies a position of trust in the firm,
he brought the business up to that point beyond
which it could not be taken by a single individual.

It was an arduous, unremitting life that was
required in those early days of one who would
succeed in the trade of newsman. Competition
was keen and profits so small that success could
only be attained by constant watchfulness to
make use of every opportunity to extend the
business. The trade of disseminating literature
contains branches which are not all drudgery. A
publisher's profession, for instance, implies plenty
of hard work, and a keen sense of the public
taste; but it also means something akin to leisure,
enriched by literary occupation. But an active

news-agent is bound to laborious routine : William Smith would suffer no one to share his authority in the house; every letter that came was opened by his own hands and the answer dictated, often it was written, by himself. Yet here and there in his correspondence, buried deep in piles of letters from irritated customers complaining of delay in the delivery of their papers, or from editors negotiating terms for a supply of their journals, there occurs a trace of more attractive material— something to hint that from this incessant daily routine there were filched occasional moments of that lettered loitering which so effectually beguiles the tedium and eases the fatigue of the journey through life. The following note, for instance, from the author of ' Ultra Crepidarius '—the prototype of Harold Skimpole—lies among letters received early in the forties; and if it be the case that Mr Smith had taken the book from the London Library for his own perusal, the suggestion is one of a wider and more sympathetic culture than might have been suspected :—

32 EDWARDES SQUARE, KENSINGTON.

A stranger is sorry to intrude this note on Mr Smith ; but if Mr Smith, without any immediate inconvenience to himself, could oblige a fellow-subscriber to the London Library with Baldelli's life of Boccacio for a few days, & if he could also be so kind as to take the trouble of directing it to this place by the parcel delivery company, it would be a great accommodation to his humble servant,

LEIGH HUNT.

William Henry Smith, senior, married Mary Anne Cooper, on June 24, 1817, at St George's, Hanover Square. For some years thereafter they continued to live over the office in Duke Street, and in that house their two eldest children, Mary Anne[1] and Caroline,[2] were born; but some time previous to 1825 the family removed to the house in the Strand, where, on the anniversary of their marriage in that year, a son was born, to be named after his father, William Henry, the subject of the present Memoir. There has been much misapprehension as to the station in life to which this child was born. It has been reported, and commonly believed, that his first employment was that of a poor newsboy. Had that been the case, there would have been no attempt on the part of his family—least of all on his own—to conceal his humble origin. But the facts of the case were otherwise, and the mistake has probably arisen from the circumstance that what we now call a " news-agent " was known sixty years ago as a " newsman," and the son of a newsman

[1] Married in 1839 to Rev. William Beal.
[2] Married to Mr R. M. Reece.

might, by a strained interpretation, be described as a newsboy. Whatever may have been the descent of his grandfather, Henry Walton Smith, the late Mr W. H. Smith was born of parents occupying the position of respectable and prosperous tradespeople.

A less eventful boyhood than William Henry's, the younger, it could hardly be the lot of a biographer to describe. Until eight or nine years of age he remained in the schoolroom with his four elder sisters, under the teaching of their governess. Then the services of a tutor, the Rev. William Beal, of Trinity College, Cambridge, were secured for him; and, when twelve years old, he went with his mother and sisters to Paris, where they remained for some weeks. Meanwhile, Mr Beal had become engaged to the eldest Miss Smith, and on his receiving from the Duke of Bedford in 1838 the appointment of head-master to the newly revived grammar-school at Tavistock, their marriage took place. This led to William's only and brief acquaintance with a public school, or, indeed, with school of any sort. He was placed there as a boarder early in 1839, being then fourteen years old, and in June his name appears as second in the second form, William Lethbridge (of whom more hereafter) being first. The following note appears on the report of the midsummer examination for that year :—

The medal for Mids^r. 1839 gained by, and awarded to, W. H. Smith of Kilburn, London.   W. BEAL.

But William Smith's name is not again found on the school‑lists after that date. The boy returned home, and another private tutor, the Rev. Alfred Povah, of Wadham College, Oxford, took him in hand.

There remains in one of the boy's letters, written from Tavistock to his father, evidence of thoughtfulness unusual at the age of fourteen, and of attention directed to a class of subject which, in after-years, was to occupy a great deal of his energy and thoughts.

Last Wednesday being a half-holiday, Mr Beal took a walk with me in the afternoon to the Union Workhouse in the neighbourhood of the town, which was quite a new sight to me. To all appearance the people looked extremely comfortable; in fact, much more so than many poor people in their own houses. I was rather surprised at seeing them so comfortable, for from the noise made about the new Poor Law I expected to find it rather a wretched place.

The influence which had prevailed so long to keep William from school, and to remove him from it after such a short experience, is not difficult to trace, neither was it without important bearing upon his after-life. His mother's

family, the Coopers, were Wesleyans of the early
and strict kind; and her' mother, a widow, used
to pay long visits at her son-in-law's house in
Duke Street. This lady was not only extremely
devout, but also painfully apprehensive of the
perils to which young people are exposed at
public schools from bad companions and worldly
influence. She it was who prevailed to persuade the Smiths to keep their only son so
long at home, and probably to remove him from
Tavistock after so short a trial, though he had
made, as the prize-list shows, such a promising
start there. Anxiety to withdraw the lad from
sympathy with the Church of England, signs
of which he showed even at this early age,
and to keep him in touch with the Wesleyan
body, had, no doubt, a good deal to do with
the domestic policy.

There may be traced in the economy of this
Methodist-Christian home something resembling
the stern Lacedæmonian spirit, exacting from
the son unquestioning submission to the father,
but also putting him, while still very young,
in authority over others. In the refusal of
the Smiths to yield to their boy's intense desire
to go to a university, there is some analogy
to the edict forbidding the youth of Lacedæmon
to visit Athens; in spite of the learning and

philosophy of that focus of culture, there was too much tittle-tattle and luxury to be reconciled with the strenuous home life. Whatever the effect of this early discipline may have been in forming the young man's character, it certainly was the cause of lasting disappointment to himself, and often, in later years, he used to deplore bitterly the circumstances which had debarred him from acquiring a wider culture.

After a couple of years at home, William was allowed to return to Tavistock school at the age of seventeen, not, apparently, as an ordinary pupil, for his name does not appear on the school-lists of those years, but rather as a private pupil of his brother-in-law, the headmaster. His time seems to have been divided between the pursuit of learning here, and attention to business in the Strand, until some time in 1844, after which date any learning he acquired was the fruit of voluntary application of his leisure.

As the lad grew in stature, his spirit struggled to emancipate itself from the narrow and rather sombre surroundings of his boyhood. At sixteen he had already expressed to his father his strong desire to go to a university and prepare for Holy Orders. Whether his mother-in-law's warning had given the elder Smith a genuine

dread of the profligacy of universities as well as
of public schools, or whether he merely looked
upon Oxford or Cambridge as an extravagance
unsuited to his own station in life, he would
not listen to his son's pleading to be sent
there; and as for the Church—he gave an em-
phatic discouragement to that idea. In fact, he
gave his son to understand that if he persisted
in his purpose of entering Holy Orders, he need
not expect a shilling from his father; whereas,
if he came into the business, he might count on
being made a partner as soon as he should come
of age.

The young man submitted his will to that
of his father, and began work in the office; but
he could not bring his spirit into sympathy with
the Wesleyan community to which his parents
were so closely attached.[1] To a youth brought
up so constantly at home, it must have been
a matter of much difficulty, and have required
the support of strong conviction, to attempt
separation from the congregation in which he had
been reared. To support himself in the effort,
and to overcome his parents' objections to his

---

[1] It is believed that the elder Smith never actually joined the
Wesleyan Society, though he constantly attended their services,
and subscribed liberally to their funds. He was, however, married
in St George's, Hanover Square, and all his children were baptised
in the Church of England.

attending the services of the Church of England, William availed himself gladly of the
help of his brother-in-law and old master, Mr
Beal, who in 1842 wrote to him—

Would you like me to name to your Father the subject
of *your*, & Augusta's and Emma's, going to church every
Sacrament Sunday? I feel very confident indeed that
both with your Father and Mamma I could gain it for you
all. With this stipulation, however, that so long as you
are under age, this shall be the *last* concession made to
you in these matters—viz., that one Sunday in a month,
and *that* the Sacrament Sunday, shall be at your own disposal, but that the other three, you all consent willingly
and regularly to go wherever your Father thinks you get
the most wholesome spiritual food.

It would have been in accordance with what
very often happens, if early restraint of so strict
a kind had brought about a reaction as the boy
grew to manhood : the impulse to escape from the
narrow field of duties precisely defined—weariness
of warnings against all that allures a youth as the
world opens before him—the flush of health and
the free instinct of our race,—these are influences
which have often in such cases brought about the
violent rupture of parental control and started
the prodigal down the slopes. The saving instrument in such cases is generally found in
warm affection ; and it implies the existence of

more endearing qualities in the parents of this young man than a stranger is able to trace in the record of their habit of life, that, from first to last, their son never wavered in his love for them, and that home influence never lost its hold upon him.   On the other hand, though almost the first use which the younger William made of the liberty of manhood was to carry out the wish he had for some years entertained, of separating himself from the Wesleyan body and joining the Church of England, the effect of early training never disappeared : throughout his life he remained serious, sometimes almost to despondency, deeply religious and attentive to regular worship, and accustomed, in intimate correspondence, to express himself with more freedom and fulness on spiritual subjects than is usually the habit of laymen in the older Churches.   This may explain many passages in letters written in after-years to his wife and sisters, and enable the reader to understand his constantly recurring request for their prayers on his behalf in whatever business he happened to be engaged on at the time.   It must not be supposed, however, that Smith was ever in the habit of obtruding his religious feelings in general conversation or correspondence. Some of those who had most constant intercourse with him in public life, though they *felt*

that they had to do with an earnest Christian,
may never, in the course of many years, have once
heard the name of the Almighty pass his lips, or
remember a single sentence of religious doctrine
—still less of controversy—escape from him.

Mr Beal's intervention seems to have been
effectual, for in 1842 there came a letter from
William to his sisters :—

Have you heard from Mr Beal on a particular subject?
Did you expect anything of the kind? I was quite surprised when I heard from him about it, and Father's
approbation too. You know of course that all things go
on well day by day. Father says that there is a slight
difference in the young generation, but you must wait till
Sunday, when, if you'll go to Church in the morning, you
shall hear it all in the afternoon, and then, by attending
Methody or other Chapel in the evening, you will cover
your double sin and go to bed a Xtian.

Not improbably the elder Smith, though himself remaining staunchly attached to the Wesleyan body, viewed without apprehension the
tendency of his children towards the Church of
England, and it is to the influence of his wife
and her relations that such active resistance as
he showed in preventing his son offering himself
for confirmation may be attributed. Constantly
and actively employed as he had been in business,

and absent from home during daylight hours, he would, as is the habit of the husbands of good wives, willingly resign into Mrs Smith's hands the chief part of the spiritual direction of his household; yet there may also be traced, in his thus yielding to Mr Beal's proposal, some of that tolerant breadth which, as men approach the half-hundred, generally mellows the view they take of religious controversy. Indeed, though the creation of the minor divisions which separate the Christian Church into so many parts lies at the door of the men, their maintenance must be placed to the account of women, who, being far more conservative in spiritual as well as in temporal affairs, resist all change and modification as dangerous innovation.

But however tolerant the elder Smith showed himself of the alteration of his children's views and their alienation from the Methodist connection, he remained inflexible in his resistance to William's inclination to enter the priesthood. In this he was evidently strengthened by the circumstances of his private affairs. He had, by diligence and active foresight, raised his business from a very modest scale to one of considerable importance and value. But as he advanced in years, incessant work began to tell upon his health. In 1845 his friend, Mr Sercombe (whose son Rupert afterwards married his daughter Louisa), wrote from Exeter —:

I feel persuaded that nothing but rest will do for you ; will you therefore allow me to suggest to you what has passed through my mind and my dear wife's, which is this. If you could by advertisement or otherwise get a respectable business man, who understands your kind of business, and who would take your morning work, . . . this would save your health, and in all human probability prolong your valuable life.

No doubt Smith felt the soundness of this advice, and the result of it is shown in a letter from young Smith to his sister, Mrs Sercombe, written in the same year :—

We have at last made an alteration—a decided and, I hope, an effectual one. Father has long felt that his late attack of lameness resulted from overwork, and therefore has so far overcome his natural predilections as to determine on doing less—on giving up packing altogether—on playing the gentleman Tradesman. In order to carry out this idea he has resolved to dine *here* [at Kilburn House] regularly at 4 o'clock, excepting on Saturdays, and he has purchased me a Horse—a very beautiful one indeed—on which I am to ride backwards and forwards—if necessary, to stay a short time after he has left, if not—to leave with him or when I choose.

The weight thus lifted from the father's shoulders was placed upon those of his willing son, who now entered upon the battle of life, the labours of which varied, it is true, in character as years brought him into different fields of labour, but were without intermission to its close. In this early begun and long-sustained work may be traced the source of that sense of weariness so often alluded to in the letters of his later years, and the strain so long endured seems to have tended to bring sooner to its close a life which might, under less trying conditions, have continued in vigour till at least the threescore and ten.

Slow as Mr Smith had been to show confidence in his son's judgment in religious matters, this rearrangement of his business was not the first proof he had given of reliance on William's capacity and common - sense. Mr Smith had shortly before this acquired some property in Cornish mines, and in 1844, while the youth was still a private pupil with Mr Beal at Tavistock, he wrote to him as follows :—

Can you tell me the cause of the Herod's foot shares being £7 each? have you any knowledge what has been paid for the *set*, because 256 at £7 each is about £1790— a goodly sum. Think about this, & let me know your opinion. I do not think anything is wrong, for otherwise Mr P. has my utmost confidence, but we are all apt to run too fast when we get excited. Coolly think over this matter, but do not think that I have any intention to withhold entering into this matter, but I wish to draw your attention to a full consideration of the matter and also to mining in general. I suppose you will go to the Green Valley.

I do not see anything in your letter respecting the state the Miners are in—has any provision been made for the welfare of the nobler part? It will not do for me to attend a Place of Public Worship myself, & yet put men in such a situation that they have not the means of religious instruction, and I am sure you will see the inconsistency of subscribing to Missionary Societies, & at the same time being the cause of making my fellow-countrymen heathens. I hold my hand at the present till my mind is set at rest on this subject.

Do not think that I am in any way displeased respecting Herod's foot—far from it. I think as far as you have gone you have done perfectly correct, but the other part must not be neglected.

Nothing could illustrate more clearly than this passage the nature of the training which gave a lasting bent to the character of young Smith. His father, though a peculiarly shrewd man of business, with a quick eye to the main chance, and constantly on the look-out for good investments for his savings, was also scrupulously righteous, and conscientious as to the sources whence he should draw his profits.

It must not be supposed, however, that old Mr Smith was close-fisted or ungenerous. Persons still living testify to his liberality and consideration for others. On one occasion, when extensive additions were being made to the offices in the Strand, and were on the point of completion, he happened to meet on a Saturday the contractor for the work, who wore an air of depression and anxiety. Smith asked him why he was so down-cast. "Perhaps you would be downcast, Mr Smith," was the reply, "if you had come to Saturday night, and had no money to pay your men. The architect is out of London, and I can't get a certificate for my work." "Oh, is that all?" replied Smith; "come into my office and I'll write you a cheque for £1000." He did so, and the contractor, then in a comparatively small way of business, now a partner in one of the most powerful firms in England, still speaks gratefully of this mark of confidence.

Neither at this time nor at any later period of his life did young Smith possess the gift of poignant expression in his letters. He wrote fluently, indeed, and, making allowance for the greater brevity which multiplied posts have brought about in later times, his early letters are certainly of more liberal measure than most modern sons and brothers address to their parents and sisters. Full of common-sense, they are not always free from a tendency to commonplace, and the homely language is often an indifferent vehicle for really dignified thought.[1] It is not, for instance, every brother who, at the age of nineteen, takes the trouble to impart such true philosophy as is contained in the following sentence from a letter written by Smith in 1844 to his elder sister Augusta on her birthday :—

Although in a very humble and apparently confined sphere of action, who can tell the effect which our influence or that of our conduct may have upon others, and its reaction throughout future ages ?

Written by the heir to influence and possession, such words might have come to be remembered as pregnant with conscious meaning ; penned as they were by the son of a London tradesman, to whom the University training which he had craved for had been refused, they signify a thoughtful sense of responsibility beyond what might have been reasonably expected.

In the previous year, 1843, William had already, on the invitation of Mr Reece of Furnival's Inn, accepted the office of one of the secretaries of the Great Queen Street Branch Missionary Society, an institution of which the importance was cer-

---

[1] In spite of the profusion of his correspondence at all times of his life, Smith possessed two virtues of a letter-writer—he wrote a distinct hand, almost ladylike in neatness, and he hardly ever, even at his busiest, used contractions.

tainly not underrated by its members, for Mr
Reece, in making his proposal to William, mod-
estly describes it as "the noblest and most
deeply interesting enterprise that either the
Church or the World—in this or any former
age—ever witnessed!"

There was a time when the opposition to his
strong desire for ordination seemed about to be
removed. His father, weary of incessant work,
contemplated the sale of his business and retiring
upon the substantial means which he had gained
in trade.

I am most sincerely delighted [wrote Mrs Beal to her
brother in 1844] at the encouraging prospect of affairs.
You have now certainly far greater likelihood of realising
your long-cherished hopes and wishes. All I can say is,
may it please God to grant your desire, and that you may
live to be the useful minister of a nice little parish of your
own. . . . I am very, very thankful dear Father has determined to relieve himself, but shall not be able fully to
believe he will sell the business he has so long cherished,
until I hear of some very decided move in that direction.
. . . Some occupation that will be interesting and not
burdensome must be provided. I am quite sure he cannot
live inactive after the life of work and bustle he has
passed.

Mrs Beal's incredulity was justified by the
result. Mr Smith overcame his sense of weariness, pushed his business with redoubled energy,

and became more resolved than ever to make his son an active partner in the concern.

Don't be afraid [wrote young Smith to Mrs Beal in 1845] that I am becoming a Puseyite, a Newmanite, or Roman Catholic. If you think me really higher than I was, I have given you a wrong impression. I am only confirmed in my dislike for Wesleyanism as now carried out by preachers and people, and in my decided preference for the Church, and to a certain extent I judge of systems and principles by their results in the lives and ideas of those who hold them. I think the extremes of parties are decidedly wrong; and, besides, I should be careful how I held views which would give just occasion to certain parties to exclaim against what they would state was the inevitable result of a departure from Wesleyanism, for the sake of the Church itself. I am sometimes so much annoyed by these people that I should really say some unpleasant things to them, if I did not remember that they would be carefully treasured up and used at another time against the Church as an illustration of its principles, the aggravating cause being of course forgotten, or never mentioned.

Sisters are a little strong in their views now and then, and if I become a Roman Catholic they will go first; but there is no fear. We are all quiet enough and low enough to please even you, when we get amongst Church people, but now the very reverse is forced down our throats. . . . Nothing has transpired respecting the business or the change that appears to wait me. The increase of clerks promises a little ease, and, accordingly, Father does not say much of selling now. His idea was that after selling the business he would find sufficient employment for his time in attending to the business of the public companies with which he is connected, and in looking after his other property. . . . I don't think, however, that even if I go out of it he will really sell the business; he may probably do less—perhaps take some one in, as Cyrus, whom he could manage completely; but he would never give up the position of master in the concern, nor when the time for action came would he like to give up altogether the influence and income which the business gives.

I shall endeavour to be perfectly content whatever may be the result of all these things, for I feel I should not be justified in doing that which would seem to anticipate the ordering of events. The position which I desire to occupy is of far too responsible a character to be regarded merely as an occupation. I shall not therefore be satisfied unless a clear opening presents itself, and if it does, I hope I shall be enabled to fulfil conscientiously the duties to which I shall then feel I am called.[1]

You need not fear I have any desire to tie[2] myself up for life. It is the opposite tendency that induces Father to suggest the subject so frequently, to *our* great amusement. He thinks that if I entertain such thoughts now, I shall then be settled to something like business for life. But whether I take orders or not, I shall certainly not think of anything like matrimony for some years to come.

---

[1] This lofty tone of Christian fatalism remained with Smith throughout his life. It is the note on which Samuel Johnson continually dwelt. "To prefer," he wrote to Boswell in 1776, "one future mode of life to another, upon just reasons, requires faculties which it has not pleased our Creator to give us." Again, in 'Rasselas': "'Very few,' said the poet, 'live by choice: every man is placed in his present condition by causes which acted without his foresight, and with which he did not always willingly co-operate.'"

[2] By marriage.

It would destroy all hope of mental improvement, and make me undoubtedly " soft."

How great was the sacrifice which young Smith was called on to make to his father's will, in resisting the strong vocation he felt for the Church, may be gathered from passages in a journal kept through part of these years. In 1846, the year he came of age, he wrote :—

August 6.—The past twelvemonth has been one of great importance to me, and as far as man may be permitted to judge, determined the particular course of life I shall lead, and the object to which my best energies shall be devoted.

The decision on these most serious matters was not, perhaps, in accordance with the hopes and desires I had long cherished.

Those who have a natural claim upon my respect and obedience so strongly opposed the schemes I entertained, and in such a feeling, as to render it impossible for me to carry them into effect.

It is true that many friends (whose opinions were freely and impartially given, and who, by their position, their knowledge of the world, and the soundness of their motives, were well qualified to give them) said that they thought I was fitted for, as I was inclined to, the high and exalted position of a Minister, and they judged my strong wishes in the matter to be an indication of the will of Providence. But it is not so, at least apparently, for he whose power is absolute in the matter—under Providence itself—by the strong expression of his wishes and intentions obliged me to yield my own desires and views, and adopt his instead.

By this I do not mean that he acted otherwise than from the kindest wishes, as he no doubt considered the course of life he contemplated for me the best and most useful, and that, in fact, for which I am designed.

However it may be, I now, as a man, am called upon to fulfil obligations imposed upon all men to their Maker and to each other. I may not idly regret the disappointment of long-cherished hopes which, it may be, I have not been justified in entertaining, but it is my duty to acknowledge an overruling and directing Providence in all the very minutest things, by being, in whatsoever state I am, therewith content. . . .

My conclusion is, then, that I am at present pursuing the path of duty, however imperfectly ; wherever it may lead, or what it may become, I know not.

Bitterly as the young man felt the disappointment, he did not allow it to destroy the attraction which ecclesiastical matters possessed for him, and the tenor of his after-life was accurately forecast in one of Mrs Beal's letters expressing sympathy for him in the turn affairs had taken :—

In your present situation there is nothing to prevent your being very useful. I know more than I once did the difficulty ministers find to get willing, intelligent, and suitable persons to co-operate with them in carrying out many benevolent designs : in this you may render many important services. You know that you used to agree with me that if a man had but the inclination he might be as useful out of office as in it. I trust in future years you will find this to be your experience.

There is no trace in the letters or journals of this period of his abrupt severance from the sect. in which William had been brought up. On the contrary, for some time after he had become a member of the Church of England, he continued to attend Wesleyan services, though with a growing distaste for that form of worship. Thus, during a tour which he took in the autumn of 1846, after he was of age, with his mother and four sisters, in the English Lake district, he wrote from Kendal:—

Sunday, 2nd August.—Attended St Thomas's Church in the morning,—Mr Latrobe, an excellent man, duly valued; Trinity Church in the afternoon—the old church, of immense size, having five aisles; and the Methodist Chapel in the evening. To perpetuate my remembrance of *this* service would be unkind.

On January 29, 1847, he wrote to Mrs Beal:—

I am going on very comfortably with Father now, seldom or never going to Chapel, or asked to do so.

Another letter to the same, written a month later, gives the impression made on young Smith by a well-known individual:—

I have had an interview with the great George Hudson, the Railway King. The 'Times' wrote for a man to come up to town, on my representation, who knew something of the railways down in the North, and we went together to see this great man, and to remonstrate with him concerning some errors in the arrangement of the trains. We were with him about half an hour, and had a good opportunity of seeing his character, of which I have not formed a very favourable opinion. I think he is a cunning, clever man, but very deficient in everything that is noble and commanding respect; very much of a bully in conversation if he thinks he can succeed; if not, possessed of little courage, if any. At first he was disposed to treat me very slightingly, and I felt rather angry, and in the course of conversation brought in the names of the conductors of the 'Times' and 'Chronicle,' which had such a magical effect upon the honourable gentleman that both my companion and myself could hardly refrain from laughing in his face.

It has been a matter of much consideration how far it is expedient to unveil the most secret and sacred thoughts of the man whose narrative fills these pages. One shrinks from putting on permanent record anything that might be but the fruit of a transient mood or merely evidence of a youthful phase of thought ; yet no estimate of William Smith's character and work would be faithful which did not show how, from very early days down to his latest years, he was constantly penetrated with deep religious feeling, and unremitting in the practice both of private prayer and public worship. There are those who believe that this is incompatible with the higher intellectual power ; that the bolder spirits are those which show themselves somewhat impatient of church

services and incredulous as to the efficacy of
prayer : not the less would such as these have
cause for complaint if the leading motive of all
Smith's actions were kept in the background. It
will be for each one to form his own judgment of
the degree in which the man's usefulness, and
the confidence he gained from his fellow-men, was
affected by his undoubted piety.

Smith's early journals are full of religious meditation, expressions of deep regret for failings,
and gratitude for deliverance from evil.[1] But
there would be little profit in quoting extracts,
differing not much from the sentences in which
many a serious-minded youth must have committed to paper his perplexity and hope, his
ardour and disappointment. Yet there has been

---

[1] Like all men of prayerful natures, Smith was subject to moods
of deep despondency. One is reminded by the tenor of many notes
in his handwriting of similar expressions made use of by Dr
Johnson — his prayerful reflection, for instance, on his fifty-sixth
birthday : "I have now spent fifty-five years in resolving, having,
from the earliest time almost that I can remember, been forming
schemes of a better life. I have done nothing. The need of doing,
therefore, is pressing, since the time of doing is short. O God !
grant me to resolve aright, and to keep my resolutions, for Jesus
Christ's sake. Amen." In making reference to Smith's devotional
habit of mind, one is tempted to echo the comment passed by
Boswell on the passage above quoted : "Such a tenderness of conscience—such a fervent desire of improvement—will rarely be
found. It is, surely, not decent in those who are hardened in
indifference to spiritual improvement to treat this pious anxiety
of Johnson with contempt."

preserved on a loose slip of paper something so characteristic of the writer, something that may give, once for all, so clear an insight into his ardent, yet withal methodical, devotion — not merely the sentiment of adolescence but the enduring practice of his life—that there seems no reason to withhold it. This document, written about the time Smith came of age, contains a list of the subjects for which he prayed daily. They are as follows :—

1. For repentance. 2. Faith. 3. Love. 4. Grace to help. 5. Gratitude. 6. Power to pray. 7. Constant direction in all things. 8. A right understanding of the Bible, and a thorough knowledge of it. 9. Deliverance from my easily besetting sin—watchfulness. 10. Grace that blessings and talents—God's gifts—may not be the means of withdrawing my heart's service from God the Giver. 11. My wife—if it is God's will I should have one. 12. Like blessings for my Father and Sisters, according to their several necessities. 13. My friends. 14. This place. 15. Missionaries. 16. All for whom I ought. 17. Pardon for all ignorance and sin in all my prayers. Remember the 4th February, and pray that I yield not to temptation.

Never, surely, did the boyhood and youth of one whose parents were, if not in affluent, at least in easy circumstances, pass with so little provision for amusement as did those of William Smith. Games generally bulk largely in a school-

boy's letters, but in the few that have survived
from the brief school-days of this boy, there is
not even a passing reference to football or cricket.
The only exercise which he seems to have been
at liberty to enjoy—and that from very early
years—was riding.   Each year, however, after
leaving Tavistock, he used to take an autumn
holiday with his mother and sisters.   In 1844
and 1846 they went to Rydal; in 1847 they
made a tour in Scotland; and in 1848 and 1849
they travelled in Ireland.

The absence of active recreation does not seem
to have been compensated for by a decided appe-
tite for literature.   True, he was at some pains—
after his desire to go to a University had been
sacrificed to his father's wish for him to enter the
business—to carry on such studies as his limited
opportunities allowed, and for a couple of years
after he came of age he used to study with a private tutor; but he used books not so much from a
love of literature, as from a desire for knowledge.
His letters are not those of a bookish man; and
long afterwards he remarked once to Mr White,
who still holds an important, confidential appointment in the head office, " I don't read, I
appropriate."

But he had one darling occupation—one, too, in

the pursuit of which he had the good fortune to be encouraged by his father. He was passionately fond of music, and learned to play with some skill on the organ. This taste was dominant with him throughout his life, and the last addition to his country seat at Greenlands in 1885 included the conversion of the kitchen into a large organ - room, in which was placed a fine instrument by Willis.

It is perhaps fruitless to speculate what his life might have been, and to what level he might have risen, had William Smith been allowed to follow his inclination in the choice of a profession. There are few parents who think it wise to thwart the decided prepossession of their sons for definite callings—few that do not rejoice when such prepossession for a worthy vocation is shown. Still, looking back over the circumstances surrounding Smith in boyhood and manhood, it is difficult to see matter for regret in the obstacles placed in the way of fulfilling his ambition. One cannot but see that his was a character requiring external pressure to develop it: had he become a clerk in Holy Orders, he might have filled a rural incumbency, with diligence indeed, and with profit for his own soul and the souls of his parishioners, but his light would not have shone before men, showing how pure and lofty principles can be successfully carried into the highest and most complex conditions of modern government.   His private friends and parishioners might have gained something, but the public could not but have failed to lose much.   In the last year of his life, in reply to a letter from his old friend, the Rev. H. H. D'Ombrain, vicar of Westwell, congratulating him on his appointment to the Wardenship of the Cinque Ports, an honorary post reserved for the highest in the service of the State, Smith wrote: "Our courses in life have been very different, but if I had had my choice at twenty-one, I should have been as you are."   There comes to mind a story told of old John Brown, the minister of Haddington, to whom a conceited young fellow, who thought himself too good for his calling, had expressed his ardent desire to be a minister of the Gospel. "I wish," he said, "to preach and glorify God." "My young friend," replied the cool-headed old divine, "a man may glorify God making broom besoms; stick to your trade, and glorify God by your walk and conversation."

To some such conclusion Smith's own strong common-sense seems to have led him.   Forty years later — in 1885 — he was writing to his daughter Emily, now the Hon. Mrs W. Acland, from Balmoral, where he was Minister in attendance on the Queen :—

Your account of yourself reminds me of my own feeling when I was young. I thought my life was aimless, purposeless, and I wanted something else to do; but events compelled me to adhere to what promised to be a dull life and a useless one; the result has been that few men have had more interesting and useful work to do—whether it has been done ill or well—than I have had.

Man proposes and God disposes, and His dispositions yielded to and accepted turn out for our happiness.

One of Smith's most constant correspondents during his early years was William Ince (now Canon Ince, of Christ Church, Oxford). Interspersed with copious reflections on serious subjects, especially on the development of the Tractarian movement, which Ince, as a Low Churchman, regarded with suspicion and aversion, there occur in his letters to Smith references to matters of the day which are not without interest at the present time :—

30th Jany. 1844.— . . . Pray, are you acquainted with Keble's 'Christian Year'? If not, I would advise you to get or borrow it of some one, as it contains some of the most melodious verses and beautiful sentiments that have been produced in modern times, and you may have it without much fear of being suspected of favouring the party to which its author belongs, as it is read and admired by all—even his bitterest opponents.

30th March 1846.— . . . As for political parties, they

appear to me to be all alike. One when in power pursues the very same line of policy which it denounced when out. Great broad principles are abandoned, and mere expediency is the guide of conduct.

In writing to Ince about this time Smith observed :—

Your Bishop [Wilberforce] has come out in the House of Lords in good style—independently—like a man, and although he may have made a mistake or two, they are nothing to the spirit which is in the man. He will do you in Oxford immense good—make men who never thought of thinking for themselves (or acting, rather) first admire his energetic character, and then copy it. . . . I am amused, even among people who are a little educated, to observe the easiness with which a man first starting a subject can induce all the rest to follow in his steps— taking the same view of it. I suppose it must be so, or the world would be in a terrible mess. For my part, how- ever, I should be inclined to examine any conclusion, all the more because other men had arrived at it; and I do not think that even if I had thought, and expressed the thought, with them on a previous occasion, it would show either a dishonourable or a weak mind if, on further information and more consideration, I dissented from them and acted accordingly.

Here is another extract from Ince's letters :—

Dec. 8, 1848.—We had a grand treat here last week in Jenny Lind's concert; nobody has talked of anything else since; every anecdote of her stay and every word she uttered are most assiduously treasured up. Her singing was certainly most enchanting, and besides its own intrinsic merit was enhanced by the simplicity and art-lessness of her manners, so utterly free from all affecta-tion, and so indicative of goodness. She sang two or three songs to the servants at the Angel where she staid, sang some pieces from the Messiah in New College Chapel, and, when asked by the Bodleian Librarian to sign her name in the book provided for distinguished visitors, refused, saying, "No; Oxford is so great and I am so little."

The circumstances of Smith's boyhood and youth forbade the planting of many friendships at that season when the tender rootlets of affec-tion creep silently and fasten themselves deeply into the fabric of a human life. With Ince his friendship was enduring; he was almost the only one of whom he could have exclaimed with Charles Lamb: "Oh! it is pleasant as it is rare to find the same arm linked in yours at forty, which at thirteen helped it to turn over the Cicero *De amicitiâ*, or some other tale of antique friendship, which the young heart even then was burning to anticipate."

CHAPTER II.

1846–1854.

DISAPPOINTMENT IN CHOICE OF A PROFESSION—RESIDENCE AT
KILBURN HOUSE—YOUNG SMITH ENTERS THE BUSINESS, AND
ON COMING OF AGE BECOMES HIS FATHER'S PARTNER—HIS
INFLUENCE IN THE OFFICE—BEGINNING OF THE BOOKSTALL
BUSINESS — ACQUIRES MONOPOLY OF THE NORTH-WESTERN
RAILWAY STATIONS — HIS DEALINGS WITH *EMPLOYÉS* — EX-
PANSION OF THE BUSINESS—WORK ON THE COMMITTEE OF
KING'S COLLEGE HOSPITAL.

NOTWITHSTANDING the agitation of alternate
hopes and fears as to the realisation of his
dream of becoming a clergyman, young William
Smith had shown no want of willing application
to the business of news-agency, upon which he
entered at the age of sixteen. While it is impossible to doubt the reality of his religious
conviction and the large place which it filled
in all his schemes for the future, it is equally
impossible not to admire the resolution with
which he acted on Candide's maxim — *il faut
cultiver notre jardin.*

There is an entry in his journal for August 1846, highly characteristic of his thoughtful and precise habit of mind :—

The last few weeks have been marked with very important and serious events. First came the decision affecting my future life, of the results of which no one can form any estimate. Then my coming of age on 24th June was a serious event, as, with the liberal means afforded me by my father, and the general though tacit concession of freedom of thought and action, . . . the acknowledgment that I am a man—all have opened up fresh responsibilities and duties, without removing any that previously existed. . . . On the 30th ulto., Mr Ford waited upon us by appointment to take our joint instructions as to the Partnership, which gives me £500 a-year clear, board and lodging, a comparative interest in the capital of £2000 — for seven years, but liable to six months' notice on either side. These terms, with which was coupled an express declaration that they were only temporary, as a prelude to much greater concessions, are extremely liberal and considerate.

Somewhere about the year 1840 his father had bought Kilburn House, a pleasant suburban villa, then standing in ample private grounds, though it has now disappeared under the advancing tide of bricks and mortar. This became the home of the family instead of the house in the Strand, and every week-day morning at four o'clock, summer and winter, the brougham used to come to the door to convey the father or son, or both of them, to the Strand office, to attend to the despatch of the papers by the early mails.

You are correct [wrote young Smith to Mrs Beal in 1847] in supposing that I have been *prevented* from writing to you. I never remember such a period of excitement and hard work. I have been *in* town with Father, once at 3 o'clock in the morning, and every other day since the beginning of the season before 5, excepting Mondays and Thursdays; and we have already had 9 special express engines to Liverpool, Manchester, and Birmingham, and they will run every day this week. All this I have *mainly* to arrange, and I can assure you it has worn me not a little. Constant excitement and anxiety during the days, and short and disturbed sleep at nights as the consequence, are gradually making me as low and nervous as I was a' few months back.

But exclusive reliance was not placed on the mail-coaches for the transmission of news. Light carts with fast horses were employed when the newspapers were late of coming from the publishers, to overtake the mails; and in addition to these, when any event of unusual importance took place, or when something of interest happened too late for insertion in the papers of that day, Smith had his own mounted messengers, riding sometimes a couple of hours in front of the mails, distributing printed slips among his agents and customers in provincial towns.

or son, or both of them, to the Strand office, to attend to the despatch of the papers by the early mails.

You are correct [wrote ——— Smith to Mrs Beal in 1847] in supposing that I am being prevented from writing to you. I am at ——— this a period of excitement and hard work ——— been in town with Father, as I ——— and every other day ——— the beginning ——— excepting Mondays and Thursdays ——— but 9 special expresses ——— Liverpool, Winchester, and Birmingham, and they ———. All this I have ——— and I can assure you ——— Constant excitement and ——— during the ——— short and disturbed sleep at night in the ——— are gradually making me as low and nervous as I was a few months back.

But exclusive reliance was not placed on the mail-coaches for the transmission of news. Light carts with fast horses were employed when the newspapers were late of coming from the publishers, to overtake the mails; and in addition to these, when any event of unusual importance took place, or when something of interest happened too late for insertion in the papers of that day, Smith had his own mounted messengers, riding sometimes a couple of hours in front of the mails, distributing printed slips among his agents and customers in provincial towns.

The Hoe at Kilburn

Not seldom it would happen that, when the House of Commons sat late, the publication of the 'Times' was delayed until after the departure of the morning mails, by reason that it was the only journal which gave a full parliamentary report. Smith's men would be all ready to receive it and carry it into the country, thus enabling readers to get their paper on the day of publication, instead of waiting, as they would otherwise have had to do, till the arrival of the mail on the following morning. By this means, on the death of King William IV. in May 1837, Smith was enabled to carry the news into the country some hours in advance of the mails, and that not only into this country, but into Ireland, for he chartered a special packet to convey the papers to Belfast on the same day. By this boldness and activity, by never grudging expense in a matter of business, and by the excellent organisation of his staff, he had secured the confidence and favour both of publishers and country customers. "First on the road" was his maxim, and it brought his house ultimately to the position of first in the trade, for it enabled him to take full advantage of the change of system and rapid development of newspaper traffic consequent on the creation of railways.

Some years after the exploit mentioned above,

1842, writing to his son, Mr Smith had ex-
ultingly said :—

I gave our Opposition a little taste on Saturday. I got
the M^ng Papers into Liverpool about 2 Hours before the
time of the 6 O'Clk. arriving. I had lost ground a little
there, but this has brought me right again. If our friend
K.[1] intends to continue the opposition he has begun, he
must turn out a little of his money.

Entering upon his first duties at the Strand
office in 1842, young William Smith received an
allowance of £200 a-year from his father. When
he came of age in 1846, he was taken into the
business on the terms noted above. At that time
the property was valued at £80,527, 8s. 6d., and
the new firm was registered as Messrs W. H.
Smith & Son, the title by which it is still
known.

From the day that young Smith took the position of junior partner, new life made itself felt
in the place. Old Mr Smith's temper had not
improved with age. The early work now, as
was natural, devolved on the junior partner; his
father used to drive over from Kilburn later in
the day, and woe betide the *employé* whom he
found neglecting or mismanaging his task!

Things go on pretty smoothly [William writes to his

---

[1] Clayton, the largest news-agency of that day, and until 1854.

sister Augusta in the first few months of his partnership].
Father is of course a little testy, but generally manage-
able.   He came down on Monday for half an hour,
walked into the Counting-house, bowed to the people,
then walked up-stairs, had his leg dressed, and then got
into the carriage (which was waiting for him all the time),
vowing "the place stunk—couldn't breathe"—and he
"would not come down again for some time—it was
wretched—such a noise too."

There is no doubt that the senior partner's
rule, though just, had become increasingly harsh
of late years, and one who remembers the events
of these days in the Strand house speaks warmly
of the milder influence which prevailed as soon
as young Smith entered upon authority.   Often,
when some clerk or workman was smarting under
a prolonged chiding, which might have been well
deserved, but was made almost unbearable by
the fiercely sarcastic tone in which it was delivered by the old man, the son would wait his
opportunity to pass near the culprit, and, paus-
ing with a kindly look in his good brown eyes,
tell him in a low voice not to take too much to
heart the injurious words addressed to him—that
his father had a touch of gout on him—did not
mean all he said,—and so on.   The effect was
wonderful in sweetening the daily toil; the men
soon came to know that, with resolution and
business capacity not inferior to his father, the

son was of finer fibre and gentler disposition. His hand was not less firm on the reins, but it was more elastic.

But the new partner's presence was not long in making itself felt far outside the walls of the counting-house and workshops. The business began to spread far beyond its original scope. Hitherto it had been strictly confined to that of distributing newspapers, a trade in which Clayton's was still the largest and leading' house: it was by extending their operations to another and a wider field, that Smith & Son were ultimately able to turn the flank of their powerful rivals.

As railways began to cover the land and travellers multiplied, bookstalls began to be a familiar feature of the principal stations. Sometimes they had been started by the enterprise of local booksellers, who generally combined a display of refreshment for the body with that of food for the mind. Newspapers and novels were ranged in amicable jumble with beer-bottles, sandwiches, and jars of sweets. No regulations controlled the privilege of selling on railway platforms, and miscellaneous vendors pushed their humble trade at their own pleasure. Then the railway companies began to find bookstalls a convenient means of providing occupation for men disabled, or for the widows of men killed, in their

service ; and in the early days of railway travelling, when the longest stretch of rails was no
more than thirty miles, and nobody wanted more
than a newspaper to while away the journey, this
answered all that was required. But, as journeys lengthened and travellers multiplied, more
copious literature came in demand, and it is not
surprising that complaints began to be heard
that the people who were allowed the privilege
of supplying it were often illiterate, and almost
always untrained to the business.

Another objectionable feature soon became manifest : to supply the demand of travelling readers,
dealers furnished their stalls with literature of indiscriminate character. Cheap French novels of
the shadiest class, and mischievous trash of every
description which no respectable bookseller would
offer, found purchasers ; indeed, it became notorious that some people sought for and found on
railway stalls books that they would have been
ashamed to inquire for from tradesmen with a
character to lose. Attention was called to the
disreputable nature of this traffic by letters to
the newspapers, and the directors of the principal
railways, recognising the necessity for its regulation, began to advertise for tenders for the rent
of stalls on their stations.

In this hitherto unpromising soil young Smith

was not slow to discern the prospect of a rich harvest; but in opening negotiations with the railway companies for the right to erect bookstalls, he had to encounter his father's opposition, who was disinclined to go beyond what he looked on as the legitimate business of the firm—the circulation of newspapers—and sceptical as to the profits to be derived from bookselling, pointing to the ill success of private adventurers in that line. Howbeit, the young man ultimately got his own way, and the first decisive step in the course, which he had initiated by buying up the ventures of local men on liberal terms, was accomplished when he concluded a lease with the London and North-Western Railway Company, giving the firm exclusive rights for the sale of books and newspapers on their system.

The companies, naturally concerned more about the profits of their shareholders than about the morals or mental development of their passengers, paid more regard to the amount offered in the tenders than to the respectability of the tenderers; consequently the quality of the wares offered by Smith & Son at the London and North-Western stations soon came into favourable contrast with that of the salesmen on other lines. An article which appeared in the 'Times' of 9th

August 1851 brings this out so clearly, and
throws so much light on the principles on which
Messrs W. H. Smith & Son started and maintained their new business, and the vast advantage which it was the first to ensure to the
travelling public, that it may be permitted to
make somewhat lengthy extracts from it. After
dwelling on the revolution effected by railways
in social habits, the writer went on to say :—

Men cannot move their bodies and leave their minds
behind them. . . . When disciples are restless, philoso-
phers must needs be peripatetic. Are we turning this
rushing and scampering over the land to real advantage?
Is the most made of the finest opportunity yet offered to
this generation for guiding awakened thought and in-
structing the eager and susceptible mind? . . . Could it
be possible that the conductors of our railways, all powerful and responsible as they are, had either set themselves,
or permitted others to establish on their ground, store-
houses of positively injurious aliment for the hungry
minds that sought refreshment on their feverish way?
Did they sell poison in their literary refreshment-rooms,
and stuff of which the deleterious effects twenty doctors
would not be sufficient to eradicate? We resolved to
ascertain at the earliest opportunity, and within a week
visited every railway terminus in this metropolis. It
was a painful and humiliating inspection. With few
exceptions, unmitigated rubbish encumbered the book-
shelves of almost every bookstall we visited, and indicated only too clearly that the hand of ignorance had
been indiscriminately busy in piling up the worthless

mass. The purchasers were not few or far between, but the greater the number, the more melancholy the scene. Were all the buyers daily travellers? Did they daily make these precious acquisitions? If so, it was a dismal speculation to think how many journeys it would take to destroy for ever a literary taste that might have been perfectly healthy when it paid for its first day ticket. . . .

As we progressed north, a wholesome change became visible in railway bookstalls. We had trudged in vain after the schoolmaster elsewhere, but we caught him by the button at Euston Square,[1] and it is with the object of making him less partial in his walks that we now venture thus publicly to appeal to him. At the North-Western terminus we diligently inquired for that which required but little looking after in other places, but we poked in vain for the trash. If it had ever been there, the broom had been before us and swept it clean away. . . . When the present proprietor of the Euston Square book-shop acquired the sole right of selling books and newspapers on the London and North-Western Railway, he found at the various stations on the line a miscellaneous collection of publications of the lowest possible character, and vendors equally miscellaneous and irresponsible. . . . At one fell swoop the injurious heap was removed. At first the result was most discouraging. An evident check had been given to demand; but as the new proprietor was gradually able to obtain the assistance of young men who had been educated as booksellers, and as public attention was drawn to the improvement in the character of the books exposed for sale, the returns perceptibly improved, and have maintained a steady progressive increase greatly

---

[1] The terminus of the London and North-Western line, where Messrs Smith & Son had erected bookstalls.

in excess of the proportion to be expected from the increase of travelling up to the present time. . . . Unexpected revelations came forth in the course of the inquiry. It has been remarked that persons who apparently would be ashamed to be found reading certain works at home, have asked for publications of the worst character at the railway bookstall, and, being unable to obtain them, have suddenly disappeared. . . . Cheap literature is a paying literature, if judiciously managed. A host of readers are springing up along the lines of rail, and imitators of the North-Western missionary will not long be wanting at every terminus in the kingdom. Railway directors will find it their interest no less than their duty to secure the co-operation of intelligent men, and bookstalls will crave for wholesome food, which our chief purveyors must not be slow to furnish.

In this great work of purifying the sources of information and amusement, it must not be supposed that the " North-Western missionary " was acting solely upon principles of self-interest. There was plenty of demand for the kind of literature which he was determined to discourage. It is on record that already as much as £600 had been paid as the annual rent of a bookstall at a London terminus, and the profits accruing from the old traffic were jeopardised by a sudden change.

It cannot have been an easy matter to compile an *Index Expurgatorius*. From first to last, letters came in from correspondents indignantly complaining of the profligacy of some of the books sold. Thus in 1853 a gentleman wrote expressing surprise that Byron's 'Don Juan' was on sale at some of the stations, calling upon Smith to prevent "such a vile book as that to pollute his stalls," and indicating his intention to follow up this letter with another on the subject of Alexandre Dumas's novels. As late as 1888 Smith was reproached by another correspondent for allowing the 'Sporting Times' to be exposed for sale.

There was, besides, more than the custom of the trade and a depraved public taste to be overcome in setting the bookstall business going : young Smith had also, in this matter, an enemy of his own household, for this branch of the business never, from first to last, found favour in old Mr Smith's eyes. Often, so long as he continued to visit the Strand, when he saw a pile of books in the counting - house, he would gruffly order their removal, or if he met a man carrying a parcel of them, he would ask him what he meant " by bringing such rubbish into my premises."

It is surprising how soon the son's quiet confidence succeeded in establishing the bookstall business. Besides acquiring the monopoly on the London and North-Western system, he continued to extend his operations on other lines of railway, and wherever he had an opportunity, bought up the local man, who was often glad to be let out on easy terms. The railway companies and the public soon became familiar with the bookstalls of W. H. Smith & Son, and the business became so extensive, that in 1849, only three years after its creator had entered the firm, it became necessary to appoint separate departmental managers. It was to the well-known firm of wholesale booksellers, Messrs Hamilton, Adams, & Co., that young Smith applied for assistance, and, on their recommendation, selected for the book department in connection with the bookstalls a young man of the name of Sandifer. It was a most happy choice, and the enormous development of the department, and its popularity with the public, must be largely credited to the unfailing sagacity with which, for upwards of forty years, it was conducted by Mr Sandifer.[1]

From this humble beginning there took its rise what must now be looked upon as a great institution. At first, each bookstall clerk had to make a weekly return to the head office of every book sold of one shilling and upwards in value; it often happened that one such list was easily written on half a sheet of notepaper. But once

---

[1] Mr Sandifer continued manager of this department till his death, after a short illness, in 1887.

started in the hands of a powerful firm, and con-
centrated under control of a competent manager,
the enterprise, which had proved so. disastrous to
many isolated local traders, began to advance by
leaps and bounds.　One after another the great
railway companies ceded to Smith & Son the exclusive right to erect bookstalls at their stations.
It was not easy to meet the requirements of such
sudden expansions as were caused by acquiring
the whole of the London and South-Western system about 1852, that of the London and Brighton
a few years later, and that of the Great Western
in 1862.　To man and supply with literature
so many new stations involved taking on an
immense number of new hands, as well as considerable capital expenditure.　But the junior
partner had a quick eye for capabilities, and was
constantly on the watch to secure the services of
young men in the great wholesale houses, who,
as the firm of Smith & Son rose in reputation,
often came to ask for employment.　He never let
a promising young fellow past him, but was
always ready to engage him, even if, as would
sometimes happen, there was no niche into which
he could be fitted at the moment.[1]

---

[1] This faculty of detecting "form at a glance" (if it may be
permitted to borrow from the phraseology of a system so foreign
to Smith's habits and character as the turf) never left him. During
his later years it happened that he attended a meeting of fifteen

Sometimes a young man, "too big for his boots," would show an inclination to sniff at being put in charge of a railway bookstall. The trade had an indifferent reputation at first, and such an appointment was not looked upon as that of a legitimate bookseller.

" We'll raise it, Mr ——," replied young Smith to one who had offered some such objection—" we'll raise it. I am not at all sure that it may not be made as respectable as Paternoster Row."

These young men were educated to gauge the literary taste of the various districts. Some curious information, showing how this varied according to locality, is given in the 'Times' article quoted from above.

Stations have their idiosyncrasies. Yorkshire is not partial to poetry. It is difficult to sell a valuable book at any of the stations between Derby, Leeds, and Manchester. Religious books hardly find a purchaser at

---

or twenty persons, held to promote a certain object, in the house of his colleague, the Right Hon. Edward Stanhope, M.P. One of the gentlemen present, at the request of Mr Stanhope, acted as secretary during the proceedings, which lasted about an hour. Twelve months later, Smith went to Mr Stanhope and asked the name of the gentleman who had acted as secretary on that occasion, for he said he had been so favourably impressed with his business-like qualities in the short time he had witnessed them that he wished to meet him again, in order, if a second interview confirmed his impressions, to offer him a high and lucrative post in the house in the Strand.

Liverpool, while at Manchester, at the other end of the line, they are in high demand.

One secret of young Smith's influence upon young men, and the ascendancy which he gained over them, was the patience he showed in waiting for development of character and powers. So long as he saw a man willing—so long as his shortcomings could be explained by inexperience and not by negligence—he was most slow to discourage him by rebuke : he used to say that he preferred, even at the risk of temporary loss of profits, to let a man find out his own mistakes rather than check him at once. No one knew better than Smith the truth of the adage, *ex quovis ligno non fit Mercurius;* but no one bore more constantly in mind that to be carved into an effigy is not the only use to which timber may be put, and that, of the two, a gatepost is more often of service than a god.

It was remarkable how soon each new hand entering the employment seemed to imbibe the spirit pervading the concern,—to become jealous for its character and zealous in its interests. No doubt this may be accounted for in part by the system of allowing the clerks a liberal percentage on the sales at their stalls ; but it is not possible to discourse with one of the staff who knew the business in its beginnings, without acquiring the

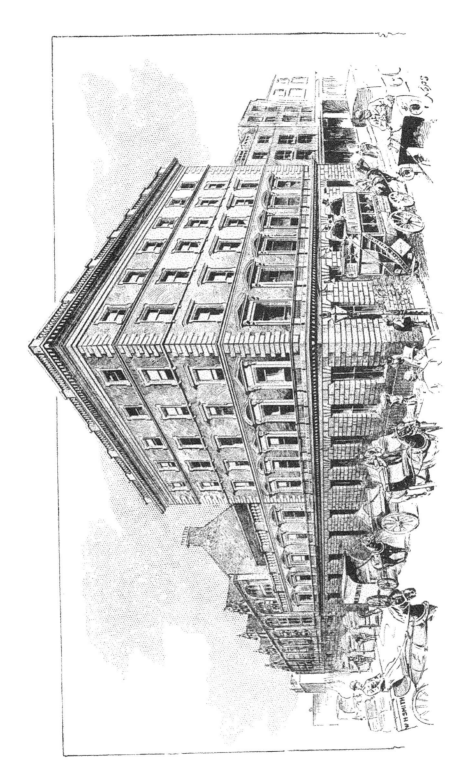

conviction that, in large measure, this *esprit du corps* had its origin in the personal influence of the junior partner.

When the Milanese critic Lomazzo chose cognisances or emblems for the master-painters of the Italian Renaissance, symbolising their various genius, he assigned to Michael Angelo the dragon of contemplation, and to Mantegna the serpent of sagacity, but for Raphael he reserved the image of man—the type of intelligence and urbanity.[1] It may seem a strained analogy that suggests itself between the characters of two men whose life-work differed as widely in kind as their social environment, but, in truth, the biographer of each has to record traits and method of influence upon others closely similar. Vasari wrote of Raphael that his kindly nature prevailed, even more than his art, to endear him to men ; he dwells on his gentleness, his modesty, his courtesy, his anxiety to help others—above all, his freedom from jealousy,—a sin besetting artists not more closely than statesmen.[2] These are precisely the qualities which distinguished Smith above his fellows, whether in the days when he was busy building up the great business in the Strand, or in after-days, when he was

[1] Symonds, Italian Renaissance : The Fine Arts.
[2] Vasari, Lives of the Painters, vol. viii. pp. 6, 60.

called on to undertake some of the highest offices
in the State.   Indeed, had he lived in an age
when men were named according to their personal
qualities, no more fitting appellation could have
been devised for him than Smith—the Smoother.[1]
Further, there was something in the concord pre-
vailing among all classes in the employment of
the Strand house, a concord established by the
younger Smith, and enduring now that he has
gone to his rest—something in the devotion to
and confidence in their chief, felt and expressed
by every one in that vast workshop, that calls to
mind the spirit described by Vasari as animating
the painters, sculptors, builders, decorators, en-
gravers, and other handicraftsmen who worked
under Raphael in his Roman *bottega*.

But it would be a mistake to suppose that
Smith was indiscriminate in indulgence.   His
principle was, once he had chosen and appointed
a man to his duty, to put complete trust in him.
That trust was seldom betrayed, and Smith was
ever slow to be convinced that it had been for-
feited; but in the rare instances when he was
justly offended, he never gave a man an oppor-

[1] There is no reality in Dean Trench's specious derivation of
"smith = one that smiteth"; the laws of comparative philology
are against it, and point to the real affinity with "smooth." A
smith is therefore not one who smites but one who smooths—a
polisher.

tunity of deceiving him a second time. In visiting neglect of duty, he was as stern as his father, though not so unreserved in rebuke. Many years ago, when travelling on one of the southern lines, he observed that, as the train entered an important station, the bookstall clerk did not turn round and face it according to his instructions, but remained inattentive, and engaged in conversation with some acquaintance. The man was not only reprimanded, but his promotion was seriously retarded by the act of negligence which his employer had witnessed. He has since proved in a higher sphere that he was thoroughly capable of discharging more important duties.

A clerk in the counting-house, who had been dismissed for gross misconduct, appeared before Smith one morning to plead for forgiveness.

"Think of my mother, sir," he said; "she has no one to depend on but me, and if you dismiss me without a character, I shall be unable to support her."

"You should have thought of your mother before, sir," was all the answer given by Smith.

If the inflexible justice with which he meted out punishment to wrong-doers sometimes approached severity, it was no more than the reflex of the perfect confidence he reposed in his men until they did something to forfeit it.

A notable feature in the history of this house has been the rareness of instances of men employed in it setting up in business for themselves. The liberality with which they have been treated —their confidence in the known practice of their employers to advance their interests as the prosperity of the business grew, have given them such a feeling of security as to deprive them of the belief they could do any better on their own account. It is but fair to observe that the constant expansion of the trade has tended not a little towards this result. Promotion has been kept moving at a rate which would have been impossible in any business less constantly under the influence of the flowing tide. Neither in newspaper circulation nor in bookstall literature, nor in the other departments into which, as will presently be mentioned, the business came to be extended, has there ever been a check in the demand: the volume of transactions has ever been on the increase, there has been no embarrassing fluctuation in prices, and the cold shade of depression which has fallen from time to time on nearly every industry has never yet darkened the house in the Strand; consequently the relations of employer and employed have never been subjected to the heavy strain involved in a reduction of the rate of pay. It may occur to some employers, less favoured by the turn of events, that it is easy, under smiling circumstances such as these, to keep a large establishment in good - humour, and to retain the devotion of old servants. No doubt there is much practical reason in this : the influence of wise management, willing service, and prosperity mutually react on each other ; but if any one of these conditions is interrupted, the fruits of the others are apt to be wasted.

Young Smith did not suffer close attention to business to prevent him taking an active part in philanthropic work. The services which he rendered to King's College Hospital extended over more than forty years, and are summarised in a resolution of condolence passed by the Committee of Management after his death in 1891, wherein they affirm that—

They are bound in gratitude to recall the long, varied, and important services which Mr Smith rendered to King's College Hospital. The munificent contributions made by him personally, and by the firm of Messrs W. H. Smith & Son, would alone ensure a grateful remembrance of his name. But the Committee are still more indebted to him for the personal guidance and support which he rendered to the Hospital, ever since he joined the Committee in 1849. . . . Since then, he served the offices of Auditor in 1862, and of Vice-Chairman from 1862–1864. For some time after his resignation of the latter office, he continued to attend the meetings of the Committee, and in February 1874 he was elected a Vice-President. After his public duties prevented him from taking any active part in the management of the Hospital, he was always ready to give his advice and assistance on any occasion of anxiety or difficulty. . . . For all these benefits his name can never cease to be remembered with gratitude by the Committee and the friends of the Hospital, and the memory of his connection with it will ever be cherished as one of its chief honours and encouragements.

CHAPTER III.

1854–1893.

EFFECT OF THE REPEAL OF THE NEWSPAPER STAMP - DUTY—
GROWTH OF THE BUSINESS — SMITH & SON BECOME SOLE
AGENTS FOR THE 'TIMES'—FAILING HEALTH OF THE SENIOR
PARTNER — INCREASING WORK — ITS EFFECT UPON YOUNG
SMITH — THE FIRM BECOME CONTRACTORS FOR RAILWAY
ADVERTISING — EXTRACTS FROM LETTERS AND JOURNAL—
THE PRINCIPLES OF PRIVATE LIFE CARRIED INTO BUSINESS
AFFAIRS—THE LENDING LIBRARY SET ON FOOT—PUBLICATION
OF CHEAP NOVELS — ITS SUCCESS AND ABANDONMENT —
PRESENT ASPECT OF THE STRAND OFFICE—EARLY MORNING
WORK—DESPATCH OF NEWSPAPERS.

IT is now time to trace some further steps in
the development of the Strand business, and
record circumstances which contributed to its
success.

Besides the expansion of newspaper traffic re-
sulting from the rapid increase of the population
of the United Kingdom, and perhaps in a greater
degree from the spread of education, the business
of journalism, and its handmaid, news-agency,
received a sudden and extraordinary impetus by

the abolition of the newspaper stamp-duty by Mr Bright's Act of 1854. The immediate effect was a reduction in the price of newspapers, and an enormous increase in the demand for them.

The standing which the energy of the elder Smith had already secured for his business in the days when he worked it single-handed, the indefatigable pluck which he had shown in carrying out his principle of " first on the road," and the perseverance which the new firm had maintained in deserving the confidence of the public as well as of publishers, enabled Smith & Son to reap the full advantage of the sudden expansion of the trade. On June 21, 1854, the most signal proof was given of their pre-eminence in this respect by a circular issued on that day from the ' Times ' office, intimating that the proprietors of that powerful journal had determined that for the future " all papers required by Messrs Smith & Son for distribution in the country shall be delivered to them by the Publishers before any other Agent is supplied. ' The Country' is understood to include all railway stations, and to exclude London and the Metropolitan districts, as defined by the Post Office. Messrs Smith & Son will distribute for the London Agents, at a fair price, the Papers required by them for the service above defined."

The importance of this document, which really amounted to a charter of monopoly in agency for the principal journal in the world, can scarcely be overestimated, and the effect was practically to place the firm out of reach of the competition alike of Clayton's and all others which had exercised the elder Smith so sorely in bygone years. It did even more than this, for it obliged every whole-sale agent to come to Smith's for his supply of the 'Times.'

The relief afforded to newspaper proprietors by Bright's Act of 1854 put them in a position to deal worthily with the Crimean War, which broke out in the autumn of that year. Telegraphic communication had been established since the last great European war, and the 'Times' was the earliest to take advantage of it by sending out the first of the class of war correspondents, Dr W. H. Russell, whose graphic despatches enabled people at home to follow day by day, not only the events of the war, but the fortunes of every regiment engaged in it. This gave an immense impetus to the circulation of this enter-prising journal, and, of course, was to the advan-tage of the firm which had become their sole country agents.

The business had by this time grown to a scale far beyond the failing powers of old Mr

Smith; the scheme and details of organisation
devolved entirely upon his son, who from that
day forward was practically the managing head
of the firm. It is true that the old gentleman still continued to busy himself in the office
as often and as long as his health permitted.
He used to drive down in his brougham from
Kilburn about nine in the morning, attended
to correspondence, and pored over the ledgers,
till, as sometimes happened, he fell down in a
swoon. His presence, however, far from help-
ing business, was a hindrance to it, for the
breakdown of his health, while it left his will
as imperious as ever, had told disastrously on his
temper. Yet his son, however sorely he must
have been tried sometimes, never failed in loyal
support to his father's authority. One day a customer came into the office to complain that a bill
which he had already paid had been sent in a
second time. Old Smith vowed that such a thing
was impossible, and maintained that the bill had
not been paid. The customer was equally confident that it had been settled, lost his temper,
and roundly abused his would-be creditor, upon
which young Smith left his seat, and, saying
quietly to the justly irate customer, " I can't
allow any one to speak to my father like that,
sir !" led him to the door, and assured him that

strict inquiry should be made into the matter. The result was to prove that the account had been settled, as had been alleged.

On another occasion, after considerable transactions had taken place with the great printing house of M'Corquodale, old Mr Smith insisted upon going over the accounts himself. Although it had long been his custom to spend much time examining the books and accounts of the firm, he had not the gift of following any but clear debtor and creditor statements of simple transactions; complicated details always threw him into a state of hopeless perplexity, and the irritation he felt at the consciousness of his want of capacity in this respect sometimes found vent in a momentary explosion of wrath against those who happened to be nearest. So, having landed himself in a maze of bewilderment over these accounts, he suddenly brought his fist down on the book with a bang, and exclaimed hotly that his son and M'Corquodale were in a conspiracy to ruin him. Young Smith rose and, laying his hand on his father's shoulder, said earnestly : " Father, you know that I would rather lose my right hand than see you robbed." The ebullition was over in a moment.

The labour thrown upon the willing shoulders of the junior partner soon became more than one man could transact. For several years it was his practice to rise each week-day at four in the morning, swallow a cup of coffee, and drive to the Strand office, by 5 A.M. People still in the business can remember how he was then the central figure in the paper-sorting office, with coat off, shirt-sleeves rolled back, and hands and arms deeply dyed with printers' ink off the wet sheets; and they speak warmly of his admirable method. The newspapers were often delivered so late from the printing-houses as to cause much anxiety, yet there was a complete absence of the fuss and hustling from which, under other management, the staff had sometimes had to suffer.

One of these early morning starts from Kilburn was marked by an unpleasant incident which might have had serious consequences. It was the duty of a servant to put some coffee ready overnight for his master, who, on rising, lighted the spirit-lamp, so that by the time he was dressed, a hot cup was prepared for him. By a sleepy-headed blunder one night this servant put into the pot, not coffee, but cayenne pepper, either wholly or in part. Smith, not observing in the dim light any difference in the mixture, gulped down half a cupful before he discovered the mistake! He afterwards described the sensation as nothing short of excruciating.

But if he was ungrudging in the length and
severity of his own labours, he soon gave practical proof of his consideration for the reasonable
recreation of others. This was before the time
when much had been heard of the early-closing
movement, yet he was one of the earliest and
most practical advocates of it, for he very soon
brought about a shortening of the hours in the
Strand office. Saturday half-holidays were almost unknown in the "fifties"; young Smith
took a leading part in establishing what is now
an almost universal and beneficial rule in good
trading houses. He organised periodical excursions on the river for the whole staff in the
Strand, and provided intellectual recreation for
them for after-work hours. A monthly parliament was set up for the discussion of questions
affecting the working classes, but it soon languished and died, for the *employés* of the firm
found they had no grievances to discuss. How
long, it may be asked, would interest in the
debates at Westminster endure, if there were
no grievances, no Supply, and no foreign
policy?

Devoted and capable as he was, young Smith
began, about the year 1854, to find the strain
of constantly increasing work getting beyond his
powers. In this year he renewed acquaintance

with an old Tavistock schoolfellow, William
Lethbridge, then an assistant master at Rossal
school. Smith invited his old friend to pay him a
visit; the result was that their early intimacy was
renewed; Lethbridge became interested in the
details of the newspaper and bookstall business,
and in the end was admitted into the firm as
a partner.

Previously to this, a totally new branch of
business had been entered upon, which was beginning to reach proportions hardly inferior to
those of the bookstall trade. Advertising may
be said to have been in its infancy at the commencement of the railway movement, but the
instincts of trades-people began to awake to the
opportunity afforded by the blank walls of railway stations of making known to travellers the
merits of their goods. It seemed to them expedient that as, in the latter days, men began
to run to and fro, so should their knowledge
(of the excellence of Heal's bedsteads and Brog-
den's watch-chains, &c.[1]) be increased. The first
stages of what has now become an enormous system were as modest and ill-regulated as those of
the bookstalls: the course adopted was the same;

---

[1] These two firms were almost the first to avail themselves of the
great impetus to advertisement given by the Great Exhibition of
1851, and to start pictorial advertisement.

the companies began to advertise for tenders for
the use of their walls, and in almost every case
Smith & Son were the successful tenderers.

But it was some time before the firm could feel
satisfied of the prudence of their new undertaking. The initial outlay of capital was very
heavy, and for a time the returns were insigni-
ficant. Old Mr Smith fidgeted and fumed at the
rent paid to the railway companies, and at the
cost of providing frames for advertisements, of
printing, agents, and bill-posters. But young
Smith's sagacious confidence enabled him to
overcome all opposition, and in 1854 the balance-
sheet of this branch showed a slight profit
on the year's transactions, with prospects of indefinite improvement. The expenses during
that year amounted to £9800 (including £7100
paid as rent to the railway companies), the receipts came to £9930, producing a net profit of
£130. But the corner had been turned, the
future was big with indefinite increase, and the
anxiety caused by the absorption of so much
capital was once and for all at an end.

The business in 1854 thus consisted of three
great branches, each in process of swift and sometimes sudden expansion—the newspaper agency,
under direct control of the younger Smith; the
bookstall trade, managed by Mr Sandifer; and

the railway advertisement department, under Messrs Moore and Small. A fourth branch, hardly less important than the others, was to be added in the course of a few years; but before alluding further to that, it may be instructive to examine into the effect all this incessant work, and the splendid success attending upon it, had upon the mind and habits of one whose early inclination had been for a very different sphere of action.

Had the press and strain of business, and the excitement of fortunate enterprise, driven from his thoughts those subjects upon which, as a youth, he had pondered so deeply and constantly? Had the flush of achievement and the seduction of increasing gains blotted out those higher views, or loosened the strict principles which guided him into manhood? By no means. It is only necessary to turn over some of the letters written by Smith at this period, and especially the private notes (they are not consecutive enough to amount to a journal), intended for no eye but his own, to be convinced that he was still deeply devout, and concerned far more about another and better world than he was about the affairs of this one.

To read his character aright—to learn that a tradesman may be sagacious, industrious, ambitious, and successful, and yet never lose sight of the object set before him by a simple unfailing faith—it is necessary to quote a few sentences showing the matters upon which his mind, as soon as he was released from business, continually revolved. His sister Augusta was always a favourite correspondent, and the letters he addressed to her while he was at school were the first of a series which extended through his life till within a few weeks of its close. Here is part of one written in pencil during a journey to Dublin.

3. 3. '53·

MY DEAR GUSSY,—I am flying along the London and North-Western by Express Train somewhere near Tring at this moment, probably near Rugby before I have done. . . . Father wishes me to stay in Dublin a fortnight, but I don't think I ought to be away from home more than three days at the outside, and I therefore think of leaving Dublin again on Friday, even if I have to return next week.[1] I have not told him so, because it is best to let him think he is having his way. Although in really good health, as far as I can see—and you know I have as nervous a disposition with regard to him as any one can have—he chafes more under the small annoyances of business, so as to become nervously irritated beyond anything I ever remember, giving three people notice to leave in one day, and suchlike things; but he is most kind and considerate to me. Still all this occasions

---

[1] Messrs Smith & Son had at this time a branch office in Dublin.

anxiety to me, and I am almost afraid of going away, not knowing what violent changes may take place in my absence, in his desire to get rid of the business. I find, too, that his excitement is much greater when I am away, and increases in proportion to the length of time, as everything comes before him. . . . I trust Providence, who makes a way for us in the greatest difficulties, will make our way straight before us. If it were not for the perfect confidence I feel that this *must* be so—cannot be otherwise—I should sometimes be very unhappy; for with the positive certainty of great changes impending, I know not what may be the next step I ought to take.

I sometimes feel that Father's happiness in his later days, and the comfort of the family, depend on me, and then I feel and know I am absolutely blind, and can really do nothing whatever of my own judgment; but I know also that if I, and we all, desire absolutely and without reservation to be guided aright, that guidance will be granted to us, and we need not and ought not to fear or doubt in the darkest night of uncertainty and human difficulty. I do sometimes tremble lest I should fail to do a man's part in the order of God's providence, for although He orders, guides, and directs, there is still the responsibility of action with us after all, and therefore I pray that my eyes may be opened to comprehend what He would have me to do, and I am assured that a way and means and strength will be given for any and every occasion. The confidence that all things are absolutely right, however painful and difficult now, turns what would otherwise be troubles into sources of thankfulness—so I feel of all the unsettled circumstances of the past and present. They are necessary to some good and right end, if we (for I believe there is a power in Man to thwart Providence) will have it so.

I have gone on writing this without quite intending it, just as I would talk with you; . . . but there is solid pleasure in the conviction that we are of one mind in these things: wherever we are, we can think of each other, and we can pray that we may each, individually and as one family, be directed in all things by a wisdom which can do no wrong, and whose purposes are, I entirely believe, both present and future happiness with regard to us. Do not think I am at all low or sad. With the exception of very transient occasions, I never felt greater reason for cheerfulness.

All this was written *currente stylo*—evidently without premeditation or reconsideration, for there is hardly a word altered from first to last. It is the genuine, spontaneous expression of the writer's meditation — unadulterated communion with a sister to whom he was accustomed to talk and write without reserve. There may be some readers, impatient of religious *épanchement*, disposed to smile at the simple faith so openly confessed; but even to these, if they have any desire to understand the man, it is necessary to know what he thought of, and how he expressed it.

Journals are, as a rule, tainted with the suspicion of self-consciousness: one fancies that the diarist harbours, and does not shrink from the prospect of ultimate, though perhaps posthumous, publicity. Nevertheless, there is in Smith's journals something so apart from vainglory—so much in contrast with his daily arena of prosperous, bustling commerce—that a few extracts must be made from these time-stained pages.

Saturday, March 17, 1855.— . . . I know the Sin which most easily besets me, and have now solemnly vowed never again to give way to it, even by thought and by desire, and I register this my resolve, made, not in my own strength, but in humble dependence on one who is able to save all who trust in him, and who did not teach his disciples to say in vain, "lead us not into temptation, but deliver us from evil." . . .

Monday, March 19.— . . . The world has had the dominion in its cares and anxieties. I have also been depressed and not sufficiently trustful for my future domestic life. It is very difficult for man to draw the line between the intelligent exercise of the personal duties and responsibilities devolving upon him—his own part in working out the designs of Providence and that anxious care which becomes Sin. Let me remember the word— "being careful for nothing, but in everything by prayer and supplication, with thanksgiving, let your requests be made known unto God, and the *peace* of God *shall* keep your hearts," &c.

Tuesday, April 10.—A day of many mercies and of one trial; but I will praise God for all his mercies, and pray to him for more, and I shall not be disappointed, for none ever asked in faith and was sent empty away. The Lord increase my faith and enable me to pray always. . . .

Thursday, April 12.—I have passed through a day of much care and anxiety and occupation. It has also been marked by a step which may affect my future life. Oh that I could more entirely trust in Him who has the disposing of events, who ordereth all things well; but I deplore for myself that· depression as to things material and temporal w^h arises from a want of trust in Him who ruleth. May I trust in him with all my heart, and possess the Peace which passeth all understanding! . . .

Monday, April 16.—I am thankful that I have not been so desponding to-day as I have been on former days, but, on the other hand, I am aware of ideas and schemes within me which may not proceed so entirely from a desire to render glory to my God as they ought to do. I pray again that he may direct me in all my ways, for no earthly good can be less than evil—unless it be blessed by Him.

Enough! we have in these passages, taken at random from among much else of similar tenor, not the sentimental lucubrations of a self-conscious idler or the vague apprehensions of a morbid-minded youth (Smith at this time was thirty), but the key-note of a laborious useful life, which, though far from purposeless in material concerns or wanting in sympathy for fellow-men, was directed resolutely yet humbly towards a lofty and distant goal. The sceptic, even if he does not envy the confidence, cannot impugn the manliness of this simple faith, nor doubt its sincerity; while he who shares it, however imperfectly, must be encouraged by the proof given that there is nothing to prevent one

who is an earnest and anxious Christian being
also a good man of business and a citizen of the
world.

But, after all, however pious, and even blame-
less, may be the private life of an individual—
however wisely he may moralise, and however constantly he may ponder on motives of conduct—
however strict may be his observance of religious
ordinances, he cannot but earn mistrust unless
the effect of it all can be clearly traced in his
worldly action. So it is natural that one should
scrutinise closely the extent to which the principles, so clearly and constantly professed in the
family and congregations, moulded the conduct of
the Smiths in their business. It was marked
very plainly, indeed ; and through all the years
which have passed since the time described, the
character and regulation of the house have been
in consistency with the profession of its founder.
Men in the employment speak enthusiastically of
the justice, consideration, and liberality with
which they have always been treated ; but these
virtues are no monopoly of Christians, still less of
strict Methodists, or members of the Church of
England. The point on which more importance
is laid by these bodies than by any other section
of the Church, except, perhaps, the Presbyterian
Church of Scotland, is the observance of the

Lord's Day. Men may hold what views they please about the best means of keeping it holy; each one may hear the voice of his own con- science, if he listens for it, telling what it is right to do for that end, and what it is wrong not to refrain from doing. But all men would agree, and would be just in agreeing, in condemnation of those who, holding certain observances to be necessary or conducive to their own salvation, should call upon men for service incompatible with their respecting the same observances.

It has always been a rule in Smith & Son's that no work should be done on Sundays. To this rule there is on record only a single excep- tion. This occurred in September 1855, shortly after the battle of Alma : the despatches con- taining the nominal list of killed and wounded arrived late on Saturday night, and after consulta- tion with his father, young Smith called upon the staff to sacrifice their Sunday rest in order that special supplements might be distributed in Lon- don and the provinces.

In contrast to this incident, and to show that this was done, not to enhance the reputation of the firm or to conciliate customers, but to put a speedy end to the doubts, fears, and— alas !—to the hopes of many distracted families, it is only necessary to mention another incident which happened some years later.   Messrs Smith received a command to supply one of the Royal Family with newspapers.   Among other journals on the list accompanying the command was the 'Observer,' published then, as now, on Sunday morning.   The command was complied with, but it was explained that, as Sunday work was contrary to the rules of the firm, the 'Observer' could not be supplied.   This was followed by a visit from an indignant official, who seemed at a loss to understand how a regulation of a firm of news-agents could stand in the way of a Royal command; but even the threat of withdrawal of the whole order did not avail to cause a departure from the rules of the house. To this day, though Sunday papers have in the meantime multiplied many times, and are, moreover, a peculiarly popular form of literature, those who desire them have to obtain them elsewhere than from Smith's agents.

The last branch of the business of Smith & Son which remains to be described took its rise, not unnaturally, out of the bookstall business, which, before 1862, had been established on well-nigh every important line of railway in England, and in the demand made by people living in remote rural districts for a supply of books on loan. This was some years after old Mr Smith had retired from the business, which he did about 1858, and the active partners, consisting of his son and Mr Lethbridge, felt no inclination for an experiment which, while it called for a heavy capital expenditure, did not promise a very remunerative return. However, it was always a leading principle with the younger Smith [1] that when any section of the public expressed a desire for the kind of literature it was his business to supply, and it was in the power of the firm to comply with it without hazard of serious loss, it was their duty to make the endeavour, even should the prospect of gain be doubtful. Negotiations, accordingly, were set on foot with that firm which held the same pre-eminence in the circulating and lending library business as Smith & Son did in that of news-agency and bookstalls, with the view of acting as agents for Messrs Mudie in such provincial towns as were in want of a supply. But the negotiations came to nothing, and the result was the foundation of Smith & Son's circulating library.

Whatever may have been the misgivings in Smith's own mind about this new venture, once

---

[1] From this point, when the elder Smith disappears from active life, it will be unnecessary to use terms to distinguish between father and son. When "Smith" is spoken of in future, it will be the son who is indicated.

he had made up his mind to it, he did not allow them to interfere with the liberal investment of capital. To one long connected with the house, who expressed doubts as to the prudence of risking so much, Smith remarked : " God blesses all I touch. I think there must be some truth in the motto on my father's seal — *Deo non fortunâ fretus.*" [1]

The enterprise has proved successful, not, indeed, in the extraordinary degree attained by the other branches of the business, for it is still the least remunerative department ; but Mr Faux, who presides over it, has charge of the circulation of more than 300,000 volumes.

It had always been one of Smith's rules not to have the smallest property in any publication. He held it important to be free to deal impartially with every publishing house, just as in the early days of bookstalls he had avoided bringing himself into competition with local tradesmen, but preferred to act in concurrence with them,— often, as has been shown, being in a position to relieve them of a business which they were carrying on at a loss. This was the origin of the establishment of the branches in Birmingham, Liverpool, and Manchester. But a time came when the supply of bookstall literature ran

[1] "Freighted not by fortune but by God."

low; Murray's "Traveller's Library" was proving rather heavy for the tastes of those it was chiefly designed to attract; there was a dearth of harmless, yet lively publications; the quality of cheapness in novels had hitherto been inseparable from that of nastiness, or, at least, of worthlessness : the receipts from the bookstalls, so brilliant at first, began to show a decline; something had to be done to restore their popularity. A decided step was taken, which, for the first time, enabled people to buy the best romances at a trifling cost. The copyright of Lever's novels was acquired by Smith & Son; Mr Sandifer, the manager of the bookstall department, was commissioned to buy paper, contract for printing, receive designs for covers, and, in short, undertake all the necessary steps in setting out on a heavy publishing venture. But, inasmuch as the firm were only concerned to supply a want felt by a peculiar class of customers—the travelling public—and as they did not wish to engage in competition with established firms,—these books were issued by arrangement with Messrs Chapman & Hall, whose name, and not that of Smith & Son, appeared on the titles.

The success of the venture was immediate and unmistakable. A new vein had been struck; the copyrights of other authors were acquired, and

Sandifer's enthusiasm knew no bounds as the steam-presses flew and the well-known "yellow-backed novels" multiplied in the land. The profits were immense : the books sold off as fast as they could be printed at 2s. a-piece, and the cost of production was only 9d.

But Smith did not feel happy about all the consequences of this splendidly successful enterprise. The cheap novels had taken better than he had either expected or intended ; they were driving other works off the stalls. It was the object, of course, of every clerk, seeing that he received commissions on sales, to give the most saleable books the preference, and one morning Smith stood on the platform at Rugby in mournful contemplation of the effects of a revolution which he himself had created. The bookstall at that station was a coruscation of yellow novels and white newspapers ; volumes of essays, secular and religious, travels, science, poetry—all were thrust into odd corners or out of sight, for the public would have nothing but fiction. Smith sadly shook his head, but, true to his principles, would not discourage the clerk in charge by expressing any distrust of his discretion : the management of the stall had been committed to him, and he must not be interfered with.

Messrs Ward & Lock were the next firm to

come upon this field of enterprise, and as soon as they and others proved able to conduct the business successfully, Smith felt that his mission in that respect had been accomplished—namely, the stimulation of a supply of cheap and sound literature—and the issue of these works was stopped. The copyrights acquired by the firm were sold in 1883 for £10,000.

The scale to which the business of Messrs W. H. Smith & Son has grown at the present time has made it necessary to acquire much of the adjoining ground. The frontage is still in the Strand, but the counting-house and offices are at the back in a splendid new range of buildings, having their entrance in Arundel Street. Although Mr W. H. Smith retired from active partnership in 1877, he continued to take a warm interest in the proceedings of the firm and the welfare of their *employés* down to the close of his life, but he was not permitted to see the completion of the new buildings. The book department keeps up the supply for the railway bookstalls, and may be seen at its busiest at the close of each month, when the magazines come out. The lending department contains, as has been said, upwards of 300,000 volumes in circulation. The workshops for making bookstalls and frames for railway-station advertisements are in Water Street. It is a singular part of the system that all damaged or dilapidated bookstalls, even in remote parts of the country, are packed up and sent here for repair.

In Water Street also are the extensive stables, kept with the regularity and little short of the discipline of a cavalry barracks. Here stand between fifty and sixty horses for the service of the red newspaper carts, and the bloom on their coats speaks plainly to good condition and careful grooming. At the entrance to the yard hangs the drivers' rolster, showing the date and hour when each man comes on duty. The printing-house, where the railway advertisements are prepared, is at some distance off, in Fetter Lane.

Of all the busy scenes in busy London, there is none more brisk and orderly than that which may be witnessed any morning, Sundays excepted, throughout the year in the packing department of 186 Strand. On the first four working days in the week, when there is not much except the dailies to deal with, work begins shortly after 3 A.M.; but on Fridays and Saturdays the pressure is increased by the weeklies, and then the start is made an hour earlier. Few of those who know the Strand and Fleet Street only in the hours when the side-pavements are hidden with swarms of busy men, and the thoroughfare is blocked with vehicles, can have formed any idea of their aspect at daybreak in summer, or imagine the singular beauty of the view eastward from a point, say, opposite 160 Fleet Street. The perspective of varied house-fronts on either side converges on St Paul's Cathedral, a shapely, soft - toned mass against the pale sky; and looking westward from the Law Courts, the eye surveys a scene, not so impressive or harmoniously composed as the other, yet far redeemed from commonplace by the quaint churches of St Clement Danes and St Mary-le-Strand, and that block of houses, long threatened by the plans of the city improver, which shuts out Holywell Street from the Strand. Save a policeman or two, and here and there a belated wanderer creeping home, there is not a human being in sight, till, as the bells ring out half-past two, the first of Smith & Son's well-known scarlet carts comes clattering down the narrow thoroughfare laden with piles of the 'Illustrated,' the 'Queen,' or some other great weekly journal. This is followed by others, till, at three o'clock, the street is crowded with vehicles, each bringing its load of "raw papers" to be carried into the office and sorted into parcels for the country.

Inside matters present an appearance in which the casual visitor might, in default of a clue, despair of tracing either method or motive. The place is like an ant-hill; men are running about in every direction carrying bundles on their shoulders, as aimlessly to all appearance, and as ceaselessly, as ants do their white pupæ when something has disturbed them. Sometimes they pause to swallow a mug of excellent coffee, which, with bread and butter, is supplied for the workers. But the simplicity of the system is apparent once it is explained. A stream of bundle-bearers comes in from the street, each tossing down his parcel on a large table on the right side of the hall ; these are " raw papers "—papers, that is to say, as they come from the publishing office. Then each of the parcels for the country is passed round, checked by a list, and receives its proper contents, which are again checked before the parcel is sent forward to be packed. Watching the packers, one is impressed not only by their swiftness and dexterity — for an inexperienced hand would find it a very difficult matter to tie up securely in a single sheet of paper a parcel weighing 50 or 60 lb., composed of newspapers of various size, shape, and substance—but also by the amount of knocking about these apparently fragile parcels afterwards endure with impunity.

One part of the secret is the excellence of the stout twine used, and the peculiar slip-knot employed, which enables the packer to draw the cord almost as tightly as if by machinery. The amount of this twine used is prodigious: in the twelve months of 1892 the consumption was 9,264,410 yards, or 5271 miles (at the rate, that is, of about 100 miles

Knot used in tying parcels of newspapers.

a-week), weighing over 59 tons. The parcels, when finished, are carried or wheeled out to the street, packed into vans, and driven off to the different railway stations.

One very remarkable feature in this busy scene is the absence of noise. No loud or hasty accents of command are heard. Mr Monger, the head of this department, who has been connected with it for forty years, moves quietly through the throng; any instructions he has to give are made in a gentle, almost confidential tone; expostulation or altercation seem quite unknown;

the contents of each parcel as it is brought in or
sent out are announced by the bearer ; good humour and goodwill seem to be in the atmosphere.

It is pleasant to stand and watch the work on
a balmy summer morning, when the cool air flows
in through the open doors, and the electric lights
are quenched by the broadening day ; but it is
far otherwise on some mornings in winter. Rain,
cold, and, above all, fog, turn this early work into
a test of endurance, and the thickest clothes will
not suffice to neutralise the discomfort of the
piercing draughts.

There is an archaic survival in the packing-hall
of one of the elder Smith's regulations : the clock
is always kept five minutes fast ; but many a
householder can testify to the futility of this
shallow device. Of course the effect upon punctuality is purely negative, and it is long practice
and strict discipline which has given to Smith &
Son's drivers the faculty of almost unerring precision in catching trains. At these early hours
the streets are clear of traffic, and the men are
able to calculate to a nicety the time required ;
so that, while it very rarely happens that a train
is missed, neither is there any time lost at the
stations.

At four o'clock Smith's vans begin to arrive
at the Strand house from the various offices of
the dailies, bearing mountains of ' Standards,'

'Daily News,' 'Daily Telegraphs,' &c., which are treated in the same way as the weeklies. The 'Times' is now, as of old, the latest to go to press and the latest in arrival.

The necessity for punctuality in the delivery of dailies is, of course, much, more imperious than in that of weeklies. A slight hitch or accident in one of the huge printing-presses, which, with deafening roar, are vomiting forth folded sheets as fast as men can carry them away, might cause a failure in the supply or a glut at the Strand office or the railway stations, which would dislocate the whole morning's work. Consequently Messrs Smith & Son have a man at each of the great newspaper offices, superintending the loading of carts and the despatch of papers to the different packing-places. For only part of the work of packing dailies goes on at the Strand. Smith's carts carry the newspapers direct from the printing offices to the railway stations, at some of which, as at Paddington and King's Cross, the packing is done in rooms provided for the purpose, or, as at Waterloo Station, on the platform; while on other lines, such as the London and North-Western and Midland, the raw papers are loaded into railway vans, and the sorting and packing is accomplished by Smith's men during the journey.

Sometimes it seems to the bystander as if, say, the 5.15 A.M. newspaper train from Euston *must* be despatched without some of its load. The minute-hand of the clock is within a few seconds of the quarter past, and the 'Times' has not arrived. The signal to start will be given directly—Manchester, Liverpool, all the North, must do without their 'Times' till mid-day. Suddenly a cry is heard—" The 'Times'!" a passage is cleared on the platform, a rush of barrows comes round the corner, and the last bundle is flung into the van as the train moves off.

Compare this with the experience of an old *employé* of the firm, Mr Elliman, who died not many years ago. In the early days of the business the daily papers were not published in time for the morning mails, but were despatched by the evening post. Old Mr Smith saw the inconvenience of this arrangement to his country customers, so it became Elliman's daily duty to take in hand the entire supply of the 'Times' for Manchester and Liverpool round to the starting-place in John Street, Adelphi. Owing to delay in publication, it would sometimes happen that he missed the coach, whereupon he had to hurry up to try and catch it at the Angel, Islington; if he missed it there, he had to saddle a horse and gallop after it to the change at Colney. His orders were to get the paper into the country at all hazards, and it even happened more than once that he had to pursue it as far as Birmingham. How could it pay the firm, it may be asked, to be at such expense in the delivery of a handful of newspapers? Well, it was by energy such as this that old Mr Smith secured the pre-eminence over all other newspaper agents.[1]

To illustrate the prodigious development of the business started on so humble a scale by Mr Smith, senior, there may be given here the summary of business done in the newspaper trade in the Strand office of W. H. Smith & Son, during a single day of the present year, Tuesday, February 14, 1893. It was, it is true, an exceptionally heavy day, owing to the demand caused by Mr Gladstone having on the previous night introduced his Home Rule Bill.

Total number of papers despatched	374,218
Quires	14,393
Weight . .	44 tons 0 cwt. 2 qrs.

The average weight of newspapers despatched on a Tuesday morning is about 35 tons. The extra

---

[1] During the present year (1893) an Austrian gentleman requested permission, which was readily granted him, to inspect the premises and proceedings of Messrs W. H. Smith & Son, as he desired to start a similar business in his own country. He seemed a little disheartened when he learned through what humble and unpromising ways the ascent to such a vast business had been made.

supply on account of the Home Rule Bill therefore amounted to

Copies of newspapers .	75,140
Quires . . .	2,890
Weight . .	9 tons 7 cwt. 1 qr.

The firm continued the endeavour to be "first
on the road" long after the establishment of the
railway system. The 'Newcastle Journal' for
February 26, 1848, contains the following statement :—

A special newspaper train was run by Messrs W. H.
Smith & Son from Euston to Glasgow *via* York and Newcastle on February 19. It made the journey of 472½
miles in 10 hours and 22 minutes: detentions amounted
to 50 minutes, making the actual travelling 9 hours and
32 minutes, being at the rate of 50 miles an hour. It
reached Glasgow two hours before the mails which left
London the previous evening. It left Euston at 5.35 A.M.,
reached Edinburgh at 2.55 P.M., and Glasgow 3.59 P.M.
Lord John Russell's financial statement was the exciting
topic reported in the papers on the occasion.

One other department of this establishment—
the postal—is also in full work during the small
hours. The work seems small in bulk compared
with the despatch of railway parcels ; but many
busy hands are at work—folding, pasting, wrap-
ping—many thousands of newspapers are thus
despatched, and the precision with which the addresses require to be kept involves an immense

amount of patient attention. These addresses are all printed in Water Street, and preserved in proof-books, of which there are no less than fifty-six requiring to be gone through carefully every day. If a customer writes directing the discontinuance of a journal which he has been receiving, and the address is not at once removed from the proof-book, it may be that the newspaper will continue to go to him for years at the expense of the firm. One such instance was lately discovered, where the ' Field ' had been sent to some one in the country for more than twenty years after he had countermanded it.

It is well remembered by men still employed in the business how, when the younger Smith entered the firm, he excelled in this department, and had the reputation of being only second to his father in dexterity of folding papers for the post.

Surgit amari —— there is a source of bitterness among the postal hands here. The embossed postage on the newspaper covers had, for many years, the name of Messrs W. H. Smith & Son tastefully woven round it in a wreath, and the staff were proud of this distinction, which was shared by no other firm. When the late Mr Cecil Raikes became Postmaster-General, he laid his veto on the continuance of this custom, which had forthwith to be discontinued.   Mr Smith, at that time First Lord of the Treasury, could of course offer no remonstrance against his colleague's scrupulousness. If it had been an enemy that had done this—but it was the act of a Conservative minister!

There is a scrap-book kept in the office containing some literary curiosities — flotsam and jetsam of the long history of the firm.   One of these is an envelope, on which the London postmark shows the date 1864, and the only indication of its destination is contained in the cryptogram—

thisel log,

near abseelengly.

It almost implies that the Post-office officials were gifted with second-sight or thought-reading power, which enabled them to convey this missive to

Cecil Lodge,

near Abbots Langley,

where Mr Smith resided at that time.
' Another envelope, dated 1888, is addressed to

Mr W. H. Smith,

The Stationer,

Downing Street,

London.

CHAPTER IV.

1855-1865.

SMITH IS ELECTED TO METROPOLITAN BOARD OF WORKS—HIS MARRIAGE IN 1858 TO MRS LEACH — OLD MR SMITH RETIRES FROM BUSINESS—PHILANTHROPIC WORK—THE BISHOP OF LONDON'S FUND—FRIENDSHIP WITH LORD SANDON—SMITH CONTEMPLATES STANDING AS A LIBERAL FOR BOSTON—AND FOR EXETER—IS BLACKBALLED FOR REFORM CLUB—BECOMES CONSERVATIVE CANDIDATE FOR WESTMINSTER—HIS ADDRESS TO THE ELECTORS—THE ELECTION—AND ITS RESULT.

SMITH's first connection with public business seems to have been in 1855, when he was elected a member of the Metropolitan Board of Works. But before this date he had entered upon undertakings quite disconnected with his professional work in the Strand, and, among other duties, he performed those of a member of the managing committee of King's College Hospital from 1849 onwards. Except his autumn holidays, which were generally spent abroad, he allowed nothing to interfere with the routine of attendance in the Strand, and was always ready to devote such intervals of leisure as it afforded to useful or philanthropic schemes. His duties in connection with King's College Hospital brought him acquainted with Mr Robert Cheere, one of those most in the management of that institution, and it was that gentleman who introduced him to the family of Mr Danvers, who had been clerk to the council of the Duchy of Lancaster since the days of George IV. Mr Danvers had several daughters. Smith was received on friendly terms by the Danvers family; and a friend of his, Mr Auber Leach, who held an appointment in the old India House, used also to visit them in Lancaster Place, and, becoming engaged to Miss Emily Danvers, married her in 1854. Miss Emily Danvers and her younger sister were married on the same day in the Chapel of the Savoy. But the wedded life of the elder sister was tragically short, for Mr Leach died in January 1855. The young widow then returned to live with her parents in Lancaster Place, where her baby, a girl,[1] was born.

Smith continued on most friendly terms with the Danvers family, and, as time went on, it became evident that he was much more susceptible to the attractions of Mrs Leach than

[1] Now the Hon. Mrs Codrington, widow of Rear-Admiral Codrington.

to those of her unmarried sisters. In short, it soon appeared, not only to himself but to others, that he was becoming deeply attached to the young widow. Never was there a more complete refutation of the seer's mournful pronouncement in 'A Midsummer Night's Dream' :—

> " Ah me! for aught that ever I could read,
> Could ever hear by tale or history,
> The course of true love never did run smooth :
> But either it was different in blood,
> Or else misgraffed in respect of years,
> Or else it stood upon the choice of friends ;
> Or, if there were a sympathy in choice,
> War, death, or sickness did lay siege to it,
> Making it momentary as a sound,
> Swift as a shadow, short as any dream,
> Brief as the lightning in the collied night,
> That in a spleen enfolds both heaven and earth,
> And ere a man hath power to say ' Behold ! '
> The jaws of darkness do devour it up ;
> So quick bright things come to confusion."

Smith's life had hitherto been useful, dutiful, and successful; it had been warmed with the steady glow of domestic affection, but it had also been almost painfully laborious and lacking in that relief which can only be conferred by something more ardent than sisterly affection— something more inspiring than devotion to aged parents. It was now to receive the complement essential to happy human circumstance ; and in winning the affection of Mrs Leach, Smith achieved the beginning of what proved an enduring and— if one may venture to pass judgment on such a sacred tie—a perfect union. Henceforward, in prosperity or anxiety, in health or sickness, in happiness or in sorrow, all his hopes were to be shared, his cares lightened, his projects aided, by the presence in his home of one to whom he never failed to turn for counsel. There are some things too deeply hallowed to be treated of on printed page, and of these are the letters which, during three-and-thirty years, passed between this husband and wife ; but those who only knew him in business or in public affairs can form no true estimate of Smith's character unless they take account of the love he bore his wife, which this correspondence shows to have been ever growing warmer and more impatient of separation till his time on earth was accomplished.

.The happy conclusion of the courtship is told in a brief note to his sister :—

STRAND, *Feb.* 25, 1858.

DEAR GUSSY,—All right. It is done for ever. Come and help me to buy the ring.—Ever your affectionate
WM.

Smith would have been untrue to his character had he concealed the serious strain that ran through all his happiness. On returning from a

visit to his betrothed, then staying with some
friends at Bedford, a few days after their engagement, he wrote to her :—

March 4, 1858.—On my way up in the train I could not
help thinking over the change that has taken place in my
prospects during the last few days, and then I came to
think of myself and to fear that I had not been sufficiently
ingenuous with you.   There are some points in my character which I am not afraid to tell you of, because you
love me enough to try to do me good, and even to love me
through them all; but you ought to know them, that your
prayers may help me, and that your influence may be ex-
erted to correct them.   Very likely I do not perceive the
worst myself, but I know this.   I have not the strong
determination to do always that which is right, by God's
help, which I admired so much in Auber, and which I see
in so many men around me.   I am inclined to be easy
with myself—just as a man who would postpone a duty
because it is an unpleasant one, and the opportunity for
performing it passes altogether, and I very often neglect
to do a thing I ought to do because it is unpleasant and
would pain one to do it.

In good truth, in some things I have really a *weak*
character, and I want you to be the means of strengthening it, and will do so a great deal more, for although it is
one of my failings to desire the good opinion of the world
at large, I must be true and transparent to you, for my
own soul's sake and for *our* happiness in this world as
well as in the next.

The wedding took place in April of the same
year.   Before this event, old Mr Smith had

finally retired from active business, and his son
was practically head of the firm—very much, it
must be admitted, to the comfort of all parties;
for it had grown to dimensions far beyond the
capacity of its founder, whose health, moreover,
had failed so far as to make him a serious hindrance in the transaction of important details.
Neither the happiness he had found in marriage
nor the increased responsibility he had to undertake in the business prevailed to diminish the
son's dutiful anxiety on his father's account.
His letters are full of directions to his sisters
about what is to be done for the old gentleman's
comfort :—

I would gladly [he wrote to Miss Augusta Smith in
December 1858] take upon my shoulders the house at
Bournemouth, if he fancied the change; or he might come
somewhere eastward, to Worthing or St Leonards, if he
fancied the change, which are both warm. Don't talk to
him about anything *you* consider impracticable, but think
over what I have said, and then write to me. Only
remember that expense on Father's account is no consideration with me, and if he disliked spending the money,
I would willingly incur ANY cost or responsibility myself
that you thought would add to his comfort or safety.

It was not only in concern for his father that
Smith showed that the new source of happiness
he had found was not to quench the warmth of

domestic ties. To the same sister he wrote after his engagement :—

> MY DEAREST GUSSY,—Not less dear that I have found one whom I can love with a different and—you won't grudge her—a stronger affection. Indeed I am sensible already of the fact that love begets love even for those who were much loved before. One's capacity is increased —but I must not go on, or the paper will be exhausted with that which may perhaps appear foolishness to some.

Life went smoothly, if uneventfully, with the Smiths for some years after their marriage. They lived in Hyde Park Street ; he became more and more occupied in educational, ecclesiastical, and philanthropic work. At a meeting held at the Bishop of London's Palace in 1861, Smith was first brought into acquaintance with Lord Sandon, at that time member for Liverpool—now Earl of Harrowby—who describes him as being then a man of very taking appearance, with very dark hair and bright eyes, and a calm and resolute look. At this meeting the Bishop of London's Fund was first set on foot ; Lord Sandon moved, and Smith seconded, the chief resolution. An inner working committee was formed, of which Lord Sandon was appointed chairman, and on which, among others, Smith had as colleagues Mr John Talbot,[1] the Rev. Canon Rowsell, Lord

[1] Now M.P. for Oxford University.

Radstock, Mr John Murray, the publisher, the Rev. W. S. Maclagan,[1] the Rev. J. W. Bardsley,[2] the Rev. F. Blomfield,[3] Mr J. A. Shaw Stewart, and Mr Redmayne of Bond Street. Mr G. H. Croad, who is now Secretary to the London School Board, joined this committee in 1866. Under this committee London was divided into districts—Smith having charge, as was fitting, over that of the Strand, in conjunction with the Rev. J. W. Bardsley. He as well as the other members of committee were oppressed with concern on account of the dreadful condition of the dwellings of London poor, which, though they may still be judged far short of what they ought to be, were at that time in a state calling far more urgently for reform.

This common work, in which they were associated for five years, brought about a close intimacy between Smith and Lord Sandon, which was to ripen into a lifelong friendship. Twenty years later, when, in 1882, Sandon left the House of Commons to take his seat in the House of Lords, he wrote to Smith, referring to this friendship as—

One of the charms of my public life, which has only

---

[1] Now Archbishop of York.   [2] Now Bishop of Carlisle.
[3] Now Bishop of Colchester.

strengthened under the strain of business and the advance
of years, and must now become more and more precious
to my heart as time goes on.   An intercourse such as
ours, of more than twenty years, with a constant similarity of aim, unbroken by a single disagreement, and of
those who, while working together on the same public
platform, have enjoyed the confidence of an unreserved
private friendship, has certainly been one of the blessings of my life.   I can only say—long may it continue!
though, to my bitter regret, we cannot sit together any
longer on the well-known benches.

While he lived in the parish of St John's,
Paddington, Smith took an active part in the
promotion of church and school matters.   The
Rev. Sir Emilius Laurie, at that time rector of
St John's, has furnished the following notes of
the benefit derived by the parish from Smith's
eager liberality :—

In Mr Smith I found a model parishioner—wise in
counsel, generous in all his impulses, hearty in his support
of all good work.   St John's parish, at the commencement
of my incumbency, was hardly up to date.   The church
itself, though a modern one, needed reconstruction, if not
rebuilding; and the very insufficient school-buildings were
held only under a yearly tenancy, liable to be put an end to
at any time on the usual notice.   In the somewhat serious
work of providing new schools in a crowded district, Mr
Smith's aid was simply invaluable.   The £500 subscrip-
tion was the least of the benefits conferred, though in
raising £12,000 for site and building, without any external
help, such assistance was not to be despised.   What struck

me most, however, was the readiness with which, amidst
the engrossing calls of public life, Mr Smith gave his full
attention to every question of detail, the tact with which
he dealt with opposition, and the free hand with which he
overcame difficulties which from time to time arose.   An
example of this occurred in the course of the rebuilding.
The new schools obstructed some ancient lights in two
adjoining houses.   The owner objected, and threatened
legal proceedings, but expressed his willingness to sell.
The law was against us ; so, alas ! were the figures—for the
price asked was high. Mr Smith stepped in and bought
the houses, and would have bought half the parish, I
believe, rather than leave a good work undone.

Mr Smith was prepared also to deal on a still larger
scale with the church.   Occupying, as he said, one of the
finest sites in London, it was poor in architecture, inconvenient and ill-ordered in its internal arrangements.   Mr
Smith thought that a church in such a position should
cost not less than £30,000, and towards this he offered to
give £20,000.   Plans were prepared by Sir F. Blomfield,
but it was found that, although built upon the Bishop of
London's estate, no room had been left for enlargement, and
we had to content ourselves with a modest reconstruction,
at a cost of £7000, leaving Mr Smith's benevolent donation
free for parishes in which the need was greater than at
St John's. . . . The Church of England owes, I believe,
much to Mr Smith.   How much he gave to it was known
only to himself. ·

It is a common complaint that the House of
Commons is not now, and has not been for at
least a generation, what it used to be under a
restricted franchise.   To listen to the talk of

some people might dispose one to the uncomfortable belief that political integrity evaporated with the abolition of pocket boroughs, that statesmanship languished when sinecures began to be extinguished, and totally disappeared with the establishment of household suffrage, and that public spirit — all powerful when the majority of the public had no voice in the direction of public affairs—took flight on the appearance of bloated registers. The divine right of those who have never felt the pinch of hunger nor, save as the direct consequence of their own folly, the gnawing anguish of pecuniary care, to govern those who live by toil of hand or brain, was, in the belief of people yet living, the Palladium of our liberty. To persons of this creed it may be conceded that, with the extension of popular rights, the risk of social oppression has been exchanged for a greater national hazard. Bacon professed his distaste "for this word 'people,'" and Carlyle wrote scathingly of the "collective wisdom of individual ignorances"; but neither they, nor any other thoughtful seer, thought that because power was passing out of the hands of a few into those of the many, there was any cause, for those who had time to spare from their private anxieties, to relax watchfulness

over the destiny of the kingdom, or to refrain
from manly effort to lead their fellow-countrymen in the paths of prosperity and peace. The
method of statecraft has changed with the
broadening of the constitution, but the object
remains the same. As Mr Nicholl, writing of
the Government of Queen Elizabeth, puts it
with a degree of frankness, not brutal, but
sternly masculine, " Much must be allowed to
the fashion of a time when it was as customary
to flatter monarchs as it now is to juggle mobs." [1]
Plus ça change, plus c'est la même chose—the
same qualities of patience, foresight, knowledge
of men in the past and in the present, courage
in yielding as well as in holding back, which,
under the old order, had placed certain individuals in the front rank of statesmen, must
be looked for in those to whom the guidance of
affairs should be intrusted in the future.

 -The perspective of years shuts out of view all
but the most conspicuous characters ; looking
back from one end of a century to the other,
one discerns only the loftiest personalities—the
Pitts, the Foxes, the Burkes ; the crowd of
lesser men have sunk out of view, and with
them has disappeared the memory of all that
was narrow, timid, mean, and selfish in their
careers. And so the impression, — founded on

[1] Life of Bacon, vol. i. p. 67.

a sentiment as old as — nay, far older than
Horace's

> " Ætas parentum pejor avis tulit
> Nos nequiores,"—

has gained ground, that from being the arena
of single-minded patriotism and the theatre of
eloquence, the House of Commons has become
but the coveted vantage-ground of self-seeking
busy-bodies.   We are disposed to compare our
public men unfavourably with the great figures
of the eighteenth century, but Dr Johnson himself, trained as he was to philosophical reflection, leaned to a similar disposition.   " Politicks,"
he said, "are now nothing more than means of
rising in this world.   With this sole view do
men engage in politicks, and their whole conduct
proceeds upon it.   How different in that respect
is the state of the nation now from what it was
in the time of Charles the First, during the
Usurpation, and after the Restoration, in the
time of Charles the Second."   This feeling has
been intensified by the degree of familiarity with
its proceedings which has of late been brought
about by the activity of the press.   It is difficult
to preserve the august repute of Parliament when
every unruly scene, as well as the foibles and
blunders of every member of it, are minutely
described and dwelt upon in the newspapers.   It
is not surprising if familiarity engenders its pro-

verbial offspring in the minds of the many. Yet there be some, and these not the least intelligent in the community, who still recognise in the House of Commons not only the goal of respectable and useful ambition, but also a field in which well-directed effort may, even at this day, produce valuable fruit. To such natures it is more congenial to be brought in direct contact with the masses for whom they legislate, than to study the moods and allay the apprehensions of exalted individuals : the modern Parliamentarian may have ruder experience to undergo than had the nominee of a great lord of old, but faithfulness to his task earns wider sympathy, and it is more grateful to honest pride to stoop to listen than to cringe to hear.

Any early indications which William Smith gave of political opinion were tinged with moderate Liberalism. He seems to have inclined naturally to that side of politics to which his father, as a Wesleyan, adhered. Thus, in 1854, he had written from Dresden to his father, after describing the beauty of the town and surrounding country :—

There is only one obvious drawback in all this—that the King and the Government appear to be and to do everything—all that is great, beautiful, and even useful appears to proceed from the Government, and the people are nothing—reversing the picture as it is in England.

The idea of entering Parliament seems first to have presented itself in a concrete form to William Smith at the age of thirty-one. In 1856 he received overtures from the Liberal party at Boston with the view of ascertaining if he were willing to stand in conjunction with Mr Ingram, who at that time represented the borough. He appears to have been ready to accept the invitation on certain conditions, clearly set out in a letter, of which a draft remains in his own handwriting :—

The most important question after all is whether or no the Party is strong enough to return a Second Member on the principles on which alone I can stand, and which are politically and religiously liberal.

His definition of Liberal principles which follows might scarcely satisfy thorough-going Radicals of the present day, for although he was in favour of abolishing Church Rates he was opposed to Disestablishment; though advocating the promotion of popular education by fresh legislation, he would not have it made compulsory; though holding the opinion that naval and military expenditure should be reduced (the Crimean war had then just been brought to a close), it must not be brought below the point of complete efficiency; and he could not look with favour on the introduction of vote by ballot.

Then in the following year, 1857, overtures were made on Smith's behalf with the view of his becoming one of the Liberal candidates for Exeter; but the idea was abandoned for the same reason that prevailed in respect of Boston —namely, that the party was not strong enough to return two Liberals.

Nothing, therefore, came of either of these projects, and the next that is heard of Smith in connection with party politics is a little incident which occurred in 1864. A personal friend of his, Mr Lawson[1] of the 'Daily Telegraph,' happened to be calling one day at the House on Lord Palmerston, who was then Prime Minister, and remarked to him that there was "a young man in the Strand who would be heard of some day, and should be seen to, as he would make an excellent candidate."

"Ah," replied the Premier, "I wish you'd tell Brand[2] about him, will ye?"

Mr Lawson did so, but apparently nothing was done, for some time afterwards Smith came up to him in the street, and said—

---

[1] Created Sir Edward Levey Lawson, Bart., in 1892.

[2] Henry Brand, Esq., M.P., the chief Whip of the Liberal party, afterwards Speaker from 1872 to 1884, when he was created Viscount Hampden.

"My dear Lawson, do you know what I have gone and done. I've accepted an invitation to stand for Westminster."

"Delighted to hear it," was the reply; "you're the very man of all others we should like to have. Rely upon me to do all in my power for you."

"Oh, but I am the Conservative candidate, you know."

"Whew! that alters matters rather," exclaimed Mr Lawson, for the 'Daily Telegraph' was then the leading Radical paper. "Then, rely upon it, I'll do all I fairly can to keep you out!"

And he was as good as his word, although it is pleasant to record that it made no difference in their friendship, which continued warm to the end.[1]

---

[1] Mr Lawson was the cause of Smith's only experiences as a betting man. When Mr Disraeli was forming his Government in 1874, Mr Lawson happening to meet Smith in the street, asked him what office was going to be offered to him. "None," replied Smith; "I neither deserve nor expect one." "All the same, you will have the refusal of one," said Lawson. "Not I," persisted Smith; "I assure you there is no such idea." "Well," exclaimed Mr Lawson, "I'll bet you twenty guineas that within three weeks you will be a member of the Government." "Done!" said Smith, and in less than three weeks he was Secretary to the Treasury, and paid his debt of honour.

Again, in 1877, Mr Ward Hunt, First Lord of the Admiralty, being seriously ill, Mr Lawson met Smith in the lobby of the House, and said, "Well, I suppose you will be going to the

Now, in speculating on the influence which, within eight years, had changed Smith from a moderate Liberal into a moderate Conservative, there is to be remembered something besides the fact that Lord Palmerston had in the interval gone to his place, and the restraint which he had so long exercised upon his followers had been removed. While Smith may be credited with a large share of what the Stoics called ἐποχή, or suspension of judgment—a quality peculiarly distinguishing his character in later life— there is also to be taken into account the effect of a rebuff he had lately received, sharp enough to have discouraged a much less sensitive nature than his. Smith's name had been for some time on the candidates' book of the Reform Club; when he came up for election the haughty susceptibilities of the Whig members of the committee were set in arms against the admission of a tradesman, and he was blackballed. This apparently trivial act—lightly done and as lightly dismissed from thought—was perhaps to have

---

Admiralty soon." "Nonsense!" Smith answered; "what put that into your head?" "Nonsense or not," said Mr Lawson, "I am willing to have another bet about it: I'll lay you fifty pounds that within six weeks you will be in the Cabinet." Again Smith accepted the wager, and within the stipulated time Mr Lawson called at the Admiralty to congratulate the First Lord on his appointment, and receive payment of his bet. "It must seem funny enough," observed Smith, "to you, who remember me working in my shirt-sleeves, to see me installed here."

a more lasting effect on the course of politics for a quarter of a century than anybody could have foreseen at the time.

To one trained like William Smith, himself a hard-working man, in constant and close intercourse with working men, the summons to enter Parliament came with no unwelcome sound. The part he had taken in social and religious schemes had already accustomed him to apply energy to objects beyond the confines of trade, and had brought him into intimacy with members of Parliament like Lord Sandon, Mr John Talbot, and the Hon. Wilbraham Egerton; while the standing his firm had attained made the choice that fell upon him no extraordinary one. On March 31, 1865, he wrote to his sister Augusta :—

I remember Father has very often talked of the famous election contest in Westminster when Sir Frances Burdett stood; and when the Troops were firing in St James Street, my Father, as a boy, had to run into courts and by backways to escape being shot.

Would it interest him to know that that little boy's Son — myself — has been seriously invited to stand for Westminster by a body headed by the Twinings, Stilwells, and Sambroke, and that the subject is being seriously considered—upon this understanding, that whether I decide to stand or no on private grounds, upon which I am quite uncertain, I should not think of doing so at all, unless I am absolutely assured of success in a contest, if any takes place.

If I go to Parliament, it will be as an independent

man.[1] . . . None but the Committee who have asked me and two or three intimate private friends [2] know anything at all about the affair, and it will remain undecided for some time, but I shall have to give some idea of my inclination on Monday.

I should like to know what Father thinks about it, if he is well enough to be spoken to on the subject. I can afford the expense, and my business will be well managed.

And again on April 4 :—

I have taken no decisive step yet. . . . A contest would be expensive, but when a man once becomes member for Westminster, he may retain his seat pretty nearly for life if his personal or moral character is good, and he attends reasonably to his duties. I am anxious beyond everything to do what is really right, and if Father really disapproved of the step, which is much less mine than my neighbours', I would at once give up the idea altogether. But I confess I should like to be in Parliament.

In this new project Smith was to encounter no opposition from his father; on the contrary, the old gentleman, at this time in very precarious health, entered upon the project with great enthusiasm, and undertook to pay all expenses.

---

[1] By how many inexperienced candidates has this declaration not been made in all sincerity—how few have found it possible to carry it out ! To bring any perceptible influence to bear upon events, a man in Parliament must be content to act with others— to postpone or altogether forego favourite schemes, and to part with cherished illusions.

[2] Among these would certainly be Lord Sandon, the Hon. Robert Grimston, and Mr Lethbridge.

How thoroughly Mr Lawson succeeded in reconciling private friendship with Smith to public obligation to his party, and maintained the thorough-going Radicalism of his journal, may be seen by referring to the 'Daily Telegraph' of that time.   There were three candidates for the two seats—Captain Grosvenor, the representative of hereditary Whiggism, the moderate Liberal; Mr John Stuart Mill, the advanced freethinker, and, as most people then thought, the extravagant and dangerous Radical; and Smith of the Strand, professing a Liberal-Conservative faith, known to the few as a practical philanthropist and steady churchman—to the many as the owner of the bookstalls.

Mr Lawson gave the support of his newspaper to Mill; threw cold water upon Captain Grosvenor, and suggested that he should retire in order to avoid splitting the Liberal vote; and attempted to treat Smith's candidature as a farce.

The metropolitan boroughs [runs the leading article on May 6, 1865] owe it to the country and to themselves . . . not to indulge ambitious nobodies who, despairing of any other distinction, want to say they were once "Metropolitan members." . . . In the category of political nobodies we must include Mr Smith. . . . The candidates are Captain Grosvenor, Mr Smith, and John Stuart Mill. Now we have already contrasted the claims of the kinsman of the Marquis of Westminster with those of the author of 'Liberty' and 'Representative Government.'

And we should insult the intelligence of the public by
dwelling on such a point.

Smith, advocating extension of the franchise
and an amicable adjustment of the question of
Church-rates, stood as a Liberal-Conservative—
a title which not only earned for him the jealous
suspicion of the old-fashioned Tories, but was
resented by the Liberals as an unprincipled bor-
rowing of their own peculiar plumes.   Smith
was in the position of Pope's moderate man—

> " In moderation placing all my glory,
>   While Tories call me Whig, and Whigs a Tory."

Thus the ' Daily Telegraph' on July 6 :—

The policy of the great Conservative party with respect
to the elections may be aptly defended on the ground of
its exact similarity to that adopted by the giver of the
banquet celebrated in the pages of Holy Writ.   In order
to secure a full complement of guests for his table, the
entertainer recorded in the parable first issued invitations
to all his friends and relations; then, when these hung
back, he brought in the halt, the maimed, and the blind;
and when he found that there was still room left, he sent
out into the streets, and compelled the passers-by to come
in.   This course of conduct exactly corresponds to the
tactics of the Tories in the approaching elections.   Their
first object is to fill the vacant seats with their own allies
and retainers; but, failing in that, they are ready to take
in anybody they can get, no matter what may be his
qualifications, or under what pretences he may be enumer-
ated among the guests of Conservatism. . . . There is one
Derby, and Disraeli is his prophet—such is the shibboleth

which every candidate for Tory votes is required to repeat. . . . Mr Smith issues an address from Westminster, so liberal in its tone that it ought to have been
dated from the Reform Club, . . . yet this gentleman is
accounted a champion of Conservative principles, simply
because he is opposed to two candidates of advanced Liberal views.

Still, sternly as the editor of the 'Daily
Telegraph' succeeded in severing the office of
censor from that of friend in this contest, there
is no doubt that the business relations between
the firm of Smith & Son and the leading journals
of the day served to impart a tone of kindly
recognition even to the most hostile articles in
other newspapers.

They might well afford to be magnanimous.
Smith's candidature could scarcely be looked on
as otherwise than a forlorn hope, having regard
to the state of parties in the Metropolis. There
had not been for many years a single Conservative member either for a metropolitan constituency or for Middlesex, and the county of
Surrey could only boast of two. Besides this
discouraging state of affairs, Smith had other
difficulties to encounter. Mr Cubitt, who in
after-years became his intimate friend, and had
at that time much influence in the party organisation of London, was dismayed at the Liberalism
of Smith's address to the electors. He consulted

Colonel Taylor, the Conservative Whip, as to
the prudence of adopting a candidate of such
milk-and-water views. " Take him," was Taylor's
advice—" take him. I don't fancy his politics
much myself, but you'll get nobody better." [1]   In

---

[1] Smith showed himself scrupulously anxious not to secure
Conservative support by posing as a member of the Conservative
party, and in order that his position should be perfectly clear, he
wrote the following letter to Colonel Taylor, the Conservative
Whip :—

April 26, 1865.

MY DEAR SIR,—I have been so heartily and so handsomely supported by the Conservative party that I am anxious there should
be no misunderstanding as to the position I should occupy with
reference to it if returned to Parliament for Westminster.

You are fully aware of the independence of party ties which I
felt it necessary to stipulate for when it was proposed by the Committee that I should stand for Westminster, but I am not sure that
your friends would gather as much from my address. It will be
well, therefore, to repeat that I am not a member of the Conservative party as such—nor am I a member of the Liberal party, but I
believe in Lord Palmerston, and look forward ultimately to a
fusion of the moderate men following Lord Derby and Lord
Palmerston into a strong Liberal-Conservative party, to which I
should be glad to attach myself.

Such an expectation may be chimerical, but I cannot help in-
dulging it, and I wish to stand by it.

In the meantime, I am pledged to oppose Baine's bill (for extension of the suffrage in boroughs), the Ballot, and the uncondi-
tional abolition of Church-rates and all similar radical measures.

May I ask you to make this matter clear to your friends who
have so generously offered their support to me, as I would rather
retire now than fairly lay myself open to the reproach of obtaining
party support under false pretences.

To this Colonel Taylor replied :—

" I consider your letter an extremely fair one, and I shall advise the
Westminster Conservatives to give you their unreserved support."

his address to the electors, dated from the Strand, April 1865, the " milk-and-water " candidate said he came forward to give the

more moderate or Conservative portion of the constituency an opportunity of marking their disapproval of the extreme political doctrines which have been avowed by the Candidates already in the field. . . . Unconnected with either of the great political parties, I should desire to enter Parliament as an independent Member, at liberty to vote for measures rather than for men. I should not be a party to any factious attempt to drive Lord Palmerston from power, as I feel that the country owes a debt of gratitude to him for having preserved peace, and for the resistance he has offered to reckless innovation in our domestic institutions.

While not opposed to carefully considered extension of the suffrage, he declared himself unable to support Mr Baine's bill, then before Parliament ; and he was prepared to resist ballot-voting, because he thought that the voter who was afraid to act openly was " scarcely worthy of the trust which he is supposed to discharge for the benefit of the commonwealth." He laid special stress on his anxiety to legislate in the interests of education and popular thrift.

Looked at in the light of that time, there was little in this address to rouse fighting spirit in the ranks of the Opposition, and at first some difficulty was found in getting together a good election Committee. The aristocratic house-holders of Belgravia and Mayfair only knew Smith as a newsvendor, and were disposed to lukewarmness in a contest wherein one of their own order could not engage with any hope of success; and, whether from jealousy or incredulity in a creditable result, many of the West End tradesmen showed little enthusiasm towards their fellow-citizen, and at first held aloof from his Committee. As time went on, however, these obstacles melted to small proportions, and a strong representative Committee, with Earl Percy[1] as chairman, having been constituted, everything pointed to a well-fought election. The Liberal party in Westminster were perplexed by the candidature of Mr Mill, which was unfavourably viewed by the party managers, and in the end Sir John Shelley, who had represented the borough for many years, retired in order to avoid splitting the Liberal vote.

The nomination took place, according to immemorial custom, on the hustings at Covent Garden, the scene of so many famous contests between parties and powerful houses. It was the last time when electors were to have the advantage of an unlimited supply of cabbage-

[1] Now sixth Duke of Northumberland.

stalks and rotten potatoes close at hand, for
with the Reform Act of 1867 came provision for
removing the hustings to a place with more
elbow-room and fewer missiles.

By the time the polling-day dawned, the hopes
of the Conservative party were high.   Smith
had made an excellent impression, and received
promises of support to such an extent as, to one
new to the infirmity of electoral human nature,
seemed to put his success beyond question.   He
was soon to be undeceived.   It will be remembered that, under the old practice of open
voting, the state of the poll was known as the
day wore on, and was published from time to
time.   The first note of warning was sent to
his wife from his committee-rooms in Cockspur
Street :—

11th July 1865.

I think you may have a disappointment. Men have
broken their promises to a considerable extent, and we
are dropping behind.   Don't be discontented ; it is all
for the best.   I will let you know later.

Another was sent to his sister Augusta :—

Things are looking a little badly for us—not very much
so, but enough to render it possible that we may be
beaten.   You must prepare my Father for it.

Then, finally, another to his sister, written

from his house in Hyde Park Street, where he had gone to carry the news to Mrs Smith :—

The close of the Poll made

Grosvenor	.	.	.	.	4384
Mill	.	.	.	.	4379
Smith .	.	.	.	.	3812

So I was 572 behind, and am left out in the cold; but although disappointed, I am not at all cast down about it. I will come to you to-morrow morning. Let me know how my Father is.

Disraeli was an adept in the art of attaching his followers to himself by tactful and timely notice of them—a faculty by no means invariably possessed by parliamentary chiefs. The following little autograph note of sympathy was despatched on the day of the declaration of the poll in Westminster :—

GROSVENOR GATE, *July* 12, 1865.

DEAR SIR,—Before I leave town to-day for my own County, I must express to you my great regret at the termination of the Westminster contest, conducted by you with so much spirit, & evidently with such a just expectation of success.

I hope yet to see you in the House of Commons, &, in the meantime, I trust you may find some dignified consolation & some just pride in the conviction that you possess the respect & the confidence of a great party.— I have the honor to be, Dear Sir, your faithful serv^t.,

B. DISRAELI.

W. H. SMITH, Esq.

Smith's reply to this was as follows :—

1 HYDE PARK ST., *July* 12, 1865.

DEAR SIR,—I am grateful to you for the expression of your sympathy with me under my defeat. Seeing that I had not identified myself with the party, I confess I felt surprise at the warmth and earnestness with which the Westminster Conservatives supported me, and the ready response to our united efforts caused me to be sanguine as to the result.

But I am amply repaid for any labour or vexation through which I have passed by the confidence of the friends I have made in this contest, and the expression of your own kindly feeling.—I have the honor to be, Dear Sir, yours very faithfully, WILLIAM H. SMITH.

Thus ended in decisive repulse the assault on the Liberal stronghold of the Metropolis. But it was not to be long before the attack was renewed. The contest had revealed Conservative feeling in a London constituency to an extent which few could have suspected. No doubt it would have been even more manifest but for the confidence which the middle classes felt in Lord Palmerston. It is true that Smith repeatedly disclaimed any wish to see that statesman dislodged from office; but the Liberals had the advantage of claiming Palmerston as the head of their party, while Smith was a follower of Lord Derby, whose name, though in high repute with landed gentry and farmers, was not one with which to conjure in the towns.

CHAPTER V.

1865–1868.

DEATH OF LORD PALMERSTON—AND OF THE ELDER SMITH—
EARL RUSSELL'S REFORM BILL—AND MR DISRAELI'S—DIS-
SOLUTION OF PARLIAMENT—SMITH IS ELECTED FOR WEST-
MINSTER—THE REVIVALIST MOVEMENT.

LORD PALMERSTON died in the autumn of 1865. The night of his death — October 18 — was marked by a phenomenon to which, in a pre-scientific or more superstitious age, there would undoubtedly have been attributed special signifi-cance, as accompanying the removal of one of great influence in the guidance of a great nation. Many persons, especially in the northern part of the island, as they watched the brilliant display of aurora borealis, called to mind the belief of the Scottish peasantry referred to by Aytoun in the stanza—

> " All night long the northern streamers
> Shot across the trembling sky :
> Fearful lights that never beckon .
> Save when kings or heroes die."

CHAPTER V

DEATH OF LORD . . . . ELDER SMITH—
EARL . . . . DIS-
SOLUTION . . . . WEST-
MINSTER . . . .

LORD PALMERSTON died in the autumn of 1865.
The night of his death — October 18 — was
marked by a phenomenon to which, in a pre-
scientific or more superstitious age, there would
undoubtedly have been attributed special signifi-
as accompanying the removal of one of
great influence in the guidance of a great nation.
Many persons, especially in the northern part of
the island, as they watched the brilliant display
of aurora borealis, called to mind the belief of
the Scottish peasantry referred to by Aytoun in
the stanza—

> " All night long the northern streamers
> Shot across the trembling sky:
> Fearful lights that never beckon
> Save when kings or heroes die."

For indeed many kings and heroes have passed from the earthly scene of their works with less consequence to the course of affairs. With Lord Palmerston's firm will and quaint, genial personality, there was lost that sense of security which made moderate men of both parties feel safer under a strong Liberal administration than under a weak Conservative one. Henceforward, step by step, in ever-accelerating descent, the Liberal party was to follow the path of reckless opportunism, till, as has come to pass at this day, it has parted with all the men who might draw to it the confidence of the educated and consciously responsible.

During this year also drew to a close the life of one who had exercised as powerful an influence on Smith's character and private life as Lord Palmerston had on his public career and political opinions. Old Mr Smith, whose unremitting devotion to business had often brought upon him the anxious warnings and remonstrances of friends in the "connection," who found it difficult to reconcile his worldly preoccupation with spiritual preparedness, had comparatively early in life paid the penalty of shattered health. Since his retirement from an active part in the firm, much of his time had been spent at Torquay and Bournemouth, and it was at the last-named

place that he breathed his last in July 1865.
A man of unbending integrity and ceaseless industry, he was a kind, if somewhat imperious,
parent, and his children loved and respected
him. In him the Wesleyan body lost a faithful adherent and generous benefactor: one of
his latest acts was a gift of £2100 to the building fund of a chapel in London.

In the year following upon Smith's defeat in
Westminster, his home in Hyde Park Street was
darkened by the first sorrow that had fallen upon
it since his marriage. His first-born son—a weak-
ling from his birth—died in February 1866, and
he records the loss in these words in a letter to
Miss Giberne :—

We are in trouble. Our little boy has been taken
from us—quite quietly, gently, slowly, and, happily, pain-
lessly; but he is gone like a breath or a shadow. A bad
cold and no strength—no power—and that is all; and
the Doctors say now that he was not a livable child—
that any illness must have knocked him down, and so
he is taken away from the sorrows to come. . . It is
a sad blank in our nursery—a quiet little sorrow which
will last with us for a long time to come. But as the
sorrow was to come, it could not have fallen more gently
and more mercifully.

Much more gently and mercifully, indeed, than
if the parents had been called on to witness a

life carried from ailment to ailment, flickering in a feeble frame, and prolonged with difficulty through painful adolescence into suffering manhood.

But in August of the same year the house was gladdened by a happier event, thus announced by Smith to his sister :—

You will be glad to hear . . . that Emily has got through her trouble safely, . . . and that we have a son again. This time the boy looks healthy and well, but I am hardly yet able to say that I am glad. I did not desire it, although we shall be very thankful if all goes well with him. I have always felt there is a greater risk with boys than with girls, and we have both been very well content with our girls. Emily, however, looks very happy indeed with him upon her arm, and if she goes on well, as I have no doubt she will, I shall begin to value the little fellow at his proper worth.

The first act of Earl Russell's Government was the preparation of a bill for extending the franchise. This was introduced on March 12, 1866, by Mr Gladstone, Chancellor of the Exchequer and leader of the House of Commons, in a speech memorable for the combined force and elegance of its peroration. "We cannot," he said at the conclusion of an elaborate explanation of the proposals of the Government—

We cannot consent to look on this addition—consider-

able though it be—of the working classes as if it were
an addition fraught with nothing but danger; we cannot
look upon it as a Trojan horse approaching the walls of
a sacred city, and filled with armed men bent on ruin,
plunder, and conflagration. We cannot describe it as
monstrum infelix, or say—

> "Scandit fatalis machina muros,
> Fœta armis : . . . mediæque minans illabitur urbi."

We believe that those persons whom we ask you to
enfranchise ought rather to be welcomed as if they were
recruits to your army. We ask you to give within what
we consider a just limit of prudence and circumspection.
Consider what you can safely and justly offer to do in
admitting new subjects and citizens within the pale of the
Parliamentary Constitution; and having so considered
it, do it as if you were conferring a boon, which will
be felt and reciprocated by a feeling of grateful attachment to the Constitution—attachment of the people to
the Throne and laws under which we live, which is, after
all, more than your gold and silver, and more than your
fleets and armies,—at once the strength, the glory, and
the safety of the land.

In spite of this powerful appeal, the bill was
coldly received by those who sat behind Mr
Gladstone. There were those who sighed

> "For the touch of a vanished hand,
> And the sound of a voice that was still."

The moderate Liberals grouped themselves
round such malcontents as Lord Grosvenor,
Mr Lowe, Mr Horsman, Lord Elcho, and Mr

Laing, and formed what soon came to be known as the Cave of Adullam, because, as was said, it contained " every one that was in distress, and every one that was in debt, and every one that was discontented." [1] On April 12 an amendment was moved by Lord Grosvenor to the effect that no bill to extend the franchise could be accepted until the House was in possession of the proposals of the Government for redistribution of seats.   This was seconded by Lord Stanley,[2] and the debate was wound up on the eighth night with a speech of extraordinary warmth and eloquence by Mr Gladstone, who declared that the Government would stand or fall by the result.   The division took place in a scene of the utmost excitement at three in the morning, the figures being—

Ayes	318
Noes	313
Majority for the Government .	5

It was generally expected that Ministers would resign, but, on the contrary, they persevered in carrying the bill into Committee.   Mr Gladstone, on being twitted with continuing in office after pledging himself to stand or fall by

---

[1] 1 Samuel xxii. 2.   [2] Afterwards fifteenth Earl of Derby.

a bill which he had only carried by a majority of five, declared that as the bill still stood, so did the Government. The bill, however, after several exceedingly close divisions in Committee, was finally wrecked on an amendment moved by Lord Dunkellin, who proposed to substitute rating instead of renting. as the basis of the franchise. On this question Ministers were in a minority of eleven. The consequence was the resignation of Earl Russell's Cabinet and the formation of a new one by the Earl of Derby, with Mr Disraeli as Chancellor of the Exchequer and leader of the House of Commons. It was the desire of Lord Derby to include some of the Adullamites in his Government, but his overtures were declined, and he had to meet Parliament early in July with a minority of Conservative members in the House of Commons, and a body of dissentient Liberals or Adullamites holding the balance of power.

In the following year — 1867 — the Queen opened Parliament in person for the first time since the Prince Consort's death in 1861, and in the Speech from the Throne chief prominence was given to a measure to " freely extend the elective franchise." To carry out this purpose the Chancellor of the Exchequer asked the House of Commons to proceed in a somewhat novel way, by adopting thirteen resolutions embodying the principles on which bills for the extension of the franchise and Redistribution of seats should be framed by the Government. But objections to this course were pressed from all quarters of the House, and after some discussion the Resolutions were withdrawn, and the bill promised. But before it could be introduced, the Cabinet had disagreed on its provisions, and three Ministers — Lord Carnarvon, Lord Cranborne, and General Peel—resigned office. Nothing but speedy destruction seemed to be imminent upon Lord Derby's Administration. Weakened as he was by the secession of three of his own colleagues, his policy was now bitterly attacked by the Adullamites—his quondam allies — who denounced Mr Disraeli's bill as more sweeping than that which, the previous year, had severed them from their proper leaders. Then was to be seen the strange spectacle of a Conservative Chancellor of the Exchequer moving a measure which, though condemned by many of his own party, and by the whole of the Adullamites, and sarcastically criticised by the Liberal Opposition, was yet allowed to pass second reading in the House of Commons without a division.

In the session of 1868 similar bills were passed for Scotland and Ireland, and Parliament was

dissolved on ⸱November 11, to reassemble on
December 10. ⸳

Smith's experience in the contest of 1865 had
the usual result of practical contact with politics:
it tended to ⸱accentuate his opinions on public
questions, and to convince him that, if he would
influence the course of events, a man must co-
operate heartily with other men, and that independence of⸳ action, carried beyond somewhat
narrow limits, must end ineffectively. Henceforward his⸳ lot was cast and his course was
steered with the Conservative party, and he
chose that line from deliberate conviction, not
because it⸳was to land him with fewest obstacles
in the House of Commons. In 1867 an invitation came to him to stand for Middlesex on
" unmistakable Liberal principles "; but he declined it because, if he stood at all, he could only
do so as a Conservative. Thereupon came an
invitation to contest the county as a Conservative, on which Smith placed himself in the hands
of the party managers, who advised him to decline. To another invitation to contest Bedford
in the Conservative interest, he replied that " my
Westminster friends have so strongly remon-
strated against the proposal to commit myself
to a candidature for another constituency at the
general election, . . . that out of regard to per-

sonal considerations . . . I feel bound to refrain from severing myself from them."

Finally, a requisition, with 3000 signatures, inviting Smith to stand again for Westminster, was presented to him on behalf of the Conservative party in the borough, by a deputation headed by the Earl of Dalkeith, M.P.,[1] and this invitation he accepted. But Westminster was not now the same constituency he had courted in 1865. The effect of household suffrage on the political complexion of such a borough could only be darkly surmised. It was true that people had begun to get tired of Mr Mill : in those days the advocacy of woman suffrage was regarded as an eccentric novelty, and if there is one thing of which the English middle class is more suspicious than of novelty, it is eccentricity. Mill had also disgusted some of his supporters by relentless prosecution of the charges against Governor Eyre ; and by espousing the cause of Charles Bradlaugh, the infidel and revolutionary lecturer, he had roused the alarm of members of all the Churches. Still, the new electors were an untried contingent, and nobody could predict what their action might be.

In his new address to the electors Smith still claimed to be a Liberal-Conservative, " unpledged to any particular party.". But the tone was more

[1] Now sixth Duke of Buccleuch and eighth Duke of Queensberry.

decided than in the address of 1865. There
was one passage to which the course of subsequent party tactics has imparted a melancholy
significance.

Foremost among the more prominent questions of the
day is that of Ireland.

I have long been of opinion that the greatest misfortune
which has befallen the people of Ireland, is that their
condition has become the patrimony of political parties in
this country, who, to obtain a fleeting popularity or a
few votes, fan the flame of popular discontent by attribut-
ing to unjust or partial legislation the existence of evils,
arising in great measure from causes within the control
of the Irish people themselves.

All through the winter 1867-68 and the succeeding summer, Smith and his friends worked
hard, holding meetings and canvassing the voters.
Mr Disraeli's profession of belief in the existence
of Conservative working men had been as much
the subject of misgiving among members of his
own party as of derision among his opponents.
But as the canvass proceeded, clear evidence was
forthcoming that there were working men of a
more thoughtful stamp than the rioters who, in
1867, had pulled down the railings of Hyde Park
and terrorised the West End.

The main question on which the general election was to turn was the Disestablishment of the

Irish Church, and those who were defending it against Mr Gladstone's attack were able, as has been the case in every one of that statesman's greater enterprises, to equip themselves with weapons from his own armoury of argument, which he had flung aside in successive changes of front. Smith was stoutly opposed to Disestablishment, because he could see in it no promise of lessened bitterness or increased goodneighbourhood in Ireland, and to Disendowment, because he recognised in it a principle which might easily be extended to every kind of property, public or private. Smith numbered among his most active supporters and advisers at this time the Hon. Robert Grimston, Mr Cubitt, and Lord Sandon.

The nomination took place on November 16, not, as by almost immemorial custom, in Covent Garden, but on hustings erected at the base of Nelson's Pillar. The candidates were the same as in 1865—namely, Grosvenor, Mill, and Smith. Smith's supporters were very hopeful; but if they were confident, he himself did not share their feeling, as may be seen from the following passages in letters to his wife :—

Nov. 10.—I don't want people . . . to suppose I sulk if I lose the battle or am too much elated if I win.

Nov. 11.—I certainly hope to succeed, but the relief of

rest will be so great that if I fail I shall be compensated by a return to home comforts.

Nov. 12.—If I go down home[1] on Tuesday evening beaten I shall not feel I am disgraced, and I intend to put a good and cheerful face upon it. It will all be for the best, and I shall be quite content to spend more time with my family and with you. . . . Everything is going well with me at present, but it is quite impossible to tell what the issue may be.

On the polling-day telegrams were despatched to Mrs Smith at intervals. Thus :—

Ten o'clock poll—Smith, 2457; Grosvenor, 1745; Mill, 1647; but don't be too sanguine.

In those days the poll was closed at four o'clock. The lead obtained in the morning by the Conservative candidate was maintained to the close. The result was beyond the expectation of the keenest Tory—even of "Bob" Grimston himself :—

Smith (C.)	7698
Grosvenor (L.)	6505
Mill (L.)	6185

—showing a majority for Smith of 1193 over Grosvenor, and of 1513 over Mill.

[1] His country residence was at this time Cecil Lodge, Abbots Langley. The pleasant old house at Kilburn had been so closely built round that it was given up when old Mr Smith retired from business in 1858. As his son once expressed it—"I can't even kiss my sister without being seen from a dozen windows."

The great day was over, marking a turning-point in the political history of London; for besides the victory in Westminster, the Tories won one of the four seats in the City of London, thus breaking the solid phalanx of metropolitan Liberalism.

His own side were very angry with Mr Mill.

It is extraordinary [said the 'Pall Mall Gazette'] that a man of his acuteness and discernment should fail even now to perceive how much he himself did, not only to bring about this result, but to jeopardise the seats of other Liberals by his patronage of Bradlaugh. . . . At Westminster the Conservatives, if they had only known their strength, could have put in two Conservatives instead of one; and if both the Liberals had been ousted, Mr Mill would have been mainly to blame.

The 'Daily News' was even more vindictive :—

From the date of his letter commendatory of Mr Bradlaugh to his journey, a few days since, to Brighton, where he delivered himself of a diatribe against the Palmerstonian Liberals, Mr Mill has neglected nothing which could prejudice against him men whom, for the sake of his party and his cause, he might at least have abstained from offending. The late member for Westminster has himself principally to thank for his defeat. The great follies of small men and the small follies of great ones may be dismissed with contempt or with indulgence; but the serious errors of a man of Mr Mill's character, intellect, and reputation are too mischievous to be passed over in silence.

The general tone of the Liberal press was not

unfriendly to the new member. Most newspapers
on that side admitted that if a seat was to be
lost, it could not be lost to a better man than
Smith ; but of course some bitter jibes were
written, and one at least of these is amusing to
read in the light of after-years :—

Westminster has shown herself incapable of keeping a
great man when she has got one, and has raised a wealthy
newsvendor to temporary prominence, and even to such
kind of notoriety as attends those whose names get some-
how embedded in the world-wide fame of an opponent.

But though the Conservative cause had tri-
umphed in Westminster, and though the monopoly of metropolitan Liberalism had been further
demolished by the return of Lord George Hamilton for Middlesex, and of Mr Bell for the City of
London, it had fared ill with the authors of
household suffrage in the country. It seemed as
if the jeers which greeted Mr Disraeli's allusions
to the existence of Conservative working men had
been justified by the result of his "leap in the
dark," for the state of parties in the new Parliament was :—

Liberals	387
Conservatives	272
Liberal majority	115

Still, the beaten Prime Minister might point to

South-West Lancashire—a genuine working-man constituency—where his chief opponent had sustained a striking reverse, the result of the poll in that division being :—

Cross (Conservative)	7729
Turner (Conservative) . . .	7676
Gladstone (Liberal)	7415
Grenfell (Liberal)	6939

Before passing from the events of this eventful year 1868, allusion may be made to one of its notable features—the Revival movement. For as long as history bears witness to human progress, there is ample evidence of the recurrence of storms of spiritual disquiet which agitate the community by mingled waves of fear and fervour, and, passing away as rapidly as they came, make way for periods of tranquillity, to be disturbed again by similar outbreaks. The form of such agitations varies as much as the *personnel* of the chief movers in them, but their general characteristics remain the same — apprehension of impending judgments, imperious call to instant repentance, fervid exhortation, and physical excitement, producing manifestations claimed to be of divine origin and spiritual nature. One of these storms was passing over the masses of this land at this time, and it is interesting to note the quiet respectful attention, not unmingled with suspicion, which it commanded from one so earnestly concerned in religious life as Smith was.   On July 20, 1868, he wrote to one of his sisters :—

Yesterday afternoon I went to hear Lord Radstock at the Revival meetings at the Polytechnic, and although he is very earnest, I doubt the ultimate value of his work.

In another letter of this date to his sister Augusta, there is a little bit of melancholy but practical philosophy.   He has been discussing a plan for affording pecuniary relief to some poor relations, and observes :—

It is a sad thing they should have this trouble in their old days, but it is just another example of the mistake of unsatisfactory marriages.   Sooner or later the inevitable breakdown occurs, and the heart had better have been broken at first, if such a thing was possible.

CHAPTER VI.

1868-1869.

PETITION AGAINST MR SMITH'S RETURN—THE TRIAL AND VERDICT —SMITH'S MAIDEN SPEECH—DEBATE ON PAUPERISM—SMITH'S MISTRUST OF CHARITABLE DONATIONS—ANECDOTES ILLUSTRATING HIS PRINCIPLES OF GIVING—THE TELEGRAPH BILL—DEBATES ON DISESTABLISHMENT OF THE IRISH CHURCH.

THE decree which banished Mill from public life and ushered Smith into it was not to pass unchallenged by the friends of the former. Before the twenty days allowed by statute for lodging petitions had elapsed, one had been filed against the Conservative member for Westminster. Under the law as it then stood candidates were much more in the hands of their agents than they are now, for there was no statutory limit to expenses, and the agent had to be supplied with money according to his discretion; and not the chief agent only, but a whole troop of assistant agents and active partisans besides.

Certainly there had been no niggardliness shown in the supply. While the published expenses of the Liberal candidates, Grosvenor and Mill, only amounted together to £2296, 2s. 7d., those of the Conservative, Smith, mounted up to the huge total of £8900, 17s. 7d. There had also been lamentable indiscretion on the part of one of Smith's warmest well-wishers, Mr Grimston, to whom, indeed, it was greatly owing that Smith had consented to come forward again for Westminster. Mr Grimston had brought up to London a tenant of his brother (the Earl of Verulam), one Edwards, in order that he might act as a sub-agent. This Edwards had already undergone eighteen months' imprisonment for his part in the malpractices which brought about the disfranchisement of the borough of St Albans. No doubt this worthy must have possessed some special qualities which caused his services to be in request, and no doubt Grimston believed he was doing his friend a good turn in securing him an indefatigable sub-agent, but in fact his zeal very nearly brought about the loss of the seat. The petition was on the grounds of bribery, treating, and undue influence by the candidate and by other persons on his behalf.

As for Smith himself, he wrote to his wife

on December 9 with a perfectly clear conscience
as to his own actions :—

From what I hear, I think it likely the Petition will be
presented, but it is not certain yet, and I do not think
they have any matter which cannot be explained honour-
ably and to all the world. I am very much less concerned about it than I was—indeed I cannot be said to be
at all so.

Parliament assembled on December 10, and
Smith duly took his seat for Westminster. The
proceedings on the petition against his return
did not begin till February 12, when the
case was opened before Mr Baron Martin at
the Sessions House, Westminster, but was afterwards removed, first to the Lords Justices' Court
and then to the Court of Exchequer,—a change
rendered necessary by the crowds of persons
seeking admittance, and by the intense local
excitement attending the proceedings. Mr
Hawkins, Q.C., and Mr Serjeant Ballantine
were counsel for Mr Smith, and Mr Fitzjames
Stephens, with Messrs Murch and Littler as
juniors, for the petitioners. The trial lasted for
seven days, and the cross-examination of wit-
nesses did not fail to produce instances of
humour of the sort peculiar to two kinds of
case—election petitions and actions for breach
of promise of marriage. For example, one wit-

ness who had applied to Smith's agent for payment of certain alleged expenses and had been
refused, said that he thereupon changed his
politics and became a Liberal, because the Conservatives were "a nasty dirty lot."

Asked by Mr Hawkins—"Give us your notion
of what a Conservative is"—a witness replied,
"I think a Conservative is a rank humbug."

"Well, what is a Liberal?"—"A Liberal, if he
acts as a man and a gentleman, is a Liberal."

"But suppose a Conservative acts as a man
and a gentleman, what do you think of him?"—
"Well but, sir, you rarely come across such a
one."

It was stated in evidence that at a tea-meeting
in the Hanover Square Rooms, a blessing was
first asked on the buns and the toast, and afterwards there was a good deal of love-making.

"But do you consider love-making a corrupt
practice?"—"Quite the contrary. I consider it
highly laudable."

And so on, after the time-honoured custom by
which gentlemen in silk gowns are encouraged
to spend their own time and their clients' money
in extracting feeble jokes in protracted cross-examination.

Though the charge against the respondent
broke down, and was abandoned by the peti-

tioners' counsel, the suspense remained intense up to the very last. Not till the closing sentences of Mr Baron Martin's summing up did he give the slightest indication of the judgment he was about to deliver. He said that

what struck against Mr Smith was the enormous amount of expenditure. That expenditure had been called extravagant on one side and profuse on the other, and it might be described by a stronger term. At any rate, it was not creditable, and its extent was almost beyond belief. . . . He had never formed any other opinion of Mr Smith than that he intended this election should be carried on legally, and that the law should not be transgressed; but intentions were nothing if bribery were done. . . . If he was convinced that any illegal act had been done by a canvasser of Mr Smith's, the election would be declared void, whatever Mr Smith's intentions were. But the connection of agency must be made out clearly, for it would be unjust to accept a light proof of agency when the law was so harsh as to make the act of one person to affect the seat of an honest man.

The judge wound up by declaring Mr Smith duly elected, though he declined, after consultation with his brother judges, to make any order as to costs.

It was indeed difficult to get round the stubborn fact that whereas the votes registered for the Liberal candidates had cost them only about 3s. 6d. each, Smith had been called on to pay at the rate of nearly 22s. for each vote. The charge against the respondent of treating broke down, and was abandoned by the petitioners' counsel; but there can be little doubt that it was Smith's personal character for integrity which alone saved him from the consequences of the lavish expenditure incurred on his behalf by agents—in fact, the judge said as much in summing up, and that it was only by giving to a candidate above suspicion of corrupt intention the benefit of all doubts, that he was able to clear him of direct responsibility. As the 'Times' remarked in a leader on the case :—

A good character has, to Mr Smith at any rate, proved better than riches. It may be a question whether the latter won the seat for him, but there can be no question that the former has saved it.

In spite of the equanimity with which, as he had professed, he had contemplated the approach of the trial, Smith's health gave way under the anxiety of its protracted proceedings : his malady took the painful form of erysipelas, and he was unable to be in court during the summing up. It was his friend, Mr Cubitt, M.P. (now Lord Ashcombe), who had the pleasure of conveying to him the propitious news.

Once safely seated within the walls of St

Stephen's, the new member for Westminster
showed a disposition and capacity for practical
business.   Importance is sometimes attached to
the maiden speech of a novice, as forecasting the
field in which any influence he is to have on the
Legislature is to be developed, and it is often
matter of concern to his friends that he should
not speak too soon, or, on the other hand, be too
long in the House without "making his mark,"
as the phrase goes.   Smith's outset was characteristic of the man.   It was neither on a lofty
theme of foreign policy nor some scheme of ardent
philanthropy that he chose to make his essay.
Choice, indeed, had little enough to do with the
matter : it happened simply that the second
reading of a bill dealing with the valuation of
property in the metropolis was moved by Mr
Goschen, then President of the Poor Law Board,
at the first sitting after the Easter recess, April 1,
1869.   It dealt with a subject concerning which
Smith was thoroughly well informed ; he had
something to say, and he said it.   It was to no
crowded senate, brimming with applause or
lowering with ire, that he addressed himself,
but to benches sparsely filled with listless legislators, reluctantly obeying the summons of Government Whips, who are ever anxious to get
some useful work through in the first few

days after the holidays, before the Opposition
shall have gathered in strength. Such was the
modest opening of a distinguished parliamentary
career.

During his first session in Parliament Smith
subsequently spoke on two or three other subjects, which furnished him with that which
Bishop Wilberforce declared makes the difference
between a good speaker and a bad one—the former speaking because he has something to say;
the latter, because he has to say something. On
May 10 Mr Gladstone gave facilities to Mr Cor-
rance, to enable that gentleman to call attention
to the question of Pauperism and Vagrancy, and
in the debate arising thereon speeches were made
by Mr Peel, then Secretary to the Poor Law
Board,[1] Sir Michael Hicks Beach, Mr Albert
Pell, and others. Mr Smith called attention to
the significant increase in the amount of outdoor relief since the commencement of the new
Poor Law in 1851, showing that in London
alone, while the population had in the interval
risen by 34 per cent, the cost of relief had
doubled. He advocated withholding all relief
of able - bodied poor, except it were coupled
with the obligation to work, otherwise the law
might be interpreted as establishing the legal

---

[1] Became Speaker of the House of Commons in 1884.

right of every man who did not, could not, or would not work, and possessed no property, to food, clothing, and shelter at the cost of those who would, could, and did work, and possessed property.

He was aware [he said] that he was touching on delicate ground, but he was not afraid of interfering with the labour market. He very much preferred the risk of such interference to the certain demoralisation which arose from giving relief as a matter of right to the person claiming it, without value given or a sense of gratitude in return.

A thoughtful, wise observation this, founded on wide, practical experience of philanthropic work, yet one which, in however many minds it may win assent, finds too rare expression in these days, when so much is heard of schemes for the endowment by the State of pauperism and old age. Throughout his life this was the keynote of Smith's code of charity : a liberal giver when the need for gifts was clear to him, he always showed an alert distrust of doles, and never subscribed to any fund, or gave to any beggar, without satisfying himself, often by protracted inquiry, into the merits of each case. A very large part—wellnigh a half—of so much of his correspondence as has been preserved (other than that on political affairs) consists of letters asking for

help and answers to inquiries about the appli-
cants.   Many years after this debate on pauperism, his friend, Sir Henry Acland of Oxford, happened to mention to Smith that he was about to
part with a yacht which he had owned for some
years and took great delight in.   Smith dissuaded
him from doing so, because it was so good for Sir
Henry's health and such an amusement for his
children.

"Well, but I have come to think it selfish to
spend so much on yachting," replied Sir Henry;
"my children are all married, it is chiefly for my
own gratification that I keep the yacht, and I
feel that the money she costs ought, in part at
least, to be devoted to charity."

"Charity!" exclaimed Smith, firing up in a
way very unusual to him,—"how much mischief
has been done in the name of charity!   Don't
you see that so long as you keep your yacht, you
employ Matthews, your captain, and the crew,
who would, if you discharged them, lose, not only
their employment, but the enjoyment of good
clothes, recreation, music, and other means of
culture which you provide for them?   In a national sense, if you withdraw this fund from
wages and give it in charity, I firmly believe you
will by so much be doing harm instead of good.
Charity is often most mischievous."

He spoke very earnestly, and Sir Henry had rarely heard him open out so much on any subject. Touching this matter of almsgiving, it may be noted here how many and various were the applications which flowed in upon Smith as his wealth increased and his name became better known. Sometimes the appeals were for thousands of pounds, at other times for a few shillings; both were treated alike, careful inquiry was made into the circumstances, and the reply depended— not on the amount asked for, but the grounds on which it was asked. Thus Miss Giberne, a constant and valued correspondent of Smith's, once wrote to him about a hawker who drove "the dearest little donkey you ever saw," but wanted to sell it and his cart on the plea of necessity. Probably the man saw in the kind-hearted lady who petted and fed his donkey the prospect of disposing of his live and rolling stock to good advantage ; nor was he far out in his calculations, for Miss Giberne suggested that Smith should buy the equipage. But both had left out of account Smith's inflexible observance of principle in the smallest things, and this was his good-natured answer :—

Dec. 16, 1876.

DEAR AUNT EMILY,—Why should I buy a donkey and a cart—yet ? I do not propose to start as a costermonger, but I may come to it, and then I will try to take care of the donkey.

At the present moment there are two horses and one pony retired from work on the premises; one or two must be shot presently, to save them from the miseries consequent on inability to work or having no work to do. There are three other ponies of the past generation, their carts and one chaise, with little more than healthy work for one, and there is a very fat and heavy boy to attend to them.   What place is there for the donkey?

There would be nothing for it but to put him to death —out of kindness lest he should be ill-treated—stuff him and place him and his cart on the lawn under a canopy, with an inscription commemorating your sympathy and affection for animals, and my weakness in yielding to it. —Ever yours aff'y.,   W. H. SMITH,
The Hard Man.

.There is no record of how Smith dealt with another claimant on his bounty who bore these credentials :—

The bearer of this is an earnest Christian young man. He is at present employed in a wine-cellar, an occupation altogether unsuited to his tastes now that he has become a new man in Christ Jesus.

And there must have been some conflict between benevolence and prudence in dealing with the following application :—

Sir i wish to know weither you are in want of a lad as i am in want of a Situation. yesterday i see there was an advertisment in the times for two youths to write a good hand i wish to know sir weither my hand writing will suit you sir i have been used to the newspaper office for 3 years but has never leant Writeing the covers sir i think with a little improvement i should suit you.

Smith avoided falling into the error of speaking too often in the House. He spoke on one other occasion only during his first session—the debate on the bill enabling the Postmaster-General to acquire the whole of the telegraphs in the country. He had been for some years a director of an electric telegraph company, and supported the bill, though he showed that the terms on which these concerns were to be ceded to the Government were by no means so over-liberal as the opponents of the measure tried to prove.[1]

Every minor question was overshadowed during the session of 1869 by the discussions on the bill to disestablish and disendow the Irish Church. This was moved by Mr Gladstone on March 1. Public interest was intensified to a degree beyond what even so radical a measure might have evoked, by the enormous wealth of the corporation which was the subject of attack, and by

---

[1] One of the arguments used by Mr Torrens against the proposed transaction was founded on what he considered Mr Scudamore's extravagance in estimating the number of telegrams to be dealt with by the General Post Office in the course of a year at 11,200,000. Last year (1892) they amounted to 69,685,480.

speculation as to the disposal of the spoil. The
property of the Church was estimated at the
following figures :—

Tithe rent-charge . . .	£9,000,000
Lands and perpetuity rents .	6,250,000
Money	750,000
Total value . . .	£16,000,000

Of this large sum the bill disposed of £8,650,000
by providing for vested interests, lay compensation, private endowments, commutation of the
Maynooth Grant and *Regium Donum*, &c., the
free surplus remaining being between seven and
eight millions.   Mr Gladstone's speech explaining
the proposals of the Government occupied three
hours in delivery, and, as has always been the
case in the perorations of his most destructive
orations, he brought his arguments to a close by
introducing some metaphor of great force and
elegance, and the expression of confidence that
the greatest advantage would accrue to the object
of his attack.

I don't know [he said] in what country so great a
change, so great a transition, has been proposed for the
ministers of a religious communion who had enjoyed for
many ages the preferred position of an Established
Church.   I can well understand that to many in the Irish
Establishment such a change appears to be nothing less

than ruin and destruction: from the height on which they now stand the future is to them an abyss, and their fears recall the words used in ' King Lear,' when Edgar endeavours to persuade Gloster that he has fallen over the cliffs at Dover, and says:—

> " Ten masts at each make not the altitude
> Which thou hast perpendicularly fell :
> Thy life's a miracle ! "

And yet but a little while after the old man is relieved from his delusion and finds he has not fallen at all. So I trust that when instead of the fictitious and adventitious aid on which we have too long taught the Irish Establishment to lean, it should come to put its trust in its own resources, in its own great mission, in all that it can draw from the energy of its ministers and its members, and the high hopes and promises of the Gospel that it teaches, it will find that it has entered upon a new era of existence—an era bright with hope and potent for good.

The Prime Minister's speech was distinguished, even among the greatest efforts of that consummate orator, by the lucidity with which he set forth a measure of infinite complexity, investing even matter - of - fact details almost with the lustre of romance. Disraeli, who rose immediately after him, bore willing tribute to the eloquence to which the House had been listening. He said that under ordinary circumstances it would have been the duty of his party to meet the motion for leave to

bring in the bill with a direct negative, but
that the result of the general election might be
interpreted into permission given to Mr Gladstone to lay his proposals before the House.
Accordingly he would not oppose, and he advised
his friends not to oppose, the introduction of
the measure; but he stipulated for a delay of
three weeks before the second reading should be
taken. Mr Gladstone protested against so long
an adjournment, but finally consented to postpone it until March 18. The second reading
was carried by a majority of 118, the motion
for going into Committee by 126, and the third
reading by 114. These crushing majorities enabled the Government to send the bill up to
the House of Lords in much the same state
as when it was first laid on the table of the
Commons.

The interest which gathered round the debates
on this measure in the House of Commons was
transferred to those in the Upper Chamber after
Whitsuntide. Would the Lords throw out the
bill, as they had in the previous year thrown out
Mr Gladstone's Suspensory Bill, or would they
recognise in this juncture one of " those rare and
great occasions on which the national will has
fully declared itself," when, as the Marquis of
Salisbury had laid down, it was the duty of

the House of Lords to yield to the opinion of the country.[1]

The President of the Board of Trade, Mr John Bright, took the unusual course of anticipating the decision which the Peers might be expected to take, in a letter to the Birmingham Liberal Association. He made use of some expressions of a kind with which the public has since been made familiar on the lips of those who claim to be known as advanced politicians; but those were days of greater reticence, and

---

[1] The duty of the House of Lords in dealing with measures which have obtained the assent of the other House has been the subject of such frequent and angry controversy in the past, and is so likely to give rise in the future to controversy not less frequent and angry, that it is worth placing on record the pronouncement of one who has long led and still leads the majority in that House. "I am not blind," said the Marquis of Salisbury, in the course of the debate on this Suspensory Bill, "to the peculiar obligations which lie on the members of this House in consequence of the fixed and unalterable constitution of this House. I quite admit—every one must admit—that when the opinion of your countrymen has declared itself, and you see that their convictions—their firm, deliberate, sustained convictions—are in favour of any course, I do not for a moment deny that it is your duty to yield. It may not be a pleasant process—it may even make some of you wish that some other arrangement were possible ; but it is quite clear that, whereas a Minister or a Government, when asked to do that which is contrary to their conviction, may resign, and a member of the Commons, when asked to support any measure contrary to his convictions, may abandon his seat, no such course is open to your lordships ; and therefore, on those rare and great occasions on which the national will has fully declared itself, I do not doubt that your lordships would yield to the opinion of the country ; otherwise the machinery of Government could not be carried on."

threats directed by a Cabinet Minister against
the Upper Chamber were then of startling
novelty.

If [he wrote] the House of Lords reject the bill, it is
possible that a good many people may ask what is the
special value of a Constitution which gives a majority of
100 in one House for a given policy, and a majority of
100 in another House against it? It may be asked also
why the Crown, through its Ministers in the House of
Commons, should be found in harmony with the nation,
while the Lords are generally in direct opposition to it.
Instead of doing a little childish tinkering about life-
peerages, it would be well if the Peers could bring themselves on a line with the opinions and necessities of our
day. In harmony with the nation, they may go on for a
long time; but throwing themselves athwart its course,
they may meet with accidents not pleasant for them
to think about.

Lord Granville moved the second reading of
the Irish Church Bill on June 14, and the
debate which ensued was chiefly remarkable for
the speech delivered by the Bishop of Peterborough (Dr Magee) against it. It has since
remained in the memory of those who heard
it as one of the most impressive orations in
modern times, and although the proceedings
of the House of Lords are somewhat remotely
connected with this narrative, some reference
must be made to what was then universally held
to be the masterpiece of the debates in either

House.[1]　The Right Reverend Prelate began by brushing aside certain arguments on which great stress had been laid by the defenders of Establishment :—

> I am free to confess I cannot regard this bill as a proposal to violate the Coronation Oath. The Coronation Oath seems to me to be the seal of a compact between two parties; and I cannot understand how because one of the parties appeals to the Divine judgment to punish a breach of the compact, both parties may not agree to an alteration of the compact. In the second place, I cannot regard this measure as a violation of the Act of Union. I regard the Act of Union as a treaty not merely between two Legislatures, the members of which may be, and for the most part are, no longer in existence, but as a compact between two nations which still exist, and have a right to modify the terms of the treaty mutually agreed on between them.

Neither did he found on the inviolability of corporate property, for, accepting the proposition that there was a distinction between corporate and private property, he used that as the very ground on which to base his stoutest

---

[1] A certain well-known Scottish baronet, then in Parliament, noted rather for the force than for the length of his contributions to conversation, rode into the Park after listening to Bishop Magee's speech. A friend inquired if it had been a success, and what line of argument had been pursued. "Oh," said Sir Robert Anstruther, "it was the finest thing you ever heard. He said that Gladstone had appealed to them in the name of the Almighty to vote for the bill, but that for his part he would be d——d if he did so."

resistance to the proposal for disendowment, and uttered the following memorable and profound sentences :—

You will always observe in history that corporate property is always the first to be attacked in all great democratic revolutions. Especially is this so in the case of ecclesiastical corporate property, because ecclesiastical corporations for the most part are very wealthy, and at the same time are very weak. . . . Revolutions commence with sacrilege, and they go on to communism; or to put it in the more gentle and euphemistic language of the day, revolutions begin with the Church and go on to the land.

The course of the speech was marked by outbursts of applause in the Strangers' Gallery, a breach of parliamentary decorum which, unusual in the highest degree in either Chamber, is peculiarly at variance with the staid and impassive atmosphere of the House of Lords. Lord Derby, in opposing the second reading, took up those weapons which the Bishop of Peterborough had flung aside, and took his stand on the Treaty of Union and the Coronation Oath; whereas the Marquis of Salisbury condemned such arguments as "involving the inexpressible absurdity that an oath taken in the days of Adam may have lasted to this time, binding the whole human race under circumstances absolutely different from those of the Paradisiacal period, and that the duties of mankind may have been settled for ever by the act of one single individual at that time, and we might never be able to escape from them."

The division on the second reading was a remarkable one—

Contents	.	.	.	.	.	179
Non-Contents	.	.	.	.	.	146
Majority for the Bill	.	.	.	.		33

It is not without interest, even a quarter of a century after these events, to examine the composition of the majority in this division. It contained a large number of Conservative peers, including the Marquis of Salisbury, the Earl of Carnarvon, and Lord Lytton, and one Bishop (Thirlwall of St David's). Thirteen English and two Irish Bishops voted against the bill, while the Archbishops of Canterbury and York and the Bishop of Oxford (Wilberforce) refrained from voting. Many of those peers who thus supported the bill on second reading did so on the understanding that it would be largely altered in the Committee stage, and this, in effect, was done on such a scale that when their lordships' amendments came to be considered in the Commons, Mr Gladstone, confident in the force of a great majority, led the

House to disagree with the Lords on all such
amendments as could be regarded as at all important.   Ultimately, after much fierce talk of
the usual character about mending or ending
the House of Peers, a compromise was effected,
and the bill received the Royal assent on
July 26.

CHAPTER VII.

1870–1871.

VISIT TO PARIS — STATE OF PARTIES IN PARLIAMENT — THE SMOKING-ROOM OF THE HOUSE OF COMMONS—IRISH LAND BILL—ELEMENTARY EDUCATION BILL—SMITH'S MOTION ON THE THAMES EMBANKMENT—DEFEAT OF THE GOVERNMENT THEREON—LETTER ON AFFAIRS IN FRANCE—SMITH ELECTED TO FIRST LONDON SCHOOL BOARD—RELIGIOUS DIFFICULTY ARISING THERE SETTLED ON HIS MOTION—ASSISTS EMIGRA- TION TO CANADA — DEBATES ON ARMY BILL, BUDGET, AND BALLOT BILL—DAMAGED POSITION OF THE GOVERNMENT— IRISH HOME RULE—MR GLADSTONE'S SPEECH AT ABERDEEN.

IN the beginning of 1870, the year destined to see the fall of the French empire, Smith went to Paris, in order to prosecute inquiries into the management of the poor in France. The thorough way in which he set about his investigation there may best be illustrated by a few extracts from letters to his wife:—

PARIS, 15th Jan*y*. 1870.

I wrote very hurriedly yesterday, as I had been kept out by my friends much longer than I expected. Maynard took me first of all to M. Dubard, an Officer of the Guard.

From him we all went to his brother: we had a long conversation with him. He is assistant to the Procureur Imperial, who holds an analogous position to our Attorney-General, and he introduced me to the Chief of the Municipal Police of Paris—a Mons. Nuss. He was very courteous, gave me a lot of information, and knew everything himself about our system, which he thinks a bad one. But first of all I had been to the Hôtel de Ville, and saw the Sous-chef in the Secretariat of the Prefect of the Seine. From him I went to the Chief of the Bureau of the Assistance Publique, and he talked to me for half an hour, and gave me permission to visit everything and to ask any questions I liked. He gave me great reports to study, and I am to return with any written questions, to which he will give written answers. Nothing could exceed his kindness and readiness to give information. From him I went to the Palais de Justice, to encounter again my friend the Procureur's adjoint, and he took me by a tortuous dirty route, by which I fancy many troubled persons have passed in troubled times to the Prefecture of Police. I have told you of M. Nuss, whom I saw there: from him I went to the Chef of the 1st Division of Police, to get permission to visit the Depôt de Mendicité, and it was his volubility which nearly destroyed me. He wanted to tell me everything, and for full half an hour he poured out a torrent of words, and every time I said " Oui, vraiment," meekly, he began again, until it got dark, and I became fairly alarmed lest I should be detained until the post had gone, and you cannot imagine the strain of mind in the endeavour to mentally translate and follow the stream of what was really very useful, only it was too much. . . . I am not surprised you tell me to keep out of harm's way. The news in the English papers looks very threatening, but since I have been here there has not been the slightest appearance of dangerous excitement. On Wednesday there was danger, and on that day and during part of Thursday the troops were consigned to their barracks, and had 92 rounds of ball-cartridge served out to each man. On Monday I begin the tour of visits to the different Institutions.

Jan. 17.

We start directly to visit one of the district bureaux de bienfaisance, then we visit one of the large Hospitals, questioning as we go ; then we go to Mr Gardiner, an English Clergyman, who has been long here, to pump him as to the condition of the Paris poor—from him we hope to get the names of some French Protestant Clergy who can give similar and independent information. I think this will be as much as we shall do to-day—and to-morrow I go to the Depôt de Mendicité at S. Denis, and I hope also to see the Head of the whole administration, to ask questions arising out of the observations we may make in the meantime. So my work will go on. I hope to finish on Wednesday evening, after dining with the Mess of the Guard.

Jan. 18.

Yesterday's work was very interesting. I arranged to see the Head of the Protestant system of charity, and I went over two of the Hospitals—one a very large one and the newest in Paris, and another for the middle-class, where people are received and treated on payment, according to the accommodation given, of amounts varying from 4 to 10 francs per day. It is an excellent institution, as one could provide for one's friend or even oneself in illness without being under the necessity of accepting charity. . .

Paris is quiet, but it is a very curious quiet, the more one sees of it.

PARIS, *Jan.* 19, 1870.

I went yesterday with Maynard to M. Husson, the head of all the poor relief of Paris, and had a long interview with him. The result was, he sent us by his Secretary to the Director of the Bureau in the Mairie du Temple; and when we went to him, he arranged that a Commissaire and a Visitor should be ready at 1 to-day to go with us to the houses of the poor, and that we should see with our own eyes the application of the system from beginning to end. After this I called on M. Grand Pierre, the Protestant chief Pastor of Paris, and had a long talk with him, and a very interesting one. The difficulty I shall find will be in digesting and arranging all this information in my own mind.

Jan. 20.

I wonder what the children would have said if they had been with me yesterday at the Hospice des Enfants Assistés. It was most interesting, but in some respects a most painful sight. One room, which was called the Crêche, for newly born infants—or infants at the breast—contained about 50 cots, and when we were there, there were about 25 babies in the room. There was a Sister of Charity and a clerk engaged in marking them—*i.e.*, each child when received has a necklace and distinguishing mark, corresponding with a register, placed round its neck—and secured so that it cannot be taken off except by pincers. There was a row of wet-nurses advancing in order with their little bundles, and the printed paper with particulars, which is affixed to the cap of the poor little baby when taken in at the door, was exchanged from this necklace. On a sort of ottoman in front of the fire lay a row of something. As I got near to it, I found it was a row of very young babies not many days old—all dressed alike as a short bundle, labelled on their caps, all turned the same way—and looking less like babies, except for their poor little mouths and faces, than anything you can conceive. There was one just dressed, which certainly had not been born many hours, which its mother will probably never see again, and which certainly had never seen its mother, for its eyes were not yet open. This side of the picture was painful, and the sense that although there was great care, it was a general and not a particular care that was taken of these poor things.[1] To-day I have been again to the Bureau de Bienfaisance, and have by the kindness of the Sisters of Charity seen the whole working of the system. I am afraid it could not be carried out at all without them. I have also been since the morning to S. Denis to see the Depôt de Mendicité of Paris, and there I saw misery enough to make one sad, especially as it was of the hopeless kind springing from past errors, infirmity, or incompetence of some kind or other in most cases, and the place smelt—stank, most abominably, as you know how. I went also this morning with the Visitor to see a poor family receiving relief in one of the old houses in Paris, and you can only imagine it—I cannot describe it.

Smith entered Parliament at a time when the Conservative party was staggering under a crushing defeat at the polls. Disraeli's "leap in the dark" had landed in disaster, from which, in the opinion of many, and especially of the country party, there was no prospect of recovery. House-

---

[1] It will be remembered that Rousseau rid himself of his children by placing them in the receptacle for *enfants trouvés*. "*Je* savais que l'éducation pour eux la moins perilleuse était celle des enfans trouvés."—'Les Rêveries,' ixme. Promenade.

hold suffrage seemed to have swamped the instructed classes, and the presence of Mr Bright
in the Cabinet, representing the extreme, and, as
they had hitherto been regarded, revolutionary
Radicals, was full of boding for all interested in
maintaining the old order of the Constitution and
the security of property. The Opposition were
dispirited and inactive; they fought the Irish
Church Bill with resolution, but even on that
question there was a want of energy on their
front bench. Disraeli was absent from the House
on account of ill-health throughout the Committee stage of that great measure; Northcote,
who should have been his lieutenant, was much
abroad on foreign missions; and Gathorne-Hardy
was accused of want of industry. Under such
circumstances as these, there always springs up
among the younger members of the party a feeling of dissatisfaction at the laxity of resistance
to the policy of the Government. It was so on
this occasion, and Smith took his place among a
small but determined · band sitting below the
gangway, a part of the House which at that
time, before the broad lines of party had been
confused by the creation of Home Rulers and
Liberal Unionists, implied a degree of independence of strict party discipline. Conspicuous
among these stalwarts were Mr Richard Asshe-

ton Cross [1] and Lord Sandon, with whom Smith soon fell into close co-operation, and these three, with some associates, soon came to be looked on as the practical leaders of Opposition. It was no uncommon thing, when matters were moving sluggishly among the Conservatives, for Disraeli to give a hint to this little group that the fire wanted stirring.

The proceedings which take place, with greater or less decorum, among the occupants of the dingy green benches in the Chamber itself, are, in a large degree, the outcome of much that goes on elsewhere, and there is no corner of Westminster Palace where projects spring so quickly into being and are nursed into maturity than in the smoking-room of the House of Commons. When James I., with royal profusion of adjectives, penned his ' Counter-blaste' against the " continuall vse of taking this vnsauorie smoake," asked, " What honour or policy can moove vs to imitate the barbarous and beastly maners of the wilde, godlesse and slauish *Indians*, especially in so vile and stinking a custome ? " and wound up by denouncing it as " a custome loathsome to the eye, hatefull to the nose, harmefulle to the braine, dangerous to the lungs, and in blacke stinking fume thereof neerest resembling the

---

[1] Created Viscount Cross in 1886.

horrible stigian smoake of the pit that is bot-
tomlesse," he could not have foreseen what an
important influence it was to have, not only on
the revenue, but on the general direction of
national policy.   In 1870 there was but one
smoking - room for the use of members of the
House of Commons (there are now three), an
ill - lit, draughty, cheerless apartment opening
upon the terrace, and this was the favourite
resort of the most active spirits in all the political sections.   Here, more than elsewhere, was
the realm of frankness : men of the most divergent views chatted together and discussed the
course of events—past, present, and to come ;
on this neutral field Cross, Sandon, and Smith
used to spend much of their time.

When Parliament reassembled in 1870, the
condition of Ireland showed little to justify the
expectation professed by the authors of the Irish
Church Act as to the conciliatory effect it was
to have on disaffected persons.   On the contrary,
the Fenian movement had become so formidable
towards the close of 1869 that the Government
had found it necessary to strengthen the force
in Ireland by the addition of several battalions,
agrarian crime increased at a frightful rate, and
there seemed to be no limit to the violence of

seditious language uttered in the National press. Nevertheless, undaunted by the ill return shown for their efforts at conciliation, the Cabinet resolved to persevere further in that direction, and thereby justify, within a shorter time than could have been predicted, the forecast made by the Bishop of Peterborough, that, having despoiled the Church of her corporate property, they would direct their next attack against private property in land; for whatever opinion may be held as to the manner in which Irish landlords had exercised their rights and the spirit in which their estates had been administered, it cannot be questioned that the effect of the Land Bill introduced by the Government was to diminish very seriously the value of landed property in Ireland. The appearance of this Land Bill was a direct fulfilment of the eloquent Prelate's forecast.

But the Conservative leaders could not be blind to the state of matters in Ireland: they could not fail to recognise that the rights and wrongs of private ownership in land had been confused by the tacit recognition in certain parts of Ireland of customs of tenure, utterly unknown in England and Scotland, and of the existence in the other provinces of precisely the same

conditions which had led to the sanction of
tenant-right in Ulster. They resolved, therefore, not to oppose the bill on second reading;
but, by attacking the details of it in Committee,
to purge it of the novel and obnoxious principles
it contained. A division, it is true, was taken
against the second reading, but it revealed the
grotesque proportions of 442 votes to 11, and
in the minority were only found two Conservatives, one of whom, Mr, now the Right Honourable, James Lowther, to this day maintains
in Parliament a consistent and dogged resistance
to almost every innovation.

In Committee the first and principal conflict
was joined upon the third clause, which provided compensation for disturbance, even in those
parts of Ireland where tenant-right was not a
recognised custom. To this clause Mr Disraeli
moved an amendment limiting compensation to
unexhausted improvements—in itself an important concession in a country where it was extremely rare for improvements to be undertaken
by any one except the tenant. The debate on
this clause was long and animated; the division
was momentous, because it marked the first step
in a long course of legislation based on the
principle of dual ownership, and Mr Disraeli's
amendment was defeated by 296 votes to 220.

Although Smith took no active part in the debates on this important measure, it seems to have been at this time that his interest was drawn to the subject of it, and led to the exertions he devoted to it in after-years, and the share it will be shown that he had in the efforts made to relieve Irish landlords from the intolerable position in which they had been left, by equitably transferring property from the owner to the occupier.

To the consideration of another bill, introduced by Mr W. E. Forster two days after the Irish Land Bill,— a measure not so startling as the other in its innovation upon recognised principles, but not of interest less complex nor results less far - reaching — the Elementary Education Bill — Smith was able to bring ripe experience as well as sympathetic assistance. His friendship with Forster, at that time Vice-President of the Committee of Council on Education (which is the cumbersome periphrasis prescribed by departmental etiquette as the title of our Minister of Education),[1] probably began in numerous

---

[1] Time, it is said, was made for slaves, and the subjects of Queen Victoria, being nothing if not a free people, show a lofty contempt for economy in that commodity, especially, as is well known, in the House of Commons. Otherwise it might be interesting to calculate how many minutes are lost in debate by observance of the rule prohibiting one member alluding to another except by mentioning

confidential conferences at the time this bill was under consideration — a friendship which endured to the last, through many heated controversies in Parliament on other subjects about which the two men held more divergent views than about education.

It is a feature to be noted in Smith's public life that he never sowed any parliamentary wild oats. Most men who have risen to distinction in the House of Commons, at all events since the Reform Bill of 1832, have brought themselves into prominence either by persistent oratory, whether excellent or mediocre ; by identifying themselves with some particular question, in which chance or choice had made them expert ; or, lastly, by threatened or actual attacks upon the leaders of their party at critical junctures. None of these proceedings marked Smith's career at any time. Though professing independence when he entered the House, he found that the only practical course was to abandon that idea, and he yielded unwavering

his constituency or his office. The custom, no doubt, had its origin in a salutary avoidance of the risk of personal altercation and even collision, which must be held to justify the use of such circumlocutory phrases as "the honourable and learned member for the —— division of ——shire" to designate "Mr Jones," or "the Right Honourable gentleman the Chief Secretary to the Lord Lieutenant of Ireland" to indicate the ruler of Ireland for the time being.

loyalty to those who directed the party with whom he found himself most in harmony : he never suffered those subjects with which he was most conversant to assume the proportions of a "hobby" or the plumage of a "fad"; least of all could he pretend to gifts of eloquence, and showed no disposition to inflict himself on the attention of the House except when he was able to contribute something solid to its deliberations. Public education was one of those subjects on the discussion of which, alike by experience and inclination, he was fitted to take an intelligent part ; he spoke, accordingly, several times during the passage of Mr Forster's measure, but invariably with a brevity, as the records of Hansard testify, almost inverse to the weight of matter contained in his speeches.

The most controversial point in the bill was that dealing with the future of religious instruction in schools, and upon this the Opposition in the House of Commons were divided. The young Conservatives, among whom were Smith, Cross, and Lord Sandon, were in favour of voluntary religious instruction, but Disraeli and Gathorne-Hardy [1] stood out for the full Church of England

---

[1] Created Viscount Cranbrook in 1878, and Earl Cranbrook in 1892.

teaching. There was, of course, a third party
in the House, stoutly advocating the total pro-
hibition of religious instruction under all circum-.
stances in public schools ; but the Government,
supported by the advanced section of the Opposition, adopted a middle course, which, while it
gave school boards power to forbid religious
teaching altogether, also empowered them to
permit schoolmasters to read and expound Scripture without the introduction of Creeds or
Catechisms.

Another feature of novel interest may be noted
in this bill—namely, the provision made for introducing ballot-voting, up to that time unknown in
this country, in the election of school boards ; and
in connection with this, Smith supported Lord
Frederick Cavendish's amendment in favour of
cumulative voting, which, devised as a safeguard
to the reasonable representation of minorities, has
since proved, as many people think, unduly favourable to them.

But the most important alteration in the bill
which Lord Sandon and Mr Smith were chiefly
instrumental in inducing Ministers to accept was
the withdrawal of the clause constituting twenty-
three school boards for the metropolis and sub-
stituting one, creating a single board for the
whole of London. The experience of Sandon

and Smith in the management of the Bishop of London's Fund had convinced them that it was important to secure the services of capable, independent, and responsible men to administer the Act in densely populous districts, and they saw clearly that there would be little to induce such persons to become candidates for seats on small local boards.

They urged with great perseverance upon Mr Forster how necessary it was, in the interests of education, to attract the best men ·to the work, and finally convinced him, not so much by arguments spoken across the floor of the House, as during repeated and prolonged private interviews in the Privy Council Office, that their view was just. The consequence was the withdrawal of the original clause, and the substitution of one establishing the London School Board as it now is. In his speech on the motion for going into Committee on the bill, Smith had urged that this principle should be observed in the formation of all school boards which should have areas coterminous with counties; but acting on the *ne sutor* maxim, as a metropolitan member he was satisfied with having secured its application to the metropolis.

The good understanding between Smith and Forster in their endeavours to settle this ques-

tion is illustrated by a passage in a letter of
the former to his wife on July 29 :—

I am very glad I was in the House last night, as
Forster, with whom, as you know, I like to work, came
to me and expressed a wish that I should hear his
statement on Education, and then I had to say a word.

Before the House of Commons parted with the
bill, Mr M'Cullagh Torrens, on behalf of the
Radical supporters of the Government, pronounced a frank recognition of the part taken
in promoting its success by the hon. member for
Westminster, " whose services in connection with
this bill he could not too strongly acknowledge."
On another matter which formed the subject of
debates during this session, Smith made more
than one speech. As long as we have the poor
with us, so long the presence of persons ready
with advice and proposals for their betterment
may be reckoned on ; but it is not always those
who best understand the problems involved who
are most ready to give advice and to put forward
proposals. Smith had worked long and hard
among the London poor: his speeches on the
second reading of the Poor Relief (Metropolis)
Bill (April 25), and on Dr Brewer's motion for
the Better Regulation of Outdoor Relief (May
10), consisted of practical arguments temperately
expressed, illustrated by examples of shamefully

bad administration of the law which he himself had witnessed.

But the most direct success which the member for Westminster achieved was of a nature peculiarly exhilarating to a somewhat dispirited Opposition, bringing about, as it did, the defeat of the Government, and securing to the people of London a result for which they ought to feel grateful at this day. In the formation of the Thames Embankment below Westminster Bridge an extent of land valued at £5000 a-year had been reclaimed from the river, which came as foreshore into the hands of the Office of Woods and Forests : on this land it was proposed by the Government to erect certain public offices, and Smith met this scheme with a motion that an address be presented to her Majesty, praying that the land, which had been reclaimed at the heavy expense of the ratepayers, should now be reserved for their advantage as a breathing - place and pleasure - ground. The Chancellor of the Exchequer (Mr Lowe) and Mr Gladstone both spoke vehemently against the motion, the former minimising the objections to the scheme of the Government as " sentimental or æsthetical arguments," the latter declaring that the address moved for would be " flatly contrary to the law of the land, which makes it the duty of the Commissioners of Woods and Forests to turn to the best profitable account the property of the Crown," and that to dispose prospectively of Crown land to the extent of £150,000 would be an invasion of the Prince of. Wales's rights of entail. Mr Locke, in supporting the motion, moved the House to laughter by declaring that "wherever you build in this country you are sure to make an eyesore of it." In the division which followed, the Government were defeated by 158 votes to 108, and the question was hung up for the time.

During this year a change was effected which was destined to have a very important and lasting effect on the character and constitution of the Civil Service. An Order in Council was promulgated, directing that in future all appointments to situations in the Public Departments (except those to the Foreign Office and certain other posts requiring professional qualifications) should be made by competitive examination. This year also witnessed the surrender by the Sovereign of the Royal Prerogative in the government of the army, and the Secretary of State for War became the official superior of the Commander-in-Chief.

After the prorogation Smith took a tour in Scotland. The terrible disasters which had already in the early autumn begun to overtake the distracted empire of France in the conflict with Prussia made a melancholy impression on his mind, and there are many allusions to that country in his letters. Writing to Mr Ford, from Tarbert, Loch Lomond, on September 12, he remarked :—

I cogitate as I wend my way along roads made most beautifully, but along which scarcely twenty people pass in the course of a day, so silent and lonely and uninhabited is this district when the Tourists have passed. . . . If it were not for newspapers, it would be difficult to believe there could be moral storms, earthquakes, among societies and peoples—the figure of iron and clay falling, crashing, and no form of order remaining, but all selfishness asserting itself—one class hiding, running away; others displaying their natural instincts as savage predatories; and all law and justice in abeyance.

This is the result of a Government *for* the people, and not *by* the people; of centralisation and bureaucracy; of a resolute resolve of every individual to live for himself, to ignore his share of the common burden of care and work for the public weal which belongs to every man; that virtue of personal service which in one way the Prussian people are showing they can give to the Prussian state, and which the French, for love of ease, love of pleasure, love of money, have insisted shall be done for them by a strong Government. And we see the result.

The unexpected happens in this year 1870, and therefore Paris may escape a siege, and it may escape being sacked by the reds, and the Republic may last for a time, but the people will not learn, they will not change; and under whatever name—whether you call it republic, constitutional monarchy, or an Empire—they will still insist on being governed, not on governing themselves, and they will use material riches and power only for increasing mental demoralisation.[1]

These sentiments will perhaps strike the reader as having a good deal of insular bias, and as showing some tendency to judge the national spirit of France by the moods and motives of the populace of Paris, and there is more interest in what follows :—

I am concerning myself about the election of the School Board for London, and if I hear favourable accounts from Armstrong,[2] to whom I have written, I shall stand, and Lord Sandon with me, as candidates for Westminster. It is a bold thing to do, but I have two great objects in view—to show my earnest interest in education, and to endeavour to prove that popular election may result in the creation of a Board in London as strong in position, character, and fitness for its work as the House of Commons itself. Forster very strongly pressed me to engage in the work, and I like him, and like to work with him.

The intention thus expressed Smith carried out successfully, being returned to the first school

---

[1] While these lines are being written, the papers are reporting the formation of the thirtieth French Ministry in twenty-three years.

[2] Created Sir George Armstrong, Bart., in 1892.

board for London—a body which fully justified by its composition the anticipation he had formed of the kind of men who would be attracted to it. With Lord Lawrence as chairman, the board possessed among its members such men of note as Mr Charles Reed, M.P., Professor Huxley, Mr Hepworth Dixon, Mr M'Cullagh Torrens, M.P., the Rev. Dr Angus (Baptist), the Rev. Dr Rigg (Wesleyan), Viscount Sandon, M.P., and Mr Samuel Morley, M.P.

The first act of the member for Westminster in the deliberations of this newly constituted body was characteristic of the man. The question of religious education in board schools, which had distracted earnest people from one end of the country to the other, and had, it was fondly hoped, been laid to rest by the compromise agreed to in Committee on the Education Bill, was revived in an acute form in the narrower limits of the London School Board. It was Smith—the Smoother, the quiet, unpretentious reconciler of conflicting opinions — who framed a resolution providing an easy escape from this formidable difficulty. The purport of this resolution was the adoption of a by-law ordering that the Bible should be read, and instruction in religious subjects given therefrom, in the board schools generally, while those interested in particular schools might show cause for exemption from the whole or part of this by-law; and in all schools it was to be understood that the spirit of the Act was to be observed, and no proselytism allowed. This proposal, though opposed by Professor Huxley and two other ardent secularists, was seconded by that distinguished Nonconformist, Mr Samuel Morley, and, being supported by Roman Catholic, Baptist, and Wesleyan members, was carried by 38 votes to 3.

Gratitude for relief thus afforded from what had promised to be a long and bitter controversy found free expression in newspapers of all shades of politics. One of those most strongly opposed to the party represented by Mr Smith had a leading article which is such a delicious example of the style dear to the English journalist in moments of expansion, that it certainly ought not to be allowed to pass into oblivion :—

Post tenebras lux! The motto, good at any time for such a body as the London School Board, is especially appropriate after the proceedings of yesterday. Mr W. H. SMITH, that sturdy and singularly sweet-tempered axe-man, has hewed his way to the light through a tangled forest of what seemed unconquerable difficulties, by dint of the sharp edge of common-sense, strongly hefted with broad human and Christian sympathy. The public knows but too well where the School Board left off on Monday.

Every member felt that a crisis was at hand, on the issue of which depended the capacity of the body for useful work in all time coming. Deep darkness and the night seemed settling down upon the Board, doomed almost ere it left port to suffer disabling shipwreck on obstacles of its own creation. In a happy moment, Mr SMITH presented himself as the pilot to weather the storm. . . . But the old leaven of anti-denominationalism was allowed to work again after all virtue—for good or ill—seemed taken out of it; and when the debate is resumed, under the auspices of Canon Cromwell, nobody can tell how far the vessel of the School Board may have drifted away from that welcome opening into blue water, which Mr Smith signalised yesterday, amid the hearty approval both of his friends and of those who but a minute before had been his foes.[1]

It would be very hard to beat the agility with which this writer skips from metaphor to metaphor—presenting Mr Smith to his readers first as the "sturdy and singularly sweet-tempered axeman," and then as the pilot weathering the storm, passing from the unusual phenomenon of a ship drifting upon "obstacles of its own creation" to the figure of the action of a sinister "leaven," working either in the "tangled forest," or in the ship, or in the sea, and thence once more to the restful prospect of the blue sea.

Smith's work in the East End had convinced

---

[1] Daily Telegraph, 1st November 1871.

him that the lot of many of the poor who swarmed in the slums of London could only be relieved by removing them to new lands, and this led him to take an active part in the affairs of the East End Emigration Club, in connection with the British and Colonial Emigration Society. On June 26, 1870, he went down to Gravesend to bid adieu to 1197 emigrants to Canada, passengers in the Ganges and the Tweed. The expenses of about 250 of these were defrayed by himself; but his interest in them was not allowed to drop with their departure, for in 1872 he visited Canada and devoted close inquiry to the resources of that country and the condition of the emigrants there.

It must always be difficult to decide where legitimate opposition in Parliament ends and factious obstruction begins. A good deal depends on the nature of the measures proposed by a Government—whether the resistance is directed against such as are genuinely obnoxious to a large party in the House, or whether dilatory tactics are pursued in discussing harmless proposals, in order to postpone progress with such as are regarded with greater aversion. If their proceedings during the session of 1871 be submitted to this test, the Opposition must be acquitted of the charge of obstruction made

against them; for although debates were prolonged almost beyond precedent, the subjects of
them were two bills of a highly controversial
and novel character, against which, if opposition
is justifiable at all, those who opposed them were
justified in employing all the force permitted by
the forms of the House.

These two measures were the Army Regulation
Bill, introduced by the Secretary of State for
War (Mr Cardwell), and the Parliamentary and
Municipal Elections Bill, introduced by Mr Forster.
It was about the first of these measures that the
hottest conflicts were joined, especially on the
clauses providing for the Abolition of Purchase
in the Army. They contained a bold proposal.
Purchase in future was to be illegal, but no
officer who had entered by purchase was to suffer
loss; the public were to be called on to refund
not only the regulation prices of their commissions, but whatever they had paid in excess of
regulation, amounting in all to $7\frac{1}{2}$ or $8\frac{1}{2}$ millions.

To summarise the arguments of the Government and the Opposition in a single sentence
from the speeches delivered on either side, that
of Mr Goschen may be quoted when, in replying
to the toast of her Majesty's Ministers at the
Lord Mayor's Banquet on Easter Monday, he
said: "We have to buy back our army, which

belongs at this moment to the officers and not to the nation;" whereas the Marquis of Salisbury, in opposing the bill in the House of Lords, declared that "if purchase had been described as a system of seniority tempered by selection, the more correct formula of the proposed system was stagnation tempered by jobbery."

This bill was before the House of Commons for four months: the rules of debate as they then were afforded no means of bringing interminable discussion to a close, till, in the second week in June, Mr Cardwell announced that the Government would only insist on the Purchase Clauses and the transfer of control of the Militia and Volunteers from the Lieutenants of counties to the Crown. When at last the bill, in this mutilated condition, reached the Lords, it fell upon worse times. By 155 votes to 130 they refused to pass it. Then followed Mr Gladstone's *coup d'état.* On the second day after the division in the Lords, the Prime Minister informed the House of Commons that the Queen, acting on the advice of her Ministers, had signed a Royal Warrant abolishing the purchase of commissions in the army.

The excitement caused by this announcement was intense. The Peers accepted a resolution proposed by the Duke of Richmond, censuring the Government on account of "the interposition of the Executive during the progress of a measure submitted to Parliament by her Majesty's Government, in order to attain by the exercise of the Prerogative, and without the aid of Parliament, the principal object included in that measure." Explanations were demanded in the Commons also, and to this day it is doubtful whether the Government were in their rights in the action they had taken ; for the Attorney-General (Sir R. Collier) and the Solicitor-General (Sir J. Coleridge) differed sharply in the grounds on which they based their defence of what had been done. Whereupon up jumped Mr Harcourt from below the gangway,[1] and, amid much laughter, in racing parlance asked the Prime Minister to say on which horse the Government declared to win — with Attorney-General on Statute or Solicitor-General on Prerogative.

Probably the best justification for this highhanded proceeding is to be found in the consideration urged by the Prime Minister that, once the question had been raised, it was dangerous to the discipline of the army to keep it longer in suspense.

Mr Lowe's Budget brought the Administration into deep disgrace with the country.   It is mem-

[1] Now the Right Hon. Sir William Vernon Harcourt.

orable, if for nothing else, for the solemn perpe-
tration of a pun by the Chancellor of the Exchequer. Casting about for some new and unob-
jectionable source of revenue, his envious eyes
fell on the match trade, which at that time
annually produced and disposed of 560 million
boxes of wooden matches and 46 million boxes of
wax vestas and fusees in the United Kingdom.
His proposal to impose a tax on matches was
accompanied by the explanation that this was to
be levied by affixing a stamp to each box, bearing
the legend, *Ex luce lucellum*—a little gain out
of light; but never did a proposed tax more
quickly kindle opposition. The match - sellers
were a feeble folk, it might have been thought ;
but they proved to be extremely combustible, and
produced a perfect conflagration of discontent.
Processions of match-girls paraded the streets, the
ill-starred pleasantry irritated the public, and,
finally, the proposal was withdrawn, and an additional 2d. on the Income-Tax substituted. The
opposition to this was led by Mr Smith, but after
a debate which lasted till two in the morning, his
amendment was negatived by 335 to 250. In
commenting on the debate and its result, the
' Times,' which in those days always gave independent support to the existing Government,
asserted that Smith's amendment was lost " not

because the majority disapproved its principle, but because they wished to spare the Administration. The merits of the last scheme of the Government were never fairly discussed. It was tacitly, if not expressly, condemned by all. The balance of reason was on one side, but the force of sympathy was on the other, and the Ministry secured a vote, not by argument, but by favour."

On May 5, on the motion for going into Committee of Supply, Smith called attention to the operation of the Poor Law within the metropolis, and moved for the appointment of a Royal Commission to inquire into the policy and administration of the law. Now, of the many members who rise "to call attention," only a small fraction succeed in obtaining it, but Smith was one of that number on this occasion. His well-known connection with practical philanthropy, combined with the alarming increase in the number of persons who were receiving relief from the rates, enabled him to make out a formidable case for inquiry, for he was able to show that, whereas in the preceding ten years of general prosperity the population of London had increased 16 per cent, pauperism had risen in the prodigious ratio of 64 per cent. But he was unable to persuade the House to adopt his resolution, which, after a long and interesting discussion, was withdrawn.

Twenty-two years later, in the present year 1893, the subject has been revived. A Royal Commission has been appointed to inquire into the administration of the Poor Law in England and Wales, and their labours have already brought to light how immensely the ratio of pauperism has been reduced by the consistency and discrimination in giving outdoor relief, the want of which formed the main burden of his complaint of the state of matters in 1871.

The Parliamentary and Municipal Elections Bill, or, to use the better known title derived from its most important and debateable provision, the Ballot Bill, was brought in early in the session, but, owing to the prolonged proceedings on the Army Bill, it was not till late in June that progress could be made with it. Mr Gladstone, who for thirty-five years had stoutly resisted the principle of secret voting, now performed on this question a complete change of front, and declared that the bill must pass before the session should be brought to a close. Midsummer Day had gone by, there was still a heavy proportion of the Votes in Supply to be got through, and the Tory Opposition was obstinate. Moreover, there stood on the Notice Paper upwards of 200 proposed amendments to the bill, half of them in names of supporters of the

Government. Under these discouraging circumstances Mr Gladstone resorted to the sagacious expedient of calling his party into council in Downing Street, persuaded them to withdraw their amendments, and to agree to a policy—his opponents of course called it a conspiracy—of silence. This proved successful; and although the Government suffered defeat at the hands of two of their own supporters, Mr Harcourt and Mr James, on the proposal to charge election expenses on the rates, they were able to send the bill up in time to be considered by the Lords. Here, however, it was destined to be thrown out by a majority of nearly two to one.

This was the closing event of a session which had proved singularly damaging to ministers; and although it is a well-known maxim of old parliamentary hands not to argue too much from by-elections, the significance of the result of those which took place during the autumn in the immemorial Liberal strongholds of East Surrey and Plymouth could scarcely be overlooked.

The Fenian agitation had been overcome, but the chronic restlessness of Irish discontent began about this time to crystallise into a form all the more dangerous to the integrity of the empire because it assumed the guise of constitutional agitation. Home Rule for Ireland began for the first time to be a source of concern to politicians, and the constituencies of England and Scotland heard with relief the following plain bold words spoken by Mr Gladstone at Aberdeen on the occasion of his receiving the freedom of that town.

You would expect, when it is said that the Imperial Parliament is to be broken up, that at the very least a case should be made out showing there were great subjects of policy and great demands necessary for the welfare of Ireland which representatives of Ireland had united to ask, and which the representatives of England, Scotland, and Wales had united to refuse. There is no such grievance. There is nothing that Ireland has asked and which this country and England has refused. This country has done for Ireland what it would have scrupled to do for England and for Scotland. . . . What are the inequalities of England and Ireland? I declare that I know none, except that there are certain taxes still remaining which are levied over Englishmen and Scotchmen and which are not levied over Irishmen, and likewise that there are certain purposes for which public money is freely and largely given in Ireland and for which it is not given in Scotland. That seems to me to be a very feeble case, indeed, for the argument which has been made, by means of which, as we are told, the fabric of the united Parliament of this country is to be broken up. But if the doctrines of Home Rule are to be established in Ireland, I protest on your behalf that you will be just as well entitled to it in Scotland: and moreover I protest on behalf of Wales, in which I have lived a good deal, and where there are 800,000 people, who, to this day, such is their sentiment of nationality, speak hardly anything but

their own Celtic tongue—a larger number than speak the
Celtic tongue, I apprehend, in Scotland, and a larger
number than speak it, I apprehend, in Ireland—I protest
on behalf of Wales that they are entitled to Home Rule
there.   Can any sensible man—can any rational man, suppose that at this time of day, in this condition of the
world, we are going to disintegrate the great capital institutions of this country for the purpose of making ourselves ridiculous in the sight of all mankind, and crippling
any power we possess for bestowing benefits through legislation on the country to which we belong ?

Such were the convincing phrases by which all
suspicion of Mr Gladstone's indulgence to these
proposals was allayed—such the proclamation of
resolute purpose to maintain the integrity of Parliament and the realm, which it was the destiny
of him who spoke them in later years to minimise,
explain away, and retract.

Greatly as the pressure on Smith's time,
thoughts, and bodily strength had been increased
by the growing share he was taking in public
affairs, there may be traced in his correspondence
and private notes the same earnest anxiety about
the spiritual life which always pervaded his
thoughts and controlled his action.   Thus, at the
close of this year, on Advent Sunday, he wrote in
his journal :—

A new Christian year—an attempt to look at my own
daily life more narrowly, to try and examine motives as

well as actions. Mr Robinson of St John's [Torquay], preaching of the story of Uzziah, referred to the dangers of prosperity, of selfishness. Uzziah prospered, although called to the throne when the kingdom of Judah was in utter defeat, because he trusted in God: and he became a leper because he defied his laws. A lesson for nations and for individuals, to be read in the history of the Jews, in the history of our own times, and borne out by my own self-knowledge.

O God, give me to think of them more, of Thy love to me, and of my *duty;* and help me to pray always with faith.

CHAPTER VIII.

1872.

MEETING OF PARLIAMENT—UNPOPULARITY OF MINISTERS—THE
BALLOT BILL—THE THAMES EMBANKMENT SCHEME AGAIN—
SMITH SAILS FOR AMERICA—JOURNAL OF TRAVEL.

MINISTERS were able to lay before Parliament on February 6, 1872, a Queen's Speech which congratulated her faithful Commons on the relative freedom from crime in Ireland, and the remarkable prosperity of agriculture in that country. The Government were unpopular in the country, but had been protected from sinister consequences by the indifference to politics which invariably springs from extraordinary prosperity. The consequences of the financial disasters of 1866 had wellnigh passed away, the anxiety of the formidable troubles in France had been relieved, and the country had entered on that cycle of prosperity, the knell of which was not to be sounded till, six years later, the City of Glasgow Bank fell with dismal crash.

But the opening incident of the session was as inauspicious to the Administration as the close of the last had been. In defending themselves against a Vote of Censure for the appointment, contrary to statute, of their late Attorney-General, Sir Robert Collier, to a seat on the Judicial Committee, Ministers, with a normal or nominal majority of more than 100, were only able to show one of 27.

In a second Vote of Censure, moved by one of their own supporters, Mr Dixon, on account of the operation of the 25th section of the Elementary Education Act, they were more fortunate, being able to command the support of many Conservatives, among whom was Mr W. H. Smith, who spoke in deprecation of premature interference with the Act.

The Ballot Bill was once more introduced by Mr Forster, and probably there never was a bill secretly more detested by the House of Commons than this one. Contrary as it was to all national custom and parliamentary tradition, men felt ashamed of compelling their fellow-countrymen to accept the protection of secrecy in exercising a right which had always been used with the utmost openness. The measure had an un-British, almost cowardly complexion, and obviously the fair corollary to it—namely, secret voting by

members of Parliament in the division lobbies—
was one that could never be claimed. Nevertheless the Opposition seem to have been afraid to
resist it lest the franchise might, in the general
election which seemed not far distant, be used
under cover of the ballot against the party which
should seek to deny this protection to electors.
Hence, in spite of the fact that such well-known
Liberals as Mr Walter and Mr Fawcett denounced
the system of secret voting, the debate on the
Second Reading was half-hearted, and the division, taken in a listless and half-filled House,
showed in favour of the bill by 109 votes to 51.
Smith, who, as has been shown by his declara-
tions to the electors of Westminister, detested
the ballot, did not vote. But when the bill,
after a stormy passage through Committee, was
put down for Third Reading, the Opposition
plucked up heart and fought hard against it.
The division showed a majority of 58 in favour
of the bill, which was framed to expire in 1880,
since which time it has been necessary to renew
it annually by including it in the Expiring Laws
Continuance Bill, which is passed at the end of
every session.

The rest of the session of 1872 was occupied
principally in discussing Mr Cardwell's scheme
for the Localisation of the Army and the Ele-

mentary Education Bill for Scotland, in neither of which measures was it likely that Smith would take an interested part. Nor did he vote on Mr Jacob Bright's motion in favour of Women Suffrage, though it was supported by a good many Conservatives, such as Mr Hunt, Sir Stafford Northcote, Sir Charles Adderley,[1] &c.

One subject, however, in connection with which Smith had taken an active part, that of the Thames Embankment, on the management of which he had beaten the Government in 1870, came up in an altered form this year. No action had been taken in consequence of the Resolution of the House when Parliament reassembled in 1871, so Smith gave notice that he intended to move that " it was desirable that the ground reclaimed from the Thames between Whitehall Gardens and Whitehall Place should be devoted to the purposes of public recreation and amusement." The experience of the previous session made the Government aware that they could not successfully oppose this resolution; a repetition of defeat was a foregone conclusion, so before the day for its discussion came on, the Prime Minister took the course of referring the question to the consideration of a Select Committee. That body reported in favour of the disposal of the ground

---

[1] Created Lord Norton in 1878.

in the manner advocated by Smith and indicated by the vote of the House, but still the winter of 1871-72 passed without any action being taken to carry the plan into effect. Indeed so tenaciously did the Treasury adhere to the principles which should regulate the administration of Crown property, that a new Committee was appointed in 1872 at the instance of the Government, which reversed the decision of the former Committee, and recommended the appropriation of nearly all the space in dispute for the erection of public buildings. Thereupon the Chancellor of the Exchequer prepared and brought in a bill to give effect to this recommendation, but the only result was that Ministers suffered another defeat, this time on the motion of Mr Harcourt, who carried a resolution against them to the effect that it was not desirable to proceed further in the matter that year.[1]

[1] The settlement of this matter did not come till 1873. Smith did not allow it to rest until the Commissioners of Woods and Forests agreed practically to his proposal, by offering to hand over to the Metropolitan Board of Works almost the whole of the ground for a payment of £3270, an arrangement which was confirmed by Parliament and carried out. In May 1875 the new ornamental grounds, thus redeemed from being built over, having been completed, were formally declared open by Mr Smith, who had by that time become Secretary to the Treasury; and it is undoubtedly to his exertions that Londoners owe the enjoyment of a pretty piece of public garden. The seats therein were the gift of Mr Smith, and it is only necessary to walk there on a summer evening to see how much they are appreciated.

Having undertaken legislative responsibility, Smith was conscientiously anxious to fit himself for his duties by every means of acquiring knowledge of the effect of different forms of government and conditions of society. To this end it was natural that he should have early directed his thoughts to the great American Republic and the British American colonies. But the necessity for a separation from wife and children, even for a few months only, weighed heavily on his mind; his thoughts centred in his home, and the only reward he sought for his labours was to escape thither as often and for as long as might be. Circumstances made it inconvenient for Mrs Smith to accompany him, but he held it to be his duty to visit Canada and the United States, and he sailed in the 'Moravian' on August 15. During his absence his letters to his wife form a consecutive journal; and although many of the details contained in them are far too minute to be of general interest in these days, when travelling is so easy and so frequent, some of the sketches in this simple narrative are worthy of preservation, were it only that

> "Hence th' unlearned their wants may view,
> The learned reflect on what before they knew."

Wednesday, August 14.—Brougham to the train, and coachman drove so slowly that anxiety lest I should lose it almost drove out of my head and heart the pain of parting.

At the station I was fortunate enough to get into the same carriage with my future fellow-passengers, the Russell Gurneys, and it was a comfort to find them almost as sad at leaving as I was. On the way down Mrs Gurney tried to induce her husband to say he would be home again by Easter, but he talked of May! . . .

August 16.—What a change a few hours had made! Last night—almost a calm; this morning—flying scud, wet decks, and sad sounds below. We have been coasting Ireland since daybreak, and have just (9 A.M.) passed the Giant's Causeway, running for Moville, in Lough Foyle.

17th.—A dirty night for our first at sea. The Irish Channel was hardly worth the name of sea, and it blows hard this morning. We are well away from land, and out in the Atlantic. . . . Quiet prevails, with interjected sighs—almost groans. Food—dry toast and tea.

18th.—Very much the same. A serious tone prevails, and we speak respectfully of the Atlantic. Very few passengers visible. Food—still tea and toast. Have come to the belief that we are all in the habit of eating a great deal too much, and that so many meals on board ship are quite unnecessary. Night—roll, roll. . . . Children cry, and their mothers can't attend to them, and we have a lively night. An old lady in the cabin has a silver bell, which she is constantly ringing to assure the stewardess that she hears the water bubbling about the ship, and she is sure it is sinking. We are all grave, and most of us selfish. Captain read service in cabin; could not venture down. . . .

20th.—Fine. Ship steady. Turn up at breakfast for the first time. A shoal of porpoises, which seem to race with the ship for some time. Music on deck at night.

No sail in sight all day. Wind gets up towards evening.
Rain comes with it. I turn in early, but no sleep in
the ship to-night. Roll, roll, roll; crash, smash, bang go
china, plates, glasses, doors—everything that can move.
The old lady's bell rings constantly, and the Captain
keeps to the bridge on deck. In the morning our party
is smaller at breakfast than usual, and we have to hold
our cups in our hands and seesaw them as we drink.

Mrs MacNabb, who has crossed many times, and has
been wrecked once, begins to tell her story over again,
and wonders whether last night's Aurora forebode storms.
No ship in sight to-day—no life but sea-birds.

21st. — Old lady very troublesome; has heard there
is iron in the ship as cargo, and is quite sure it is
rolling about underneath her, and that the ship will go
down. Fore-cabin passengers and emigrants very miserable; all wet, and many sick. We went—*i.e.*, Mr and
Mrs Gurney and I—after dinner to the middle deck with
fruit for the poor children. . . .

25th. — Sunday morning, and as bright and beautiful as a Sunday should be. The breeze fresh ahead; the
ship moving a little, but running well; every one thankful, and in good spirits. We speedily ran past Anticosti—
an island of bears, 120 miles long—and sighted the opposite
Canadian shore—the promontory of Gaspé, where the St
Lawrence may be said to commence, and from this time
we shall be within four or five miles off shore all the way
to Quebec.

The shore here for miles is rocky, covered with low
timber, and dotted here and there with little fishermen's
huts, which look like tents at a distance, but are really
wooden buildings covered with whitewash. . . . Old Captain said that he liked the Old Hundredth psalm, because
it always seemed to him that it went straight up to the

masthead—a very simple description, but a very touching one, of his own honest but unaffected devotion; and many of us felt the mysterious sympathy which links together those who are using the same beautiful words and forms, however widely they may be separated from those they love. These words meet up higher, somewhere higher than the masthead—and they go straight up there.

26th.— . . . I have not heard the old lady's bell for three days, but there is a charming old maid and her canary, who are going together to California, who have been very amusing. They came to church together yesterday, and wherever she goes, he goes.

On the 27th they landed at Quebec, and, dining that night with the Governor-General, the Earl of Dufferin, Smith made the acquaintance of his host's private secretary, Mr Jacob Luard Pattisson, a gentleman who in after-years was to render him invaluable and devoted service.

Leaving Quebec on 30th, Smith went to Montreal, and here is one of his earliest experiences there :—

Sunday, Sept. 1.—I wanted a bath early, so I told the chamber-maid last night, and she promised to speak to the man. No women attend upon men in their bedrooms in Canada, but they look after their rooms when they are out of them. At 7 I rang: boy answered. "I want a bath." "Oh, do you? Very well," and went away: at 20 minutes past no bath. I rang again. An old man came this time. I said, "I ordered a bath a long time ago, and it has not come yet." "Did you? How long?" "More than half an hour." "Oh, I don't call half an hour a long time." "Don't you?" said I; "then we do in our country." "Ah, but it is Sunday morning, you know." " Well, never mind, bring the water and the towels." " You can't have any towels. The chamber-maid keeps them, and she has gone to breakfast."

Is not this a free country?

. . . I have spent a very quiet afternoon in my room, making use of the church-service so long used by my dear love. . . .

2nd.— . . . I have told you already of the Lachine rapids, which we shot this morning, and I will now finish the day. As soon as I had posted my letter for England, Mr G. Stephen [1] called with his carriage to take us a drive round the town, which proved to be more handsome than I had supposed. Private houses with gardens, which sell for £15,000 and more, and large public buildings all built of stone, some of it brought from Caen in France, and other from Peterhead in Scotland. We visited the cemetery on the mountain. Like that at Quebec, it is very large, and a very large part of it remains in a condition of wild or natural wood, which gives a sense of rest and even solitude to the little green settle- ments interspersed among the trees. A great proportion of the names on the monuments are Scotch, who are very successful in Canada. On our way down we had a view of the St Lawrence, the Rapids, the mountains of Vermont, and the country between. It was difficult to believe we were not at home, so home-like was the view, except for the magnitude of the river. . . .

I am learning a great deal, seeing very much that is interesting, and making the acquaintance of every man of note almost in Canada; but with all this qualified enjoy-

---

[1] Created Baron Mount-Stephen in 1891.

ment and sense of acquisition, I am looking forward so gladly and so hopefully to the bright November day of my return. . . . At present my watch is five hours behind London time, so that writing now at 12 it is 5 P.M. with you, and I often imagine to myself your engagements at the actual moment I am looking at the time. . . .

Descriptions of the Falls of Niagara can scarcely contribute anything at this time of day to the impressions of those who have not visited them : nevertheless the following sentences convey so distinctly the effect of the great cascade upon one witnessing it for the first time, that they are, perhaps, worth preserving :—

Sept. 4.— . . . We went to Government Island, coming through the trees by a most natural and pretty path to steps which led down to the edge of the American Fall. I will not attempt to describe it; but no disappointment is possible to any one who can admire Nature in her grandest and also most lovely forms. The mass of water is absolutely astounding, and it seems almost impossible it can go on with such a volume and force for ever. And the colours are marvellous, owing to the very different ways in which the light falls upon the falling water and spray. It appears to the eye to be divided into sections —one part rolling over the top smoothly in deep emerald green, broken as it falls way down by streaks of white foam, and in other parts by millions of watery diamonds glistening in the sun. Then there is a white section of water,—a dead white like snow in shade, as it is itself in shade, a section in which the white appears tinged with violet, and yet another where it takes a brownish or earthy hue. No one, I fancy, ever sees the bottom of the fall; for the mass of water crashing against water and rock pulverises itself and creates a cloud which is constantly rising by the force of the draught created by the fall, but as constantly renewed. At a distance it looks like the smoke of an enormous cauldron, steam from the boiling waters below; but on coming up to it you find it to be the minutest particles of water floating in the air, lighter than a Scotch mist, and as it floats away in the wind it adds a fresh grace and beauty to the scene, as the thinnest and most graceful of veils, through which to catch glimpses of beauty and colour beyond, or as affording material for the iris or rainbow lying down as it were on the water, which may always be seen if the sun is shining. . . .

I have never seen anything approaching these Falls for grandeur as well as for beauty, for every variety of light and shade, for every effect which they give in colour upon water. At one moment there is a sense of awe, of fear. The flow is so irresistible and tremendous. It is too much to look at, as the gleams of light catch the edges of the water, and they sparkle like the diamonds in a fairy palace, and there at the bottom, eddying slowly away, lies the water, looking exhausted and almost dead after its mighty leap. It is worth the journey to America and back to see the Falls alone. . . .

5th.— . . . After dinner we were taking another stroll on Goat Island, and we encountered the lady fellow-passenger of the Moravian, who had the canary-bird which had always gone with her wherever she went for 9 years, and which came to church in the cabin on the Sunday. She gave us the gratifying news that the bird was well so far. . . .

6th.— . . . As soon as I had finished my last letter, I started out for another look at the Falls, to which one is drawn by an irresistible fascination. It had rained heavily during the night, but the clouds cleared away by 10 A.M., with a still air, steamy and hot, and a very scorching sun, giving quite another effect to the Falls, all glistening in the heat and light, with the cloud of steam or spray like a golden veil suspended in front of them.

At mid-day off in the train to Hamilton city, *en route* for Toronto. . . .

7th.— . . . There I met a gentleman who reminded me he had sat next to me at Drapers' Hall two years ago, and told me what I had said to him. He took me up to Professor Goldwin Smith and introduced me to him, and we had a long talk about the politics of Canada and the United States. The Professor says Canada enjoys a perfect constitution, complete liberty, and there is only the drawback of corruption, which exists more or less everywhere. . . .

8th.— . . . I accepted an invitation to dine quietly with Mr Gzowski,[1] a Polish gentleman who has become a very rich and influential man here. It was an hour's walk from the hotel. He told me the story of his life. He was a student in a University, joined in the insurrection, and was taken and banished for life; sent out to America in charge of the police. Arrived here, he remembered that the Governor-General's name was that of an officer who had been taken sick and was nursed in the house of his father, who had been Governor of St Petersburg. He introduced himself, was kindly received, work was found for him, and he is now one of the most prosperous men in Canada. He has a beautiful place, a

---

[1] Created Sir Casimir Gzowski, K.C.M.G., in 1890.

large library in all languages, very many pictures, and, being married to an English lady, is more English in his habits than many Canadians. We are, I think, friends for life.

Monday, Sept. 9.—Visited the great Normal Schools here, where masters and mistresses are educated and trained. A Dr Ryerson is at the head of the institution and of education in Western Canada. He knew Mr Reece and my sister Caroline very well. To educate the masters and mistresses he has procured copies of many of the best pictures, sculptures, busts of great men, and engravings of the old world. He is a talkative, old gentleman now, very kind, very attentive, but difficult to escape from. . . .

To luncheon by invitation with the Board of Trade, an association of merchants. There I was formally introduced as Mr W. H. Smith, M.P. for Westminster, England, and I had to sit down at 2 P.M. to eat and to drink, and to hear and to make speeches. Everybody very kind, very demonstrative, and very anxious to show that Canadians and Englishmen are one and the same people. In the evening I had to attend another dinner at the Club, given by a Mr Gordon and a Mr Sheddin in honour of the Directors of the Grand Trunk Railway and of myself. More champagne and more speeches—and more heat, for it is very hot and muggy here. . . .

I think I am learning a great deal, and taking in much; but really it is harder work than any one would suppose to look about one with the intention of retaining recollection of things—to ask questions and to receive the amount of information which everybody is disposed and glad to give. I am really quite lazily disposed sometimes at the end of the day, especially as we are now having great heat again.

10th.—Started at 7 for a trip over the Northern Railway, in which I am interested. . . .

I travelled over 130 miles of country outwards. .The station-houses were neat and pretty, with nice gardens attached to them, and part of the country was smiling and fertile and beautiful; but for many miles we went through forest which had caught fire and been burnt, everything having been destroyed — fences, farm-buildings interspersed here and there in the woods, and the stations themselves. I have never seen such desolation, stumps of blackened trees, some trees standing with all the leaves off, but the timber of which was too green to burn thoroughly, some burnt to half-way up, blackened and charred timber lying all round, and this extending as far as the eye could see. We touched at several lakes on our way, Lake Simcoe, Lake Huron, and, on our return, another portion of Simcoe and Lake Couchiching, where the railway is penetrating through the backwoods into the wilderness.

I saw in the distance two or three miles off an Indian settlement on the shores of this lake, which is a lovely one. The silence and comparative absence of man and the presence of the railway are strange contrasts, and in these wilds are to be found educated men from the old country, their children enjoying a free life, running about now in summer barefooted, but well clothed and fed, and schools set up for them as soon as there is a sufficient number to send. Common labourers get 6/6 a-day here, with food cheap.

The names of towns and stations are pretty and full of old recollections; Richmond Hill, Davenport, Bradford, Allandale, and others like them. We got back at 11 P.M. after a very pleasant day, and having seen a great deal of the country and of the people, but it was tiring work.

Wednesday, Sept. 11.—Another warm day. It was a golden mist in the morning, and was very thick over the lake. . . . Another luncheon was to be ate to-day in public! Champagne flowed freely. The M.P. for Algoma proposed the health of the M.P. for Westminster, and the M.P. for Westminster had to propose prosperity to Toronto, &c., &c. . . .

A good hard road is quite a rarity in Canada, and appears to be deemed a superfluous luxury. The footways are always planks, and planks are laid across at intervals to enable people to get from one side to the other, and carriages drive over these obstructions as if they were of no consequence at all, passengers inside going up in the air like corks, and coming down on their seats quite unconcerned, and as a matter of course. At 7.30 dined at Chief-Justice Haggerty's, an Irishman who came out at 17 to Canada to push his fortune, a very genial and pleasant fellow. I met Dr MacDonald again and many of the principal people in the city.

Toronto is a curious place. Seventy years ago it was bush, now it has 70,000 inhabitants, but it extends over space large enough for 20 times that population. The hotel in which I stop is in the centre of the city, near the wharf where the steamers land, and the railway stations; but it must have two or three acres of land round it, and except in about two or three streets it is very common to find open spaces lying quite waste between houses which are all numbered consecutively. A great church or a public building stands alone away from everything, and it is quite difficult to believe there is really a large population close by. They are all out of sight.

12th.—Took passage by the Athenian steamer on Lake Ontario for Kingston. We were to start at 2 P.M., and reach Kingston at 5.30 next morning. After I had secured my berth I overheard a gentleman calmly discussing with another how long the boat would last,—"her back was certainly broken,"—and she did sink unpleasantly amid-ships; but, he added, if there was no storm she would run out the season, and if there was a storm, why, there were harbours to run into every few miles, and life-buoys on board. . . . We drove (Dr MacDonald and I) after breakfast to Dr Dobbs's house—an Irish-English clergyman, a relative of MacDonald's. He received us very cordially and took us to the Lunatic Asylum. . . . After a short stay we went on to the Penitentiary, where all the prisoners are obliged to work at some trade. I was very much pleased with the discipline and system. . . .

What I am seeing here impresses me with a sense of the great changes which are coming over society. Every man, woman, and child can earn here much more than is necessary for food, lodging, and clothing, if they have fair health. The commonest labourer will get 6 and 7 shillings a-day, and food is cheaper than it is in England. The country appears healthy, but in one little town I visited in the backwoods on Tuesday there were four doctors, all of whom appeared to be living very comfortably. . . . If it were not for the different kind of houses they have, the distances between them, the very bad roads, some not paved or stoned at all, but simply the sand and earth which has existed since the flood—one would sometimes imagine oneself at home. The people are very "English," live a family life, conduct their religious services exactly as we do; dress as we do, and with one or two additions to the course, they eat and drink as we do. I am sure you would like them.

Saturday, Sept. 14.—Walked out to look round Ottawa city. It stands very prettily half-surrounded by a noble

river, from which in one part the ground rises abruptly.
On the top of this hill, looking down on the water and
over it to the wooded country beyond, are the Parliament-
house and the public offices for the Dominion of Canada.
They are worthy of the great country in which they stand.
Sir Francis Hincks, the Chancellor of the Exchequer,
took me round and showed me everything, most kindly
devoting himself to me for some hours.   In the afternoon
he drove out with me to see two large saw-mills, where
many saws worked by water-power, each saw having
eight rows of teeth, and therefore cutting eight planks
at a time, were at work.   It was marvellous to see how
rapidly great trees were devoured by these monsters
and disappeared.   The logs are cut in the woods 300
miles back, and floated down the stream to Ottawa and
other mills.   The men who cut them down spend the
whole winter in the woods, going up in September and
not coming down again until April or May, being away
from wife, children, and friends the whole time; but they
seem to like the life, and say it is healthy.

In the evening Sir F. Hincks gave a dinner in my
honour, and I had the good fortune to meet the Prime
Minister, Sir John Macdonald, the Bishop, and many other
celebrities. . . . Recollection and anticipation, what
pleasures they give us!

Monday, Sept. 16.—Started at 7 A.M. by steamer for
Montreal.   The banks of the river are very prettily
wooded, and there are plenty of wild-fowl about; but the
most curious feature at this season on the Ottawa river
is the rafts coming down from the interior.   If they are
fortunate it takes them 2½ months from the time they
start before they arrive at Quebec, and the distances
traversed by mighty rivers in America can be realised
when it is considered that these rafts go floating on night

and day with the stream for all this long time. The people live on them in little wooden houses, and they have generally a flag hoisted. . . .

At St Ann's encountered the famous rapids which gave birth to the Canadian boat-song. A fine morning changed into rain here, and I could only console myself by talking to backwoodsmen about their hard but healthy life.

We noticed that at the point where the Ottawa flows into the St Lawrence the waters do not mix but flow on side by side, the Ottawa dark brown, the St Lawrence bright green. Arrived at Montreal at 6.30 P.M.

Tuesday, Sept. 17.—Went to 382 St Antoine to find Lyndon Smith. . . . Returned and called on the President of the Montreal Bank ; found him in a state of excitement about a corner in gold at New York. Had to find out what a " corner" meant, and at last ascertained that some speculators had got hold of all the gold they could lay their hands on, and that is called a " corner" in gold. . . . Started at 3 P.M. for Boston.

Thursday, Sept. 19.—Mr P., superintendent of schools, called for me at 8.30 to take me the round of the schools. I saw one opened at 9, of 700 boys, by simply reading a chapter and repeating the Lord's Prayer. The boys were of all ranks—some gentlemen's sons, some without shoes or stockings—and yet the discipline appeared to be most perfect. The head-master, one assistant, and sometimes two, are men. All the other teachers are women, and they appear to be really accomplished ladies, some of them quite young and good-looking. I visited two of the large schools. . . . I also visited numerous libraries, Athenæums, societies, and wound up with a careful look into the Boston system of giving relief to the poor.

I have been going about seeing everything I can in the

shape of schools, charities, and public buildings, until my eyes ache, and both my ears and my tongue are tired. . . . There is much to learn, to see, to appreciate, and I may never have another chance, and so I want to absorb all I can.

Friday, Sept. 20.—Schools again, this time in very poor smelly quarters, but the children for the most part come regularly. To the High School for girls. It almost took my breath away to see girls from 15 to 19, some hundreds of them, studying at work which was beyond me. Some of them looked wan and dragged. None looked fresh, like healthy English girls, and as I was asked to say a few words, I told them English girls lived more in the open air than they did, and I hinted pretty broadly that I thought they would be the better for more fresh air and exercise, and a little less work. It was confessed that the effect of this high training was to overstock the market for teachers. . . .

New York, Sept. 22.—At 2 Dr Smith came to take me to see some missionary work going on in the city—like Field Lane in London. There was a large building in which ragged and destitute boys and girls are received, lodged, and fed, and then taught; and I listened to the superintendent's lecture to the children. This was called the Seven Points Industrial School.

He then took me on to another chapel and school in a destitute part of the city, and here a young lawyer was teaching, or preaching a real children's sermon.

There are three missions, each distinct from each other, with separate staff of clergymen, school-teachers, and Bible-women, maintained by this one church of Dr Smith's at a cost of nearly £13,000 sterling a-year.

The record of one day is very much like that

of another : this was no mere pleasure trip, but hard work from morning to night — schools, colleges, prisons, workmen's dwellings, charities, churches, banks, commercial houses, interviews with public men and merchants, took up all the time.

From New York Smith went to Albany, thence returned to Toronto, Niagara, and started on September 27 for the far West. He arrived at Chicago on Sunday 29th, and noted that it was

the place that has had the biggest fire that ever was known. It burnt an area covered with houses 5 miles long by 3 wide.

. . . The landlord of the hotel in which I stay had his house burnt, and while the fire still raged he calculated from the course it was taking that another large hotel would not be burnt. He went to the owner, and then and there bought it. No doubt he parted with it believing it would be burnt, but the fire stopped the next day on the other side of the street, where some houses had been blown up by gunpowder, and this is the house in which I am staying. When the fire was out the seller wanted to get off the bargain, but my landlord insisted on it, and gained the point. There are 16 huge hotels now building in the city, which will lodge 7000 people.

All wooden houses are to be moved beyond what are called the fire-limits of the city, and I saw one going down the street to-day on rollers to its new location.

It would be quite impossible in England, and would have been taken down to be rebuilt, but it is a business here to move houses as we move furniture. I visited the water-works, which were burnt, but at work again in a week. Fancy a city with the gas and water works all burnt in one night!

More corn and more pigs than in any other place I have ever seen; but I did not see one child at play, or one face without marks of care, anxiety, and excitement — the police only excepted, and they took life easily.

Tuesday, Oct. 1. — Called on Mr Pullman again, and was presented with letters giving me command of his cars on the railways going West, and secure provision for comfortable sleeping-berths on the road. Started at 10 A.M. for Omaha; made acquaintance with Mr Thompson, an American gentleman, in the next section of the carriage, who was going through, and had been in California before. Our route lay through the State of Illinois, which was covered with crops of Indian corn, not yet harvested. The soil very deep and rich, but as full of ague and fever as of corn. We dined in the hotel-car, the dinner being cooked by coloured men in the car as we travelled. Burlington was the first large town, made within the last 10 years, and to reach it we crossed the Mississippi on an iron bridge ¾ mile long. I stood on the platform of the car, and looked down on the great river rolling below me. There is no guard or hand-rail to these bridges, and although it was quite imaginary, there was an appearance of danger in passing over without any such protection.. . . .

We now went to bed, to wake up in the morning in the same rich prairie country, thinly settled, but bearing great crops, and capable of bearing much greater.

Wednesday, Oct. 2.—In the morning I found the hotel-car "Westminster" was attached to our train, and so I had the pleasure of breakfasting in Westminster before I crossed the Missouri on another fine iron bridge, which was only completed this year, to Omaha in the State of Nebraska. Here we changed into the Union Pacific Company carriages, in which we were to pass three days and two nights.

There was another Mr Smith in the train, going to New Zealand through San Francisco, and as the conductor was charged to be specially careful of Mr Smith, he wished to know which of us it was who could not take care of himself. I rejoiced in. avowing my weakness! . . . Our pace from Omaha was not great, averaging less than 20 miles an hour, including stoppages.

Thursday, Oct. 3.—We woke up on the borders of the desert to a most lovely sunrise. Every.hue that can be imagined in the sky, and the earth in the dim light, as like the sea in a calm as can well be imagined.

There were many antelopes in sight; some stood still and looked at the train, having got used to it. Others in large herds galloped away more gracefully and at greater speed than deer. Flights of wild-duck were common, and towards mid-day we came on villages of prairie-dogs, which are of a dust colour, and sit upon the mounds over their holes barking as we pass. There were some hundreds of these mounds within the space of three or four miles. Settlers were no longer visible. Here and there the railway had a station for water or coal, and there was of course a drinking-"saloon," made of logs covered with canvas or shingle, and letting in plenty of air. Towards the afternoon we came in sight of the Rocky Mountains, and the scenery became interesting. It was hardly beautiful, as there were no trees; but the rocks were very water-and-wind-worn, rugged, and cut into fantastic shapes. . . . At evening a few stunted pines reappeared, and there were stones which, placed one over the other, the larger over the smaller, looked as if they were granite tables. A very slight effort of imagination would have turned others into ruined castles, so well were they perched.

Oct. 4—Train near Green River.—This morning I woke up to more complete desolation than ever. We are in what is termed the great American desert, many hundred miles in extent, at an elevation exceeding that of the Engadine, cold, but not so cold as that district, but without a blade of grass to cheer the eye. On the banks of the river there are some few stunted bushes which are green, and that is all. The landscape, if it may be so termed, is a vast expanse of light-brown rock, topped by a red sand-rock. . . . But even here men and cattle and children are to be found, brought there by the necessities of the railway, I suppose, or by that wandering adventurous feeling which belongs to some Americans. The men are great gaunt-looking fellows, very rough in appearance, but not so bad as they look; and they know me as an Englishman at once by, they say, my ruddy look. I heard in the rail yesterday that Mr Allport, my friend of the Midland Railway in England, was on the road, and that our trains would meet at 1 A.M. It was a singular meeting.

Be-o-wa-e (?), Nevada, Oct. 5.—We are passing through wonderful scenery—for the last two days it has been one prolonged pass, rivers on one side, mountains close on the other; oases here and there of great loveliness, but generally utter wild barrenness; and yet there are human beings who, with millions of fertile acres lying waste, seem to prefer this savage and grand solitude. Our travelling companions are still pleasant. Some have come with me all the way from Chicago. There are four or five nice children, but they want the ruddy look of English, and have some of them a careworn look. . . .

Plains again—more alkali, more dust, more sage-brush, but no grass. Still there are inhabitants, probably looking for silver and gold rather than wheat or cattle. The Indians now appeared, and they were not beautiful to look at. The men looked lazy, well fed and clothed, with very black eyes and hair, but one-half of their faces covered with vermilion; the women dirty and miserable to a degree hardly human.

Oct. 6.—Daylight broke upon us in the Sierra Nevada Mountains, and here was magnificent scenery—mountains of granite raising their heads to the sky, with patches of snow here and there, and covered up to the snow with magnificent pine. The summit station is 7200 feet above the sea, and we had forty-three miles of snow-sheds to pass through before we reached the lower country. Unfortunately these snow-sheds shut out much of the view, which, when we caught it, was more like the Italian side of the Alps than anything I had seen in America. We now dropped down rapidly to the western side, and soon realised the fact that we were in the region of the trade-winds, and that it never rains here between April and November.

Grapes were abundant and large—dust was in greater quantities. Conduits to convey water were everywhere visible, but no water was to be seen. The sun shone vindictively, and man, who never is content, wished for shade, and consoled himself with iced water. . . . We told each other we were dirty, and looked forward to baths on our arrival. A few hours before we were shivering, and the fire in the car was lighted to warm us. Now we came to one vast wheat-field, apparently hundreds of miles in extent. If there is a good spring rain the wheat grows without trouble, and there is no doubt of the harvest. . . .

San Francisco, Oct. 7.—How delightful to be still—to have been in bed—to have had a bath—not to hear the whir, whir, whir of the train, or to feel the tremendous motion under one's feet! . . . I presented my letters. The talk was of wheat, of diamonds, and of gold. Why won't you believe we are the richest people under the sun? I politely believe my friend, but he is angry because all my friends do not understand it. I looked on the water right away seaward towards China, Japan, and Australia, and the sea broke on those rocks with the same thud and spray as those waves nearer at home, of which I was reminded. But for the sands close at hand, I might have closed my eyes, dreamt, and opened them on Devonshire rocks. The trade-wind brought its mist with it at 5 o'clock, and we drove along the firm sand while the sun went down in the richest red glory I have seen for years. It seemed to mark the sea with blood— and it might have been, for we passed the wrecks of two old ships deeply bedded in the sand—of gallant ships which had been. It was dark when we got home. And after dinner I walked to the Chinese quarter of the town. There are 25,000 Chinese here, and they live almost as completely in a quarter by themselves as if they were in Canton. . . .

Oct. 8.— . . . I spent the early part of the morning in looking for a joss-house in the Chinese quarter, and after a time I found it in an upper room in what appeared to be an ordinary Chinese dwelling-house, but the street-door was open, and the staircase covered with matting. The room was a small one; there was an altar or table opposite the door, and behind the altar an idol of some sort. Paper reeds, with incense in them, were smoking, and made the atmosphere taste and smell like a Roman Catholic church. There were candles burning in broad daylight. On the front of the table, from the top to the ground, were some very elaborate relief figures, apparently in gold or silver gilt, representing animals in one part, and men fighting in another. There were idols in the corner, which were either separately worshipped or change places with the idol who was the God of the day. One of these at the side was a very fair representation of a panther; the other was a frightful imitation of a horrible human being. A Chinaman was performing his devotions while I was there, and I stood and watched him for some minutes. He knelt down before the table, repeating some prayers, holding in his hands two oblong pieces of coloured wood marked with some devices. He threw these down with great violence on the ground at every pause in his prayer and genuflexions, and I imagine he kept on till they fell in a particular way, so as to bring luck. When this was ended, he went to a tray on the table or altar, took out a piece of paper, lit it by the candle which was burning, and then dropped it into an open iron receptacle by the side of the door. This finished his work, except that he had to go to the keeper of the joss-house, who inhabited a small apartment behind the altar, and pay him some money. This keeper had a child of two years old, I should say, and I observed, while all was proceeding, the child playing with what appeared to be young idols.

For the next hour or so I amused myself by turning over things in a Chinese shop, kept exclusively by Chinamen. They are very shrewd, clever fellows, and write and speak English well. Many of them are very wealthy, and have an important part of the trade of San Francisco entirely in their hands.

On October 9, Smith started with some American friends for the Yosemite Valley, a region so thoroughly well known from the accounts given by innumerable tourists, that quotation from his minute description of the scenery may be dispensed with. Returning on the 16th from Merced—

A seven hours' railway journey takes us back to San Francisco, and I stand on the platform of the train as we approach it, and open my mouth wide to draw in the fresh cool breeze the trade-wind sends off the sea. If you want to be grateful for fresh air, shut yourself up in a large oven for a week, and provide a constant supply of the most minute dust, which, after stopping up your nose, insists upon being taken into your lungs through the mouth, and into the stomach as well. The Yosemite is very lovely, very grand, but, as Mrs Cass said to me, I say, I won't advise any lady to go there until after I have forgotten the journey to it. . . .

I wound up my San Franciscan visit by a last stroll through the Chinese quarter. My ideas about the Chinese are greatly changed. They are a remarkably quiet, steady, hard-working body of men, as exhibited in California, and people there say they would gladly give us back all the Irish who have invaded the country in numbers, and substitute Chinamen for them. No doubt a large part of the great prosperity of the State is owing to these people. But for them the Pacific Railway could not be built, the wheat could not be harvested, the gardens would not be cultivated, and clothes could not be washed or dinners cooked. They are literally servants-of-all-work to the American on the Pacific coast.

Friday, Oct. 18.—Started at 7 A.M. for the East. I found on board the car a party of directors of the Northern Pacific Railway, to whom I had letters, and they invited me into their car, which meant frequent refreshment in iced champagne and good claret. They had returned from the Columbia River and Puget's Sound, and spoke of the resources of that district as quite equalling those of California, with a cooler climate. They described narrow bays and inlets, with mountains rising straight up from the sea, so that a ship might make fast to a tree on shore and yet lie in deep water. Any amount of timber is to be had for the cutting.

The railway is, in their judgment, to be the route to China from Europe, and they are to have a grant of 26,000 acres of land for every mile of railway they construct. Our journey to-day was almost as hot as the valley was before. The load was heavy, and the engine unequal to it on the steep ascent of the Sierra. . . .

When I went to bed we had lost three hours' time. Mr Hill and Mr Thompson travelled in the same carriage with me, so that between the directors' carriage, which I frequently visited, and my own, I had plenty of conversation.

Saturday, Oct. 19.—On the sage desert again—dust, drought, dirt in one's eyes, one's throat, one's nose, one's temper—grit everywhere, until I noticed everybody more or less cross because the man opposite was so foolish, so unreasonable, and then I began to see humour in the whole thing. . . .

October 20.—I part with my friends at Ogden, promising to meet in New York; they proceed east, I diverge a little south to Salt Lake City, the capital of Mormondom. I went to the Tabernacle to morning service—mid-day I should say. It is a very large, plain building, holding

6000 people, the roof supported without a pillar or buttress, of great span, resembling an inverted dish-cover. The organ is a very fine one, built on the spot. There is a sort of low Exeter Hall Orchestra raised step by step, one level behind the other.

There were three pulpits or stands, one on each step or stage, and the preacher, Orson Pratt, took his place at the middle one. His text was from the Word of God as revealed to Joseph Smith, page so-and-so, on the 27th December 1832, and he read it. He said the Latter-day Saints believed the Bible which he had, the Revelations to Joseph Smith, and the Book of Mormon, each and all, one as much as the other, and he went on to a defence of polygamy on the grounds that under the Old Testament dispensation it was permitted, and also that as other Christians permitted widowers to marry again, and they might therefore have two or three wives in heaven, it was certainly right to have two or three on earth. Much more was said which I shall not repeat, but the congregation received it all.

While the singing and preaching proceeded, bread and water were partaken by the members as a sacrament. I never saw such women as in that place, so plain, so vacant-looking, or so superstitious. Poor creatures! The system is described by those who have courage as a hell upon earth; and although the ground bears fruit and the valley teems with produce, the human beings who have adopted the so-called religion look either half-crazed or entirely knavish.

A meeting of Gentiles against Mormonism was held last Thursday in the streets. It was the first open meeting. Threats had been uttered that it would be broken up, and the chairman announced that the first person disturbing the meeting would be shot. It was known there was a body of men armed, prepared to obey his orders, and so everything passed off peaceably.

I spent the evening quietly in my room. There was not much to choose between the countenances of the Gentile miners who are attracted to Salt Lake by the silver-mines near and those of the Mormons. A stranger unarmed is perfectly safe. If you want to incur danger show a six-shooter revolver, and instantly every man will produce and cock his weapon. By the way, highway robbers are called road-agents in these parts. Robbers is an offensive term. And so two road-agents relieved the stage last week of the trouble of carrying some bullion from the mines near Virginia City to Rens. . . .

Oct. 21.— . . . Reached Ogden at 7, and found a drawing-room in Pullman's car had been reserved for me, and I am now writing in it while the train drags slowly and joltingly up-hill. My drawing-room is furnished with two fixed arm-chairs, a sofa which is a bed at night, and a table. I have a profusion of looking-glass, and plenty of room for my wife, who has been in my thoughts all day, but who unfortunately absents herself. . . .

Our journey has been through the same desolate country: we came through the Devil's Gate, and it really looks as if it might have been the place of combat between the Archangel and the Evil One. The rocks are weird and worn and tormented like. There are no inhabitants, few cattle, no birds—but a sun, rocks, and alkali-dust.

I have just discovered a party of Canadian engineers who have crossed from Canada to the Pacific surveying for their railway, and I am going to pick their brains. Good night.

*Tuesday, Oct. 22.—*I have become quite intimate with my English and Canadian friends in the next car—

the captain of **H.M.S.** Sparrowhawk, and Mr Fleming, the leader of the Canadian-Pacific Railway exploring expedition.

They rode across the continent to the Pacific in two months, averaging 40 miles a-day exclusive of Sundays, and this strong exercise kept up for so long a time has made Mr Fleming apprehensive lest a week on the railway should upset the health of his party, one following directly on the other. He therefore orders all out whenever the train stops, and every man runs for exercise in a manner which alarms and amazes the Americans, who never make any exertion which they can avoid. Captain Ross or Royds of the Sparrowhawk is a very heavy man, and he offered to carry the doctor of the expedition, also a heavy man, 50 yards on his back, while a young active fellow was running 100 yards, and to beat him. We had this race on the summit level of the Rocky Mountains at Sherman, 8200 feet up. I had arranged with the conductor to keep the train a few minutes longer for the purpose, and I was the starter. The fun was very great: the Captain came in first with his load quite easily, but running very fast. We then had another race of 100 yards between three young fellows; and after that the whole party played leap-frog one over the other, each man giving his back in turn.

I don't know whether I laughed more at the fun itself than at the surprise, the amazement, of the passengers in the train and the employees of the railway. They could hardly laugh. The exertion was so utterly unnecessary. When I returned to the cars I was amused at the reception I had—something between pity and "We really can't understand what sort of people you are." One man said to me, "You English always will be boys." I said, "Yes, to the very last."

I parted with my friends at Cheyenne, and took the train southwards to Denver City, a new town at the foot· of the mountains in Colorado, which is now a great mining district.

I discussed Indian troubles with an American officer on the road, and learnt that departments in America are as dilatory, as weak, and as obnoxious to those who serve under them in the New World as they are in the Old. . . .

At 8.30 P.M. I left Denver by the Kansas Pacific Railway for the East. I soon found out an Englishman, a Mr Teal, the manager of the Terrible Mine, who was going to look for his wife and family in New York. They had telegraphed their departure from England, and the message reached the clerk at his station on the 9th. He was drunk for a fortnight, and did not deliver it until the 21st. The ship arrived on the 19th, and the family are staying somewhere, Mr Teal does not know where, in New York helpless. Great is our indignation at the misuse of whisky. We smoked several pipes together in the drawing-room inveighing against it, and we were calmer after the smoke, and slept soundly.

Wednesday, Oct. 23.—Nothing but rolling prairie for miles and miles. Everybody is looking for the buffalo, and we saw many, alive and dead. They are certainly grand animals, and it seems cruel to shoot them simply for the pleasure of hunting, without using the meat.[1] We

---

[1] This noble animal is now extinct, save for a small herd preserved in the Yosemite Park. Twenty years ago it existed in migratory herds of countless thousands ; but the combined avarice and cruelty of man, aided by repeating-rifles, has prevailed to destroy the species off the face of the earth. The bisection of the buffalo prairies by the Canadian-Pacific Railway no doubt contributed to extermination, for it interfered with the annual migration

saw antelopes, prairie-hens, and wild turkeys in great numbers; but for the first 300 miles every station at which we
stopped for water—there were no passengers—was protected by one or two soldiers, who had formed for themselves
a sort of underground miniature fortress. The winds
here are so tremendous, when they blow over the prairie,
that men are glad to excavate, dig out the earth, and
form a habitation which cannot be blown away. We
looked into one of these underground huts, of which
walls, roof, and everything were earth, and although it
was very rough, it showed the occupier was well-to-do.
There was a profusion of firearms, saddles, &c., and one
or two large American trunks, holding clothes, &c.

Towards afternoon a tree or two became visible, and
we approached a small stream of water. Then large
herds of cattle, some three or four thousand in a herd,
took the place of buffalo, and wooden shanties became
almost frequent. At 10 P.M. I arrived at Junction City,
where I had to leave the Pacific train in order to go south
to Emporia. The names are great, and the laying out of
streets implies great expectations; but at present back-
wood cities do not come up to the Old World ideas of what
constitutes cities. Here and there a brick-and-stone house,
a clay-built one, thirty or forty wooden shanties, and a ·
good many open spaces covered with weeds, and there is
the city before you. But there is always a milliner or two
to be found, several lawyers, a dry-goods store, and a
schoolhouse.

Here this epistolary journal comes to an end,
and the next letter is from New York.

of the herds. Buffaloes have been known to destroy themselves by
charging a railway train in blind fury. At the present day the
only traces left of them are piles of whitening bones and horns.

Nov. 5.—My journey from Kansas was rather a hard one. I was anxious to get on, and although the country is interesting and part of it very beautiful, I am very glad it is all over, and that I am now sitting down as it were waiting for the door to be opened to let me in to England.

I got to Washington on Friday afternoon. . . . Mr Russell Gurney went with me to call on President Grant, with whom I had some minutes' conversation.[1] His secretary took me round the city afterwards, and in a few hours I saw everything that was worth seeing . . . Mr Froude is here, and I have been out with him this morning to see the polling at the elections going forward to-day. It is very interesting, and the police here are very careful of us; but I must tell you when I see you—not long after you get this. . . .

[1] After Smith's return to England, Mr Russell Gurney, writing from Washington, says : " I was amused with the account of a conversation yesterday at a party of very intelligent Americans. The question was raised whether there were any great men in America. The conclusion was pretty soon arrived at that neither in the Senate nor the House were there any, though some doubt was expressed as to Schurtz, who is, as you probably know, a German. At last it was settled that there was one, and only one, and he was Grant. I am so glad that I took you to him, as it would have been a pity if you had gone away without seeing the one great man in the country. I fear you were scarcely aware of your privilege."

CHAPTER IX.

1873-1874.

INCREASING UNPOPULARITY OF MINISTERS——IRISH UNIVERSITY BILL——DEFEAT AND RESIGNATION OF THE GOVERNMENT—— DISRAELI DECLINES TO FORM A CABINET——MR GLADSTONE RESUMES OFFICE——DEBATE ON BUDGET RESOLUTIONS——DIS- SENSIONS IN CABINET——DISSOLUTION OF PARLIAMENT——GEN- ERAL ELECTION — CONSERVATIVE VICTORY — THE POLL IN WESTMINSTER——DISRAELI FORMS A CABINET——MR SMITH BE- COMES FINANCIAL SECRETARY TO THE TREASURY — RESIGNS TREASURERSHIP OF S.P.C.K.

THE first Administration of Mr Gladstone now entered upon its fifth year of existence with the shadow of unpopularity deepening on its course. So many apprehensions had been aroused, such powerful interests harassed, that it might have seemed to Ministers that their only chance of conducting affairs towards the natural term of the Parliament lay in avoiding sensational en- terprise in legislation and in allaying rather than rousing opposition.

Aliter visum! In a fatal hour for the Government the Prime Minister plunged once more into the troubled tide of Irish politics. Already he had prevailed to destroy the Irish Church and revolutionise the tenure of Irish landed property; there remained a third question, the settlement of which he had in his electioneering speeches of 1868 declared to be essential to the conciliation of Irish disaffection. Perhaps in doing so he had yielded to the temptation, irresistible to less experienced orators, of casting rhetoric in a triple mould: it is difficult to assign any other reason for his having discovered in the state of Irish University Education a grievance more crying than the irreconcilable variance of the Protestant and Roman Catholic Churches in temporal matters. Although he can hardly have calculated on the complexity and multiplicity of opposition which was to be called into existence by the mere mention of this question in the Queen's Speech, it has ever been a characteristic of this remarkable statesman never to be so happy as when dragging hesitating and even reluctant followers through the turmoil of parliamentary war to an issue which they would fain avoid.

Such was the task he undertook in tabling his Irish University Bill. The event proved that in essaying to satisfy the claims of the Irish Roman

Catholic clergy without rousing alarm among his Protestant and Nonconformist supporters in all three kingdoms, he had put his hand to a work beyond his power to accomplish.

There is no need to dwell on what turned out to be an abortive plan : enough to say that though the design was so complete and elaborate as to command admiration for its author, long before the day fixed for the second reading it had become clear that Ministerialists were sharply divided on its policy. Professor Henry Fawcett [1] led the Opposition against the bill, and was followed on the same side by Dr Lyon Playfair [2] and Mr Horsman. As the debate proceeded, the Government betrayed their weakness by offering to leave several important points as open questions to be settled in Committee, but that was a stage which this ill-starred measure was destined never to reach. It was thrown out on Second Reading by a majority of 3—287 votes to 284.

In consequence of this defeat the Government resigned, but as Disraeli declined attempting to form a Cabinet, the opinion went abroad that the

[1] Postmaster-General in Mr Gladstone's second Administration, 1880-84.

[2] Afterwards Postmaster-General in 1873-74, Chairman of Ways and Means, 1880-83, and Vice-President of the Committee of Council on Education in 1886 ; created Baron Playfair in 1892.

only way out of the dilemma was an appeal to the constituencies. A singular feature of the situation was the promulgation by the rival leaders of the reasons inducing each to adopt the course he did, by means of letters addressed to the Sovereign. Mr Gladstone in his letter contended warmly that an Opposition which had overthrown a Government was bound to attempt the administration of affairs, a view which Mr Disraeli in his letter firmly repudiated. This correspondence formed the subject of debate in the House of Commons, in the course of which Mr Gladstone announced that the Government had resumed its functions, and Ministers had returned to their Departments. Disraeli, of course, spoke in this debate, and his peroration was a stirring and eloquent one, well chosen to make his followers draw their ranks closer together :—

I think it is of the utmost importance that . . . there should be in this country a great constitutional party, distinguished for its intelligence as well as for its organisation, that may lead and direct the public mind. And, sir, when that time arrives, when they enter into a career which must be noble, and which I hope and believe will be triumphant, I think they may perhaps remember, not without kindness, that I at least prevented one obstacle from being placed in their way : that I, as the trustee of their honour and their interest, declined to form a weak and discredited Administration.

Under these conditions matters settled down again, and there was little more excitement within the walls of Parliament during the rest of that session. Smith's name will be found in the annals of Hansard associated with various educational and metropolitan objects of discussion. He moved resolutions condemning the schemes promulgated for the management of the Greycoat School and Guy's Hospital, and called attention to some anomalies in the incidence of local taxation. But the most important action which he took was in regard to the Budget resolutions. The Chancellor of the Exchequer had a surplus, but it had been in great part forestalled by the award of the Alabama Commissioners, under which this country had been adjudged to pay an indemnity of £3,200,000. Half of this sum was to be paid during the current year, the sugar-duties were to be remitted, and a penny was to be taken off the income-tax. Smith's amendment was to the effect that, before remitting indirect taxation by the remission of the sugar-duty, the House ought to be in possession of the views of the Government as to the adjustment of local and imperial taxation.

The Government have been urged to exempt altogether from Income-tax the first £150 of everybody's income, and I believe that that course will, if the Government are bent upon touching the Income-tax at all, be much better than the course which they have adopted. A justification might be found for that course, for there is a large class among the artisans and labourers in this country who are earning £150 a-year, and are not only not paying Income-tax, but whom it will be impossible, or if possible, very undesirable, to *compel* to pay. I will venture to ask the House what the policy of the Budget really is. The policy of the Budget is to swallow up every farthing of surplus which can exist this year and next year. The policy of the Budget is to deprive the House of Commons of dealing with a question [Local and Imperial Taxation] which it has already decided to be of very grave and serious import to the taxpayers of the country. The policy of the Budget is, I venture to think, to embarrass the hands of any right honourable member who may next year or the year after stand in the position now occupied by the Chancellor of the Exchequer.

The general tenor of his complaint against the financial proposals of the Government was that, while giving relief where it was not wanted, they did nothing to remedy an admitted griev-ance. Mr Lowe with great warmth resisted the amendment, which he referred to as "a crowning insult"; but judging from comments on the debate in Ministerialist journals, he earned little gratitude outside the House for his exposition of the principles on which he had framed his Budget. The matter dropped, and the session moved un-eventfully to its close.

But if Ministers succeeded in holding their own in Parliament, the omens in the country were sinister. Since 1869 nine seats, all vacated by various Ministers appointed to permanent places or removed to the House of Lords, had been captured by Conservatives; six more had fallen into the hands of the enemy during 1873; and against this category of calamity the Liberals could only reckon gains at Bath and Truro. There were known to be grievous dissensions among Ministers themselves: Mr Baxter resigned the Secretaryship of the Treasury because he could not agree with the Chancellor of the Exchequer (Mr Lowe); Mr Lowe was removed from the Treasury and appointed Home Secretary; and Lord Ripon and Mr Childers both resigned office.

All this, of course, was watched with satisfaction by the Conservatives, who were biding their time; but they too were not without chill tremors of apprehension, arising from the adverse effect on their prospects which secret voting might have in a general election. Those in possession of what are sometimes humorously described as the "sweets of office" were far from happy, while their opponents were weighed down by the prospect of worse things which might come to pass.

Perhaps it is to this sense of uneasiness that

must be traced the beginning of that sharper
acerbity and scanter courtesy to opponents which
of late years has characterised party politics.
There was plenty of hard fighting in the days
when the House of Commons was spoken of as
the best club in London ; but a chivalrous understanding prevailed between the two parties; debates and divisions were arranged to suit mutual
convenience ; to snap a division on a great question in the dinner-hour would have been regarded
as a positive breach of good - breeding. How
greatly things are changed now many a weary
member can sorrowfully testify.

Perhaps the discredit for the first disregard
of these unwritten laws may be laid to the door
of the Conservative party. It had been an
immemorial custom with the Opposition of the
day not to oppose Ministers seeking re-election
on taking office. Elated by their success at
many by-elections, and anxious to score another
win, the organisers of the Tory party determined
to oppose Sir Henry James at Taunton on his
appointment as Solicitor-General. They failed
to oust him, but a bad precedent had been set,
which in subsequent years has been the reverse
of satisfactory in its effects.

In the autumn of this year Disraeli chose to
address a letter on public affairs to Lord Grey

de Wilton, in which he spoke of the Government
in terms which gave deep offence to many of
his own party.[1]   Writing to his friend, Mr
Ford, on October 11, Smith passed the following
melancholy comment on the incident :—

Disraeli has ruined himself, and rendered reconstruction
of parties—a new choice of leaders—almost inevitable.   I

---

[1] The letter was in these terms:—

MY DEAR GREY,—I am much obliged to you for your Bath news.
It is most interesting.   It is rare a constituency has the opportunity of not only leading but sustaining public opinion at a critical
period.   That has been the high fortune of the people of Bath, and
they have proved themselves worthy of it by the spirit and con-
stancy they have shown.   I cannot doubt that they will continue
their patriotic course by supporting Mr Forsyth, an able and
accomplished man, who will do honour to those who send him to
Parliament.   For nearly five years the present Ministers have
harassed every trade, worried every profession, and assailed or
menaced every class, institution, and species of property in the
country.   Occasionally they have varied this state of civil war
by perpetrating some job which outraged public opinion, ·or by
stumbling into mistakes which have always been discreditable,
and sometimes ruinous.   All this they call a policy, and seem quite
proud of it ; but the country has, I think, made up its mind to
close this career of plundering and blundering.—Ever yours sincerely,   B. DISRAELI.

Looked at in the light of later days, and read in parallel
columns with a great deal that is said and written now in party
controversy, it is certainly difficult to see wherein lay the grave
offence of these expressions.   The 'Annual Register,' usually a
dispassionate and impartial record of current events, emphatically
pronounces its condemnation : "The spirit and tone of this letter
call for no comment, as it carried its own condemnation and its
own punishment."   The punishment was the loss of a seat at Bath
to the Tories.

was going to speak at a dinner at Hertford on Thursday
next, but I have begged off.   I have no heart for it now,
and I don't want to talk.

In the autumn of 1873 Smith found himself,
much against his will, committed to a second
contest for re-election to the London School
Board.   He expressed a strong desire to retire,
but his supporters would not hear of it.   Indeed
his partner, Mr Lethbridge, was waited on to
induce him to persuade Smith to accept the
Chairmanship of the new Board.   "That," said
Mr Lethbridge, "Mr Smith will not do, if I
know anything of him at all."   Writing to his
wife on this subject on December 2, he says:
"I said positively that nothing would induce
me to take it [the Chairmanship] permanently,
and my friends gave way, and I think I shall
escape being nominated."

In spite of the general disfavour into which
Ministers had fallen, and the discouragement
with which Mr Gladstone's Cabinet had to contend, the year 1874 opened upon a kingdom
pervaded with general apathy in regard to political parties.   There was no apparent reason
why the Parliament should not run on to its
full term, and no anxiety on the part of the
Opposition to challenge a direct issue with a
Government commanding a majority of 90 in

the House of Commons. People were still find=
ing it so profitable to attend to their own
business, that they showed little concern about
the course of public affairs. Parliament had
been summoned to meet on February 5, but
on January 24 there appeared a manifesto addressed by Mr Gladstone to his constituents in
Greenwich, in which, after referring to the course
of events in the previous session, he announced
the desire of the Government "to pass from
a state of things thus fitful and casual to one
in which the nation will have full opportunity
of expressing will and choice as between the
political parties." He rested the claims of the
Liberal party to a renewal of confidence partly
on their past performances, and partly on their
intention of totally abolishing the Income-Tax
and relieving local taxation — the very points
which Smith had urged in his speech on the
last Budget. He further indicated an intention
of assimilating the franchise in the counties to
that in the boroughs.

The challenge, thus passionately and impuls-
ively thrown down, was promptly accepted by
the Tory champion. "Generally speaking," ran
one sentence in Mr Disraeli's counterblast—

Generally speaking, I should say of the Administration
of the last five years, that it would have been better for

all of us if there had been a little more energy in our foreign policy, and a little less in our domestic legislation.

The state of parties in Westminster was considered to be more favourable to the Conservatives than it had been in 1868, and this impression was undoubtedly owing, in a very large degree, to the hold Smith had obtained on the confidence and respect of those whom he represented in Parliament. Still, no one could foretell the result of household franchise exercised under secrecy of the ballot. If, as was loudly claimed by the Liberal Party managers, the effect of the Ballot Act was to be the release of the artisan and labouring classes from the alleged oppressive influence and constraint of their employers, who were mainly Conservative, there could not fail to be seen, in a constituency like Westminster, a heavy addition to the Liberal poll; and that this was the genuine faith and expectation of Mr Gladstone's colleagues had been abundantly shown by their extreme impatience to abolish the immemorial custom of open voting. Consequently, there was some hesitation on the part of the Westminster Conservatives to run more than one candidate for the two seats. Smith, standing alone, might be reckoned fairly secure of being returned; indeed, there came from the Liberals what was tantamount to an understanding that the representation should be divided by the unopposed return of Mr Smith for the Conservatives and Sir T. Fowell Buxton for the Liberals. But Smith himself could be brought to accept no such compromise, and it was in consequence of his strong and repeated persuasion that Sir Charles Russell agreed to come forward as his colleague.

It was a bold and, as many thought, a hazardous enterprise to jeopardise the certainty of keeping one seat in order to have the chance of winning both, for Westminster had been for generations part of the patrimony of the Whigs, but nobly did the ancient borough respond to the confidence of its young member.

In his address to the electors, this time Smith made no allusion to Liberal - Conservativism : half-a-dozen years of active political life had not been without effect in accentuating his political views, and his common-sense had led him to realise how vain, if a man is to let his influence be felt, must be all profession of independence of parliamentary leadership. He now stood as an avowed member of the Conservative party.

In concert with my political friends [ran one paragraph] I have deprecated, and should continue to deprecate, great organic changes in submission to the clamour of professional agitators, who aim at destruction rather than reform. There is, in my judgment, ample work for the energies of Parliament, without embarking upon great constitutional changes which are not desired by the people.

The result of this, the first general election under the ballot, came as a welcome surprise to the Conservatives — as an unlooked-for discouragement to their opponents. A minority of 90 in the old Parliament was converted into a majority of 50 in the new House of Commons, and no part of the kingdom contributed to this result in a proportion equal to the metropolis. In the deceased Parliament Mr Disraeli had been able, out of the twenty metropolitan seats, to reckon but two as held by his followers ; in the new one the representation was equally divided between Conservatives and Liberals. The verdict condemning the late Administration was given in Westminster with startling emphasis. The Whig 'Spectator' for February 7, 1874, admitted and explained the greatness of the victory.

The most tremendous of the Tory victories is that at Westminster, where the two Tory candidates, Mr W. H. Smith and Sir Charles Russell, have been returned, the former by a vote of close upon two to one, and that over a candidate supported by the whole strength of the

Licensed Victuallers and of the religious philanthropists, as well as of the Liberal Party in general—Sir Fowell Buxton. The return is as follows:—

Mr W. H. Smith (C)	9371
Sir Charles Russell (C)	8681
Sir T. F. Buxton (L)	4749
General Codrington (L)	3435

Now on the last occasion Mr W. H. Smith polled only 7648 votes, which is much fewer than Sir Charles Russell has polled on this occasion, while Captain Grosvenor polled 6584 votes, nearly two thousand more than Sir Fowell Buxton polls now. This is Conservative reaction with a vengeance!

There was no getting over it. In 1868 Smith's success had been accounted for by his opponents as the result of his liberal expenditure of money— there was no whisper of that now. By the Ballot Act the working classes had been freed alike from the oppressive dictation of employers and the demoralising application of wealth, and here was the use they had made of their freedom on the very first opportunity. A handsome acknowledgment of the fairness of the conditions of battle came from one of the defeated candidates.

14 GROSVENOR CRESᵀ., *Feb.* 6, 1874.

DEAR MR SMITH,—I must thank you for the courteous message you sent me by Sir John Kennaway last night. I can assure you I look back upon the late election with satisfaction on this ground, that each side has appealed only to those higher issues, national and not local or

personal, which I am sure you feel with me ought alone
to guide the contests of parties.—I remain, yours truly,

T. FOWELL BUXTON.

W. H. SMITH, Esq., M.P.

On Monday, February 16, Mr Gladstone's
Cabinet met to consider its defeat at the polls,
and determine its final act. The following day
the Prime Minister laid his resignation before the
Queen at Windsor, who thereupon summoned Mr
Disraeli and charged him with the duty of forming a Ministry. That statesman had been justly
credited with the faculty of discerning capacity in
new men : indeed, not long before the general election he had observed in public that he " piqued
himself on recognising ability "; it was therefore
a matter of common expectation that among the
new Ministers there would be found more than
one who had not previously filled offices. But
Disraeli's old chief, Lord Derby, had once remarked
that when an appointment was vacant he was
invariably urged to take in " new blood," and
that, as often as he followed this advice, he
heard complaints about " raw recruits." It must
be the experience of every Prime Minister that
it is far easier to find new men of capacity than
to get rid of old colleagues; consequently, in Mr
Disraeli's Cabinet of twelve, the only new name
which appeared was that of Mr Richard Assheton

Cross,[1] who was appointed Secretary of State for
the Home Department.   The reappearance in
eleven out of twelve of the great parts of actors
whose services had in former years been secured
by the great *impresario*, set at rest a great
deal of speculation and some apprehension.   Disraeli, though he had convinced people of his
ability for administration and dexterity as a
parliamentary leader, and though he was admitted to be the only man in the House of
Commons capable of confronting Mr Gladstone,
had at the same time failed to secure the confidence of the entire Tory party.   They had
followed him since the death of Lord Derby, not
because they trusted him, but because they
feared Gladstone.   The old country party had
grave misgivings at some of the things that had
been said and done; they had not forgotten the
"leap in the dark" of 1867, nor forgiven the
disasters in which it had landed them.   The
statesman of whose attitude at this time most uncertainty prevailed was the Marquis of Salisbury
—"the terrible Marquis," as he was then called
—who, as Viscount Cranborne, with the Earl of
Carnarvon, had seceded seven years before from
Mr Disraeli's first Cabinet, on the question of
household suffrage in counties.   Would Lord

---

[1] Created Viscount Cross, G.C.B., in 1886.

Salisbury and Lord Carnarvon go back to their old posts at the India Office and Colonial Office, or would they remain outside the Government, a source of disquiet and latent menace to any Administration which the member for Buckinghamshire might collect together? That was the question on the solution of which depended the hopes and fears of the Conservative and Liberal parties. Was the Prime Minister to succeed in healing old schisms, and take up the reins of power with a firm hand and tolerably clear road before him, or was he merely to put certain men into the offices at his disposal and continue at the head of affairs till some fortuitous combination of political sects should drive him from place?

The question was not long of settlement. Mr Gladstone resigned on Tuesday, February 18; on Friday 21, the list, not only of the Cabinet, but of Ministers outside the Cabinet, was complete. Lord Salisbury and Lord Carnarvon were back at their old posts. No one could suspect either of these two noblemen of having sunk conscientious scruples to grasp any advantage that might be gained from office: Lord Salisbury, especially, was well known to be devoted to scientific and literary occupation, and that he should have consented to destroy his own leisure in order to take over the administration of a department was accepted as a proof that an experienced statesman, absolutely independent of emolument and far above suspicion of selfish aims, recognised Disraeli as his political leader, and was prepared to yield him loyal support.

The result of the elections had been so decisive as to enable Disraeli to anticipate Mr Gladstone's resignation by preparing the way for this reconciliation of the wings of the Tory party, and thus to the public and the press there was afforded a period short almost beyond precedent for discussing the process of Cabinet-making and engendering the rumours which abound at such times. The London papers had from the first fixed upon Smith as one of the new men likely to be brought to the front ; several of them were for placing him in the Cabinet at once as Vice-President of the Council or President of the Local Government Board, places suggested by the part he had taken in discussions on educational matters and the reform of the Poor Laws. But Disraeli knew him also as the head of a great and successful commercial concern, and had early recognised his fitness for another post. And here let it be said that Smith's rise has sometimes been attributed to the friendly notices of him which had, from his entry into public life, appeared in newspapers of every shade of politics, and the inference

has been drawn that his position as the leading
newspaper agent contributed in some measure to
this display of favour by the press. A paragraph
from an article in the ' Spectator,' a Liberal
weekly journal of high standing, may tend to
dispel this impression :—

We still hope earnestly for Mr Smith, the Member for
Westminster, as Vice-President, and we believe that hope
would be very loudly expressed indeed, but for a fact that
it may be as well to deal with at once. Mr W. H. Smith,
though certain to rise some day, if not now, into the Cabinet, has one extremely strong impediment in his way.
He is the greatest news-agent in the world, and the public have a notion that he is always, and therefore, sure of
newspaper support. There never was a greater delusion.
What he is sure of is unnecessary neglect, a dead silence
about his merits as a Member, lest those who praise him
should be suspected of wanting his goodwill. He will
find this a real obstacle in his career, a great impediment
to becoming known, and the fact may as well be stated
plainly and at once. The truth about him as a politician,
however, is that he was made for the Ministry of Education in a Conservative Ministry: that he, and he only of
the party, except poor Sir John Pakington,[1] possesses the
needful knowledge, firmness, and moderation.

This hope was not destined to fulfilment.
Viscount Sandon became Vice-President of the
Council ; but there was another post in the Min-

---

[1] Sir John Pakington had lost his seat at the general election.
He was created Lord Hampton in 1874.

istry, requiring not less knowledge, firmness, and moderation than that of Minister of Education, and, in addition, calling for business capacity in a degree which might be more safely dispensed with in the Privy Council Office. Into this post the Prime Minister, with quick discernment, had already fitted his man ; accordingly, forty-eight hours after Mr Gladstone had resigned the seals of office, the following letter was written :—

Confidential.

2 WHITEHALL GARDENS, *Feb^y.* 19, 1874.

DEAR MR SMITH,—It would give me great pleasure &, I believe, satisfaction to the country, were you to permit me to appoint you Secretary to the Treasury.—Yours very faithfully,   B. DISRAELI.

W. H. SMITH, Esq., M.P.

The answer was dated the same day :—

2 HYDE PARK ST., *Feb.* 19, 1874.

DEAR MR DISRAELI,—I am exceedingly obliged to you for the expression of your good opinion, and for the offer you have made, which I gladly accept.—Believe me, yours very faithfully,   WILLIAM H. SMITH.

The Right Hon. B. DISRAELI, M.P.

Probably there never was a more admirable appointment made. Upon the Financial Secretary of the Treasury devolves not only the duty of receiving the Estimates from the various Departments, whereby he is brought into constant communication and consultation with all the executive heads, and of bringing the Estimates into final form before presentation to the House, but he is intimately concerned with the financial policy of the Government, and responsible for advice in guiding the Chancellor of the Exchequer in framing the Budget. Besides this, there devolves upon him the arrangement of the Order-Book of the House of Commons, and the task of keeping members on both sides in good humour, the importance of which is not likely to be undervalued when it is remembered how many excellent and amiable schemes involving expense have to be met with a firm but conciliatory "No!" With the single exception, of late years, of the Chief Secretary to the Lord Lieutenant of Ireland, there is no Minister, whether in or out of the Cabinet, who has to get through such an amount of hard, prolonged work as the Financial Secretary.

Nevertheless, admirably as Smith was qualified, by training, temperament, and business capacity, for this onerous office, there were not wanting those who shrugged their shoulders and looked askance on this latest instance of Disraeli's disposition to innovation. The author of 'Coningsby' had not yet "educated" his party to the point whence they could discern that the Tory party, if it was to have its share in guiding the destiny of the kingdom, would have to draw to it the confidence of other classes than that which was "acred up to its chin," and the squirearchy muttered unkind things about the Bookstall Man who was thus brought into greater prominence than distinguished class-men and persons of pedigree. On the whole, however, the announcement of this appointment was well received ; it was hailed with special favour by the great middle class, and it is perhaps not generally recognised how great was the direct influence it had in bringing them over to support the Conservative party.

A few weeks later, Smith, writing to his old schoolfellow and friend the Rev. William (now Canon) Ince of Christ Church, says :—

I am myself surprised at my position when I compare it with the time to which you refer when we were both young together, and yet I can say most confidently that I never set to work aiming at personal advancement in the slightest degree. One circumstance has led to another, and I have gradually found myself of more account in men's eyes, simply from doing the work of the day as it presented itself to me.

Smith found it necessary, on taking office, to give up a part of the active share he had taken

in philanthropic schemes.   Among others, he resigned his post as one of the Treasurers of the
Society for the Promotion of Christian Knowledge, which he had held for seven years; but
he remained Treasurer of the London Diocesan
Council for the Welfare of Young Men from its
foundation until his death.

CHAPTER X.

1874–1876.

RETIREMENT OF MR GLADSTONE FROM LEAD OF LIBERAL PARTY —DEBATES ON PUBLIC WORSHIP REGULATION BILL — BEGINNING OF SMITH'S FRIENDSHIP WITH NORTHCOTE — HE SETTLES TO WORK AT THE TREASURY — VISITS BOURNEMOUTH—MR GLADSTONE AND THE VATICAN DECREES—LORD HARTINGTON CHOSEN LEADER OF THE LIBERALS—THE SESSION—OFFICIAL VISITS TO EDINBURGH AND DUBLIN—THE SUEZ CANAL SHARES—CONSOLIDATION OF THE HOME RULE PARTY—THE BURIALS BILL—VISITS TO THE DOCKYARDS—WORK.

IF the result of the general election had come as a surprise, not less unexpected was its immediate effect upon the Minister who was responsible for having brought it about. Members of the Liberal Opposition were filled with dismay one morning—March 13, 1874—on taking up their newspapers at the purport of a letter addressed by Mr Gladstone, their leader in the House of Commons, to Lord Granville, their leader in the House of Lords.

At my age [it ran] I must reserve my entire freedom to divest myself of all the responsibilities of leadership at no distant time. . . . I should be desirous, shortly before the commencement of the session of 1875, to consider whether there would be advantage in my placing my services for a time at the disposal of the Liberal Party, or whether I should claim exemption from the duties I have hitherto discharged.

Now Mr Gladstone was at that time but sixty-four, a period of life certainly not beyond the normal limits of parliamentary activity, his health was understood to be unimpaired, and the only construction to be placed upon this precipitate act was that he was suffering from chagrin, if not from pique, at the overthrow of his party. It cannot, indeed, have been pleasant for him to reflect that, in dealing with the Irish Church and in pressing the Ballot Act through the House of Commons, he had, in order to secure support for his party, thrown overboard principles which he had cherished through many years of public life, and that, after all this sacrifice, he had failed of his reward. Of course the gain to Ministerialists was proportionate to the confusion caused by this announcement in the ranks of their opponents. A leaderless Opposition is a transcendental state of parties which a Prime Minister may see in his dreams, but hardly

ever hope to see realised.   There was the more
reason for gratitude for this unlooked-for dispensation, because Ministers could not but be
conscious that they came on the boards without any very dazzling or seductive programme.
The Chancellor of the Exchequer had inherited
a large surplus from his predecessors, and something might be expected in the way of Income-
Tax reduction and relief of Local Taxation.
But gratitude for relief from taxation is altogether out of proportion to the unpopularity
incurred when it is necessary to increase it, and
already the Opposition press was clamorous for
a programme.   Where are the measures of the
new Government? they asked, and made reply
themselves, that, like snakes in Iceland, there
were none.

But indeed the country was only too glad to
be spared fresh legislation of the heroic kind.
Trade was active ; prices were good ; to the
farmers, if some of them had already descried
American competition in the offing, it seemed
no bigger than a man's hand.   Nobody wanted
Ministers to devise an exciting programme of
new laws.   Disraeli's tact was equal to the
occasion : the Opposition was downcast and
perplexed, he was careful to give them no
point on which they could rally.   The word

was passed along the Conservative benches that they were to treat their opponents with forbearance — no more taunts about " plundering and blundering," no more recriminations, no challenges to fruitless trials of strength.

It so turned out that the principal subject of debate during the session of 1874 was a measure for which the Government were not originally responsible. The change which had taken place in the outward forms and ceremonies in some congregations of the Church of England were the development of the Tractarian movement at Oxford thirty years before. With certain priests and people a taste for highly ornate ritual had made great advances ; indeed, it was hard to reconcile some of the observances — prayers to the Virgin Mary and to saints, auricular confession, processions, elaborate vestments—with the spirit and laws of the English Protestant Church. Accordingly the Archbishop of Canterbury — moved thereto by a petition signed by more than 60,000 members of the Church of England—introduced a bill into the House of Lords on April 20, conferring powers on the Bishops to control such practices as might be complained of in their dioceses.

The bill met with opposition from all quarters.

Lord Shaftesbury, as a Low Churchman, would have none of it : he objected to the proposal to increase the power of the Bishops.

Why, in some respects, my lords [he said], the better a Bishop is as a Bishop, the less qualified he would be to act as a calm and dispassionate judge.

Lord Salisbury, as a High Churchman, speaking for the Government, disclaimed responsibility either for the bill or for the moment chosen to move a difficult question, and declared that the Government would be impartial. But he allowed it to appear pretty clearly how he would have treated the measure had he been free to take his own line with it :—

If you legislate without solving this problem : if you disregard this condition : if you attempt to drive from the Church of England any one of the parties of which it is composed : if you tamper with the spirit of toleration of which she is the embodiment—you will produce a convulsion in the Church, and imperil the interests of the State itself.

Eventually, however, it passed through the House of Lords without a division.

In the Commons the second reading was moved by Mr Russell Gurney. Meanwhile the agitation outside Parliament was growing fast, both in favour of and against the bill. Most of Mr Smith's constituents who wrote to him on the subject (and they were exceedingly numerous) strongly urged that he should vote against it.

The most remarkable feature of the debate was the reappearance of Mr Gladstone in the House in order to offer the bill uncompromising hostility, and the conflict which ensued between him. and Sir William Harcourt, who supported it, and vehemently contested the arguments of his late leader.[1]

[1] Mr Gladstone, in the course of his speech, bestowed a prolonged castigation on Sir William Harcourt, and the spectacle of these two distinguished members of the Opposition sparring with each other was of the sort to give unmixed pleasure to Ministerialists.

"I cannot say," said Mr Gladstone, "that the three canons of good taste, good feeling, and courtesy which we are accustomed here to regard, and which may be very old-fashioned, are entirely conformable to those of my hon. and learned friend [Harcourt], and therefore it is better I should decline the controversy, and rest under all the disadvantage which must necessarily attach to me if I forbear to traverse the arguments and propositions he has formally advanced. . . . He says he abhors vituperation, no doubt; but how does he define vituperation? Is it perfectly consistent with that declaration that he should describe language used 'elsewhere' as 'ill-advised railing of a rash and rancorous tongue'? If so, a gentleman who wishes to avoid vituperation, and at the same time wishes to indulge in those feelings which are commonly supposed to produce vituperation, may derive comfort from the thought that he will not vituperate though he may say anything he likes about the railing of rash and rancorous tongues.

"The fact is, that my hon. and learned friend is still in his parliamentary youth, and has not yet sown his parliamentary wild-oats. When he has done it, I have not the smallest doubt that all the great powers he has displayed—and there is no person who has

The tone of the debate on the first night was one which Disraeli was not slow to appreciate : there was evidently an immense preponderance of opinion in favour of the bill, and this, intensified by Mr Gladstone's denunciation of it, gave the Prime Minister his cue. When the debate was resumed on the second day, he spoke decidedly in support of the bill, and practically announced its adoption by the Government.

Mr Gladstone had chosen to meet the motion for Second Reading by giving notice of six Resolutions hostile to the bill; but so little was he in touch with his own party at this time, that it was not until Mr Hussey Vivian had warned him in his speech that if he proceeded with these resolutions he would not have the support of twenty members on his own side of the House, that he consented to abandon them. Then the opposition collapsed, and the bill passed without a division. In Committee an amendment was adopted by a large majority on the motion of Mr

seen his development and exhibition with greater satisfaction than I have—will be found to be combined with a degree of temper, a degree of wisdom, a degree of consideration for the feelings of others, a degree of strictness and vigour in stating and restating the arguments of opponents, and, in fact, with a consummate attainment of every political virtue, that will make my hon. and learned friend outshine and eclipse all former notabilities of Parliament as much as he promises to eclipse them in his great ability and eloquence."

Holt, giving complainants the right of appeal from Bishops to the Archbishop, which was rather roughly handled on the bill returning to the Upper House. Lord Salisbury took a strong line about it, dealing with it more in his old manner of an independent and merciless opponent than as a member of a Cabinet which was virtually promoting the measure. " I for one," he said, "utterly repudiate the bugbear of a majority in the House of Commons." Their lordships disagreed with the amendment of the Commons on this clause, and in the debate arising on this difference of opinion between the two Houses, Disraeli was at no pains to conceal that he differed in opinion from his colleagues in the other Chamber. He said: "The bill was intended to put down Ritualism, and by Ritualism he meant the practices of a certain portion of the clergy, symbolical—according to their own admission—of doctrines which they were solemnly bound to renounce." He urged the House to keep this point in view, and not to deal with the question with a view to the elements of the majority in the House of Lords.

Smith settled steadily into harness at the Treasury. Early training made those long office hours, which so severely try the endurance of

men brought up to habits of country life and
foreign travel, comparatively easy to him. He
had, however, to encounter one piece of bad luck,
which brought upon him a sharp rebuke from
his leader. After a long morning at the Treasury and some hours' attendance in the House,
the hard-worked Financial Secretary, seeing
matters going smoothly in the House, and reck-
oning on the usual forbearance of the Opposition not to divide during the dinner-hour, went
quietly home for an hour or two in the evening.
A snap division was taken, and the Government
was beaten. Next morning Smith received the
following reproof:—

> 10 DOWNING STREET, WHITEHALL,
> *May* 2, 1874.

Mr Disraeli presents his compliments to Mr W. H.
Smith, and much regrets to observe that he was absent
on the division which took place last evening at eight
o'clk., on the motion of Mr Synan; on which occasion her
Majesty's Government was, by reason of the absence of its
members, placed in a minority; and he would beg leave
to point out how difficult it must become to carry on a
Government which cannot reckon on the attendance and
support of its members.

To this the Secretary to the Treasury replied :—

I have only two words to say with reference to your
note of Saturday, and which I own was both just and
necessary. I was excessively annoyed at my absence

from the Division, and I can fully enter into your feelings of vexation.

If I had supposed it possible that a division could be taken, I should have been in my place; but I shall take very good care to avoid the recurrence of such a mortification so long as I remain a member of the Government.

In his immediate chief, Sir Stafford Northcote, Chancellor of the Exchequer, Smith's lot was cast with one with whom it was easy for him to work on terms of perfect accord. Sir Stafford was not less distinguished by personal amiability than by capacity for financial business, and the combination of these two qualities was present in a remarkable degree in both these men. The lot which brought them together in the same department formed the foundation of an intimate friendship which lasted unimpaired till the death of Northcote in 1887.

Smith passed the last day of 1874 at Bournemouth, where Disraeli had summoned him to consult about the business of the approaching session. Thence he wrote to his wife :—

> BATH HOTEL, BOURNEMOUTH,
> *31st Dec.* 1874.

I have a good fire in my bedroom, and a good sitting-room, which I share with Mr Corry. Mr Disraeli came in to see me for a few minutes, and to tell me there was another king in Europe—a King of Spain. He was very pleasant and cheerful. We are all to dine together to-night—Disraeli, the Lord Chancellor, and Northcote, who has not yet come, having missed his train, poor fellow. To-morrow I dine with Lord Cairns at his house. I have just called on Lord Sandon. . . .

Jan. 1, 1875.

We had a pleasant party at dinner—Lord Cairns, Northcote, Dizzy, and Corry—and I think the purpose for which I was asked to come will be attained. At 11, when we parted, Disraeli said, "Well, we have been holding a Cabinet Council, and we must meet again to-morrow morning." I am expecting Lord Cairns and Northcote about 11 to go into details, and in the evening we dine together at Lord Cairns's.

January is a busy month at the Treasury preparing for the work in Parliament, and the busiest man in that department is always the Financial Secretary.

TREASURY, *Jan.* 12, 1875.

I travelled up very comfortably, and guards and stationmaster were all very civil to Mr Smith, who seems to be too well known. . . . At Bristol I found Northcote in the train. He was very cheery. To-day I have seen Disraeli and Hunt. D. looks well and happy. . . . I am going now at 5 (or 6) to see Cross, and I shall have another hour and a half before I leave. I am, I think, better—less stiff. Work agrees with me.

Jan. 13.

I have had a busy day, commencing at 9.30 with G. at Hyde Park St., and going on without cessation up to the present time, 6 P.M., and I shall have at least another hour

of it; but much of the work is very interesting, and so are
the men who come to me. To-day, Sir John Duffus
Hardy, Dr Hooker, Mr Goulburn, Sir Geo. Elliot, Mr
Few, and a heap besides.

Jan. 14.

All well, but dirty, dull, depressing, damp, dyspeptic
weather. Everybody cross and grumpy except Cross. . . .
The work accumulates, but I think I am driving through
it, and I shall be glad to get down to you for a few days.

In order to realise the state of parties at the
opening of the session of 1875, reference must be
made to events arising out of the debates on Ritualism. After his intervention in these, Mr Gladstone had retired for some time from active parti-
cipation in affairs; but he returned to the controversy in the autumn by contributing an article to
the ' Contemporary Review ' for October, in which
he passionately protested against the attempt to
impose uniformity of practice upon the clergy of
the Church of England by legislation. The following passage brought upon him earnest and
even angry remonstrance from Roman Catholics
of high standing :—

As to the question whether a handful of clergy are or
are not engaged in an utterly hopeless and visionary
effort to Romanise the Church and the people of England,
at no time since the bloody reign of Mary has such a
scheme been possible. But if it had been possible in the
seventeenth or eighteenth centuries, it would still have

become impossible in the nineteenth; when Rome has substituted for the proud boast of *semper eadem* a policy of violence and change in faith; when she has refurbished and paraded anew every rusty tool she was fondly thought to have disused; when no one can become her convert without renouncing his moral and mental freedom, and placing his civil loyalty and duty at the mercy of another; and when she has equally repudiated modern thought and ancient history. I cannot persuade myself to feel alarm as to the final issue of her crusades in England, and this although I do not undervalue her great power for mischief.

Mr Gladstone plunged further and deeper into the sea of polemical theology by following up this essay by his celebrated pamphlet, entitled ' The Vatican Decrees in their bearing on Civil Allegiance,' in which he amplified and strengthened the charges made in the ' Contemporary' article, especially insisting that " no one can now become a convert to Rome without renouncing his moral and mental freedom, and placing his civil loyalty and duty at the mercy of the Pope."

. Well might Sir George Bowyer write to the ' Times ' reminding the people of England that four years and some months had passed since the Vatican Council had passed the Decree of Infallibility,[1] and that during that time, until February

[1] An amusing story went the rounds of Mr Black, at that time member for Edinburgh. At the meeting of Parliament he went to shake hands with the Speaker, who asked him where he had spent his holidays. " I have been to Rome, Mr Speaker," replied Mr

1874, Mr Gladstone had been First Minister of the Crown, and glad to receive the support of Roman Catholics in Parliament and in the country.

Why did he not [asked Sir George], in his place in the House of Commons, call attention to the portentous matters which he published last Saturday regarding the effect of the decrees of that Council on the allegiance of her Majesty's Roman Catholic subjects and the security of the realm? Why did he not propose some measure to Parliament calculated to meet the dangers which now alarm him? During all the time referred to he held his peace, and he gladly received Roman Catholic support in Parliament and the country.

While the storm of this controversy was still raging, there took place what most people looked on as the fall of the curtain on a remarkable public career. Shortly before the meeting of Parliament for the session of 1875 a letter addressed by Mr Gladstone to Lord Granville appeared in the newspapers, announcing that he could "see no public advantage in my continuing to act as the leader of the Liberal party, and that at the age of sixty-five, and after forty-two years of a laborious public life, I think myself entitled

Black, who spoke with a strong Scots accent, "and I had an interview with the Pope." "Indeed, and what did he say to you?" "Oh, he just said, 'How are ye, Mr Black? I understand you are a member of the Scottish Parliament.' Now, isn't it ridiculous to talk of *that* man being infallible?"

to retire on the present opportunity. This retirement is dictated to me by my personal views as to the best method of spending the closing years of my life." The question was urgent, Who was to follow Mr Gladstone as leader of the Liberal party? If the journals of that day are referred to, it will be seen that opinion was divided between Mr Forster, Mr Goschen, and Lord Hartington. A meeting to decide on a choice was held at the Reform Club on February 3, which resulted in the election of Lord Hartington to the leadership.

Meanwhile, work at the Treasury went on as steadily as if none of those great controversial storms were raging. John Hill Burton, in his amusing 'Book-Hunter,' remarks on the unexpected fun which a reader lights upon sometimes in unexpected places, and illustrates this by an anecdote of a law student who, consulting an index to a work on legal decisions, was attracted by the words—"Best, Mr Justice, his great mind." Anticipating an instance of conspicuous magnanimity on the bench, he turned up the passage referred to, and found—"Mr Justice Best said he had a great mind to commit the witness for prevarication." Even so, one struggling through the jungle of papers which accumulate in the drawers of the Financial Secretary finds, from time to time, examples of unconscious humour. Of these are some of the various proposals made by ingenious individuals with the object of assisting the Chancellor of the Exchequer out of his difficulties in framing a popular Budget. Thus in ·1875 came a letter explaining a scheme which the writer says has been "uppermost in his mind for some time." He proposes to meet the deficit of £700,000 by a tax on hunting-men! Needless to say that the writer was not a hunting-man, but quite eager to

> "Compound for sports he was inclined for
> By taxing those he had no mind for."

The deficit referred to was caused by the scheme of a Sinking Fund for the gradual liquidation of the National Debt, with which Sir Stafford Northcote's name will for many years to come be associated. As Northcote expressed himself in explaining his proposal to the House—

"I think we have arrived at a time when we may fairly say that, having the means, we ought to devote some of our attention and some of our wealth to a continuous effort to reduce the National Debt."

Under this scheme the total charge to be provided annually for the interest and redemption of the debt was fixed at £28,000,000, whereby the Chancellor of the Exchequer calculated that in ten years £6,800,000 would be paid off; in

thirty years, £213,000,000. That it has proved
a sound and far-sighted proposal cannot now be
disputed; at the same time it must be admitted
that its weakness is the temptation it leaves to
every succeeding Finance Minister to suspend the
payment to the Sinking Fund in years of leanness.
It is so much easier to stop paying off debt than
to levy new taxes.

The Budget was introduced on 15th April, and
in moving it Northcote paid a high compliment
to the Financial Secretary, alluding to the energy
and capacity for business he had shown in the
examination of estimates submitted to the
Treasury, and acknowledging the care and
ability with which he had discharged his
duties.

The best part of this session was taken up by
lengthy and angry discussions on the Peace
Preservation Bill, which the increasing disaffection
and lawlessness of Ireland made it necessary to
pass. Sir Stafford Northcote carried his Act for
the regulation of Friendly Societies, the outcome
of the Report of the Royal Commission; and the
only other measure which calls for special notice
as the work of Mr Disraeli's Cabinet is the Agricultural Holdings Act, for the purpose of giving
the tenant better security for capital invested by
him in the soil. It was but a permissive statute,

but its acceptance by both Houses marked a new departure in land legislation, by reason that it indorsed a novel principle, the application of which has since been made compulsory.

In December the Secretary to the Treasury paid an official visit to Edinburgh and another to Dublin. As was his invariable custom, he kept Mrs Smith informed of the most minute details of his proceedings.

EDINBURGH, *Dec.* 2, 1875.

I have had a sort of *levée*. I dined last night with Sir James Elphinstone, and this morning he breakfasted with me. Then came the Lord Advocate and the Lord Clerk Register. At 11 I was carried off to the Registry House and prosed to by Antiquarian Record-keepers. After that the Lord Advocate carried me off to his offices, and then I went to the Queen's and Lord Treasurer's Remembrancer. I have seen the manager of two Banks doing Government business, and now I am collecting myself by writing to you. I give a dinner to-night to five heads of departments, at which Sandon will be present.

DUBLIN, *Dec.* 5.

I telegraphed to you last night that we had reached Kingstown in safety. . . . We found wet snow in Dublin and frost in the Phœnix Park. At the station Beach[1] met us. . . . To-day we have been very busy, and now, 5.30, I fairly confess I am tired. We called on the Lord Lieutenant and have visited half-a-dozen public buildings, where we were received by the several officials. Talking and stand-

---

[1] The Right Hon. Sir Michael Hicks Beach, at that time Chief Secretary to the Lord Lieutenant of Ireland.

ing for six hours consecutively has fairly tired us all. To-morrow I dine with the Lord Lieutenant, and on Thursday Beach has a dinner-party.

Dec. 8.

Another busy day, and we—Sandon, Beach, Donnelly, and I—are now at this moment consulting and settling the terms of transfer of some of the large Institutions of Government. . . . S., after dining with the Irish " King,"[1] will go down to Kingstown to sleep on board the steamer and go across to-morrow morning early. I wish I could go with him, but I have yet a great deal of work to do, and as much as I shall get through during the next two days.

The session of 1876, Disraeli's last session in the House of Commons, was opened by the Queen in person. The question which had occupied the most anxious thoughts of the Cabinet had been the proposed purchase by Great Britain of the Khedive of Egypt's shares in the Suez Canal, and Smith, though not in the Cabinet, was asked to give his opinion from the Treasury point of view. This he did in a minute, of which the following is the text, taken from a draft in his own writing :—

Suez Canal.

This is so large a question that it is rather one for the Government to consider than for a Department.

Financially it is a proposal that England shall join the other Powers in guaranteeing a loan to keep the Suez

---

[1] Mr King Harman.

Canal open: the amount of the loan is estimated at one million or one million and a half, and it is suggested that the proportion to be borne by each Power should be regulated by the average of the tonnage of the guaranteeing nations passing through the Canal. Under this arrangement England would have to bear about 75 per cent of the burden, the other Maritime Nations bearing the remaining 25 per cent between them. But it would not be safe to calculate upon the largest amount as the measure of the responsibility of England if we go into the proposed Commission.

It is to decide the points at issue and to have *full power* to conclude an arrangement; it is to decide on the works necessary to be executed, and to fix the amount of the loan to defray their cost, and to sign a convention under which the Powers would guarantee the payment of interest and sinking fund in the event of the resources of the Company proving insufficient.

There is so much uncertainty in the questions with which the Commission would have to deal, that it is utterly impossible for any one to foretell the financial responsibility which may attach to the country which has the largest interest in maintaining the Canal.

I entirely agree with the Chancellor of the Exchequer that it is of great political importance to this country to keep open the communication, and I should be inclined to think it was equally important to the Government of India. I believe the Canal to be of great value to the commercial interests of this country, and a very large amount has been invested in steam-shipping constructed to pass through it; but if we do propose an international Commission with the large powers sketched by Lord Derby, the possible contingencies should be considered.

There is no disclosure on these papers of the, nature of

the proposals made to the Government by M. de Lesseps, but it is clear that his views and those of Col. Ross, as to the measures to be taken to prevent the closing of Port Said, differ widely. M. de Lesseps shows throughout a strong sense of the rights of the Proprietors, and it is no doubt his object to obtain for them a satisfactory dividend. He is a power in this matter of at least equal importance to the countries represented in the Commission. The scheme is that a Commission representing the Powers shall see to the execution of certain works which *they* may decide to be necessary. Will not M. de Lesseps dissent from the views of this Commission, unless the Company obtains some guarantee of interest on their capital? Will not the Commission, representing 12 Powers, of whom 11 between them will incur the financial responsibility of only 25 per cent of the whole amount to be guaranteed, readily conclude an arrangement leaving the burden of 75 per cent on the back of the 12th Power? May not serious political complications arise out of this partnership? We should be in the position of a man with money who had become the 12th partner in a mine which only required a small outlay to make it productive. Our partners would go on spending our money for us until we quarrelled with them. If it were possible for England to purchase the Canal outright, it would, in my judgment, be a safer financial and political operation than that which is now suggested. We should not be committed to an indefinite expenditure at the will of a practically irresponsible Commission: but I am aware that international jealousies would prevent anything of the sort, and it is useless to entertain the idea.

I submit, however, that the information given in these papers is exceedingly meagre, and insufficient to qualify a committment off-hand of so serious a character as that suggested.

Like his chief, Sir Stafford, Smith was opposed to the purchase of these shares; but other counsels prevailed, the transaction was completed, and has proved to be a brilliantly successful investment for the nation.[1] The bill necessary to obtain the money—£4,080,000—was brought in by the Chancellor of the Exchequer, and hotly opposed by two ex-Chancellors—Gladstone and Lowe. Northcote must have defended the policy of the bill with some misgiving and a good deal of secret sympathy with the " Treasury minds " of its opponents; nevertheless, he did the work manfully, and when Gladstone declared that to spend the money of the nation in this way was " an unprecedented thing "—" So is the Canal," retorted Northcote.

Another measure—popularly supposed to be the offspring of Disraeli's romantic genius—took

---

[1] On June 16, 1893, a question was put in the House of Commons to the Chancellor of the Exchequer (Sir W. Harcourt) as to the present state of the account between this country and the vendors of the Suez Canal shares. The reply of the right hon. gentleman was an eloquent, though perhaps involuntary, tribute to the sagacity of Lord Beaconsfield. It was made to the following effect:—

Price paid in 1875 . . . . . . £4,000,000.
Present value . . . . 17,750,000.
Amount of purchase-money now paid off . . 3,805,000.
Date at which we shall begin to draw dividend, July 1894.
Dividends payable during last three years, 17, 21, and 18 per cent.
Proportion of British tonnage to whole tonnage using Canal, 75 per cent.

up a deal of time out of all proportion to its importance. It was proposed to recognise retrospectively the transfer of the Government of India from the defunct East India Company to the Crown, by adding to her Majesty's titles that of Empress of India. There seemed really no reason for doing so at the precise time selected more than at any other, except that the Government happened to be without any other important work on hand; but the Opposition lashed themselves into a fine frenzy over the bill, and again the leaders of the attack on it were Gladstone and Lowe. The debates were much protracted, but people in the country showed small interest in what was little more than academic discussion and forensic hair-splitting.

More serious in its ultimate results was the organisation and activity of the Home Rule party under Mr Butt, with Messrs Parnell, Biggar, O'Donnell, and Callan as lieutenants. Both the great parties united in resisting the motion for Home Rule, and there was no difficulty in throwing it out by a majority of more than four to one; but for the first time the Irish Nationalists showed a cohesion and power of debate, destined to make them the formidable factor in Imperial politics which they have since become. One of their number, Mr P. J. Smythe, enjoyed a gift of eloquence which national fire and classical elegance combined to distinguish beyond his colleagues; and he used it to some purpose, for the Government were placed in a minority of 57 on his motion for closing Irish public-houses on Sunday.

Ministers opposed a measure — Mr Osborne Morgan's Burials Bill—and threw it out, which, a few months later, they were to include in their own programme. . Doubtless it became known to them after the division that party allegiance, not private conviction, had secured to them the support of many of their own followers in rejecting a measure which made it lawful for Nonconformists to perform their services in Church of England burial-grounds, and probably some of Smith's Liberal sympathy, though he dutifully voted "No," lay in the "Aye" lobby. Later in the session a resolution to the same effect was moved in the House of Lords, in supporting which Lord Selborne uttered a sentence worthy of commemoration. Resisting the arguments of those who opposed the opening of churchyards to Dissenters, because of the injustice of invading the property of the Church of England, he said—

I am not one of those who say *fiat justitia, ruat cœlum,* for I think the heavens are more likely to fall upon our heads if we do not do justice than if we do it.

Left in London to finish up the work of the session when his family went to Greenlands, Smith kept up the usual constant correspondence with his wife :—

HOUSE OF COMMONS, *August* 7.

One line, because it is pleasant to write to you, and to think a little of home in the hurry and bustle of work. . . . I am sitting at the Table of the House listening to Northcote defending the Suez Canal Bill. . . .

August 10.

Everything went on well yesterday at the Whitebait Dinner; both Disraeli and the Lord Chancellor appeared and spoke. The evening was most lovely, and the lights very pretty on the river; no doubt you are better off at Greenlands, but happily we can enjoy things as they pass.

Smith spent part of September and October visiting ships and dockyards with Mr Ward Hunt, First Lord of the Admiralty; and the repose at Greenlands which he so earnestly longed for was further curtailed by work at the Treasury during the autumn sittings of the Cabinet.

TREASURY, *November* 24.

I was very sorry to be obliged to run away from you, . . . but I think it was my duty to come here, and the moment I arrived Northcote sent for me and kept me discussing business for an hour. The Cabinet then met, and they have adjourned without fixing any future meeting, so that if I had not been here I should have been wanting in some parts of my work.

November 28.

Another busy day, but each day's work now leaves less to be done, and there is great satisfaction in getting through work.

Northcote goes away on Saturday, so I shall have much less to do afterwards, as all talking with him will come to an end.

December 6.

I have had a busy day again, and have had several long interviews, which have left me short time to write. Such a mixture of Post Office, Revenue, Exchequer Bills, Foreign Affairs, Kew Gardens, S. Kensington, Royal Society! My mind is very like the cross readings on a wall or a screen covered with scraps.

December 18.

I have been holding a *levée* to-day, or, as ladies would say, I have " received," until at last I am tired of talking. I hope things look peaceful, and at all events that we shall not be engaged in war. The Cabinet are cheerful.

December 19.

I have been prowling about looking for presents, but I have not satisfied myself yet. It really is difficult work. I am fearing I may not be able to get down to-morrow night. . . . I have had such a stream of people here one after another, and so many difficulties to smooth over, that I have not got on with my work as I hoped, and I do not want to have a quantity sent down to me.

I have been engaged incessantly up to this moment (6.40) by a succession of men and work, all wanting a last word or touch before Christmas. . . . I think I have bought everything excepting the cane, but I shall come down laden with parcels like a Father to-morrow.

CHAPTER XI.

1876–1878.

DIFFICULTIES OF THE GOVERNMENT—THE BULGARIAN ATROCITIES
—THE "BAG-AND-BAGGAGE" POLICY — THE JOURNAL OF A
DISCONTENTED MAN—OBSTRUCTION IN THE HOUSE OF COM-
MONS—DEATH OF MR WARD HUNT—SMITH APPOINTED FIRST
LORD OF THE ADMIRALTY — MISGIVINGS AS TO HIS OWN
ABILITY—PROPOSAL TO PUT THE POST OFFICE IN COMMISSION
—CONGRATULATORY BANQUET IN ST JAMES'S HALL — WAR
BETWEEN RUSSIA AND TURKEY—MEETING OF PARLIAMENT—
THE FLEET SENT TO GALLIPOLI — RESIGNATION OF LORDS
CARNARVON AND DERBY—VOTES OF CENSURE—THE BERLIN
CONGRESS—" PEACE WITH HONOUR."

As the session of 1876 moved to a close, affairs
began to wear an unprosperous aspect for the
Administration. The Porte had been in difficulties with its subjects in Servia, Montenegro, and
Bulgaria, and in the repression of insurrection in
the last - named country Turkish officials had
shown a ferocity which quickly awakened sympathy in this country for the sufferers. Party
politicians are ever on the outlook for any occurrence, however remote, which may be turned

to the disadvantage of their opponents, and in the Bulgarian atrocities Liberals were not slow to discern their opportunity. Conservative policy had ever favoured the strengthening of Turkey as a bulwark against the southward advance of Russia, therefore the Conservative Government must be called to account for the proceedings in Bulgaria. Mr Evelyn Ashley took the opportunity afforded, according to immemorial usage, by the Third Reading of the Appropriation Bill— always the closing act of the session—to call attention to this matter, and it was in reply to him that Mr Disraeli made his last speech in the House of Commons. Next morning it was announced that he had been summoned to the House of Lords with the title of Earl of Beaconsfield.[1] It had been known that his health had been severely strained by the more arduous conditions under which the House of Commons had begun to conduct its proceedings, and no one was surprised that he had decided to bring to a close his service of forty-three years as a

---

[1] The secret had been well kept, for Disraeli loved *coups de théâtre*. Mr Evelyn Ashley happened to meet one of Disraeli's private secretaries, Mr J. Daly, on the morning after the debate, before the latter had seen the morning papers. "Well," said Mr Ashley, "you see I drew your chief for his last speech in the House of Commons, and he has had to take refuge in the Lords." It was the first intimation received by Mr Daly of the intention of Disraeli.

member of that House. His place as leader of the House of Commons was taken by Sir Stafford Northcote.

The anti - Turkish agitation continued with great vehemence during the autumn. Indignation meetings were held in St James's Hall and in the country, urging the Government to interpose on behalf of the oppressed nationalities.

On September 8, Smith wrote from Greenlands to the Prime Minister :—

DEAR LORD BEACONSFIELD,—I cannot help saying I am very sorry to have to address you in this way, but yet I am satisfied the step you have taken was absolutely right and necessary, if we were to retain your guidance and direction, for I am sure you could not have borne the strain of another session in the House of Commons.

We shall, however, miss you very much, and the night will be dull and triste without you.

To say this, however, was not my intention in writing. I was asked to-day to go to a meeting at Slough to support Mr Fremantle, but I thought it better not to go, as in. the present critical condition of affairs I could hardly have avoided reference to the East, and I do not feel I have either the information or authority to speak.

In the present excited state of the public mind, one might easily say too little to satisfy one's friends at home, and too much for the difficult work in which the Foreign Office is engaged.

It is very possible I may be asked again, but I shall refrain unless I have a hint from you.

If at any time you wish to see me, I can easily drive

across the country on receiving a note or a telegram; but I am at the Treasury, for the present, on Mondays and Thursdays.—Believe me, yours very truly,

W. H. SMITH.

The EARL OF BEACONSFIELD.

Perhaps precipitate folly and sagacious forbearance could not be brought into sharper contrast than in the utterances of two persons representing opposite views on this question. " Perish our English interests," shrieked Mr Freeman in St James's Hall, " and our dominion in India," rather than we should protect the abomination of Turkish rule. Baroness Burdett Coutts, on the other hand, than whom no individual has ever shown wiser capacity for administering to the wants of her fellow - creatures out of her opulence, wrote to excuse herself from attending a meeting at the Guildhall on September 18, and employed words which, by their dignity and thoughtfulness, deserve a high place in political literature.

If the voice of England be potential and can influence the world's destiny, such a consideration should make us very careful as to how far and for what definite results the voice of the people shall be raised. As one of them, I feel the responsibility which rests upon us very strongly. Naturally, as a woman, I must be timid as to the result of this great agitation. I earnestly pray that in the measures taken to alleviate distress we may be calmly

led, and not increase, rather than diminish, the distress
of nations by urging on the Government an amount of
interference better calculated, perhaps, to light than to
extinguish a firebrand—a firebrand which may pass far
beyond Europe, or might even come near our own dear
shores.

Mr Gladstone, who in taking part in the debates on Eastern affairs had maintained an attitude generally favourable to Lord Derby's Eastern
policy, and had undertaken a defence of the
policy which led to the Crimean War, suddenly
dashed into the fray, unable, it would seem, to
resist the opportunity of taking the Government
at a disadvantage. He published an article in
the 'Contemporary Review' advocating the ex-
pulsion of the "unspeakable Turk, bag and bag-
gage," from Europe. The country was moved
in such sort as to make intelligible the fervour
which, in an age generally supposed to be less
enlightened, made the crusades possible.

Retrospect upon these excited times must lead
men to credit Lord Beaconsfield with a singular
degree of courage in adhering to a line of policy
which for the moment was widely unpopular.
He believed, and he manfully declared, that the
interest and honour of this country were alike
involved in refraining from embarrassing Turkey,

and before very long the tide turned in favour of a temperate and forbearing policy. People who had been carried away by the heat of Mr Gladstone's invective began to reflect for themselves. Several Liberals of standing — among others the Duke of Somerset, Mr Forster, who had lately returned from the East, and Lord Fitzwilliam—pronounced firmly against the "bag-and-baggage" scheme; and it was announced by the Prime Minister that a Conference of the Powers was to be held at Constantinople, at which Great Britain would be represented by Lord Salisbury.

The popular understanding of the Bulgarian difficulties was not without its effect upon the majority of the Government in the House of Commons. By the time Parliament met for the session of 1877, five seats had been lost to the Conservatives at by-elections. But there the reaction was stayed; and although the Constantinople Conference had failed, and Lord Salisbury was on his way home before the Queen's Speech was delivered, the Government were able to enter upon the parliamentary campaign without serious apprehension. Mr Gladstone's motion of want of confidence in Ministers was rejected by a majority of 131 votes.

On April 5, the Financial Secretary wrote to the Prime Minister :—

DEAR LORD BEACONSFIELD,—I hope you will be satisfied with our financial work.

The Chancellor of the Exchequer will have a surplus of £440,000 on the past year, and a safe estimate of the revenue for the coming year will give a small surplus over the expenditure without any increase of taxation. As this result is not expected out of doors, it will, I think, be the more satisfactory to our friends and to the country.—Yours very truly, W. H. SMITH.

The note from the Prime Minister in reply was one of those rewards which come to lighten a life of conscientious toil :—

HUGHENDEN MANOR, *April 7, '77·*

MY DEAR MR SMITH,—I thank you for your Budget Report, & heartily congratulate you & the country on the result. After forty years' experience of parliamentary life, I can sincerely say that I never knew the affairs of the Treasury conducted with more thorough sense & efficiency than while they have been under your management & control.—Yours sincerely, BEACONSFIELD.

During all his foreign tours, it was Smith's practice to send to some correspondent at home letters forming a consecutive itinerary. As is usually the case in such literature, much of the interest is ephemeral; but a few passages may be quoted from his description of a visit to Normandy which he paid with Mrs Smith in the

Whitsuntide recess of this year. In it he endeavoured, with but partial success, to pose as an unwilling victim, and the document is entitled—

The Journal of a Discontented Man.

May 18.—My wife insists on a little holiday, and I must go with her. Where will I go? What trouble! I do not care: just where you please: only decide. Well, then, we will go to Normandy. I ask for a deck cabin: they are all engaged. I go out to get some money, and my eyes and mouth are filled with dust and dirt. The high wind must make dirty weather in the Channel, and the boat is sure to be crowded. No deck cabin, no shelter; how miserable we shall be!

We started. A crowd in Regent Street. Bohren's cab with the luggage is passed—the man driving slowly. He is sure to be late. We arrived first at the station, and instantly fall on the R——s, who are also off to France for a holiday. It is impossible to be alone. We talked, and then—weary of each other—three out of the four fall asleep. I became more composed when I reflected on the miseries of friendship and of society.

On board the steamer came a crowd, all of whom were disagreeable to me, and some particularly so. I had deposited my wife on the sofa in the ladies' cabin and secured a sheltered seat for myself, when the steward came and intreated me to give it up for a lady. Of course I consented; what tyrannical power attaches to this fanatical subserviency to the sex-female. Why should not a man retain a comfortable seat when he had once got it?
. . . Half-way across, the lady tottered up from her seat in some sort of trouble and made a rush for the cabin.

Presently the gentlemen sitting on either side of me groaned and began to kneel on the seat with their heads doing homage to the sea. . . . We got into harbour nearly an hour late of course, and of course the water was low and we were landed near the end of the jetty. When *is* the water high at Calais ? . . .

May 19.—The lumbering carts bringing in market people filled my disturbed sleep with dreams, until I fairly woke under the influence of the horrible cries of a quiet street in Calais. If half-a-dozen old women were being squeezed to death, the screaming could hardly be worse. My wife however slept like an Angel, as I am sometimes inclined to think she is, so I smothered my resentment against the sea, breakfasted, and descended into the street for a cigar. There I instantly fell on another M.P., who would be a good fellow if he was a Tory. We introduced each other's wives and parted smiling, only to fall on another, the ——, Bart., who inquires how Mrs Smith could leave her children, Lady —— having left hers. I gave him an answer—we did not speak again.

Our seats had been taken in the train by Bohren, but a very fresh English husband and wife appropriated one of them, and although roundly abused by the French guard, the woman retained the seat; but I had the satisfaction of looking straight at the husband all the way to Amiens, and of making him feel uncomfortable. At all events I began to be happier.

We ought to have had 20 minutes for luncheon at Amiens, but the train was late, the Rouen train was waiting, and so we were hurried into it without any food. Was I not right to be angry ? . . . And now it rained heavily, and the country looked dreary and very like England. Does it not rain in England ? Was it necessary to leave the comforts of home to see Rain ?

We reached Rouen—everything wet, every place cold and dreary. Our inn is, of course, Hôtel d'Angleterre by way of sarcasm. Our room is several inches lower at the door than at the window, and there is not room to swing a cat. . . . We descend to dinner, hungry and tired. Presently up trots a small French poodle, shaved up to its neck, with very dirty hair over its head, and red, bleary, weak-looking eyes. It looks at me, and exercising a sound discretion, prefers my wife, jumps up on a chair by her side and begins instantly to beg. This is intolerable!

Of course the fish, the chicken, the meat, are all offered in succession to this insufferable dog. I say severe things, but it is of no avail. How I hate most dogs, and all little ones! A big hound walks in. My wife offers it something and pats it. The little one—a tenth of its size—jumps down and barks furiously at the hound, which slips and flounders on the polished floor, turns round and goes out, chased by the little poodle, who returns triumphant to the chair by the side of my wife.

May 20.—More rain.

May 21.—No rain, but a sharp, cold north-east wind—as cold as England. Again I ask, Why should I travel to France to meet rain and east wind, which are to be had plentifully in England? Could not get a carriage to-day, because it is a holiday and everybody is out. These holidays are a nuisance. At last we are allowed by a driver to get into his carriage, and we proceed slowly to Bonnesecours, a church on a high hill two miles from Rouen, overlooking the Seine, which is here about half as pretty as the Thames at Richmond. . . . Many holiday folk in the cemetery, which is a cheerful way of spending a happy day. . . .

May 22.—Once more rain, but we drove to the old clock in an archery over the street, the Palais de Justice, which contains the old Parliament chamber, and through other old places to the railway, whence we started to Caen. Rouen has a river, two quays, three old churches, fair wide streets, an infinite number of narrow lanes and old houses, and all round it are manufactories and tall chimneys. The climate is detestable, and the people rough as Englishmen. From Rouen to Caen—more chimneys, more rain. At Caen—still more rain, bitterly cold.

From the hotel in a close carriage almost dark to the Church of Ste Etienne, really a grand old Norman building, with grotesque capitals to the round pillars, supporting the roof of a wide nave. In the gloom before the high altar a plain slab marks the place where William the Conqueror was buried. I am not discontented with this church. It was worth coming to Caen to see ; but I now understand why William came to England—his own climate drove him away in simple desperation. . . . We returned to a grand *salon* and poor bedrooms, lighted up, however, by fires, round which we crouched. Great enjoyment, which might possibly have been exceeded at home.

May 23. — More rain — more north-east wind. . . . Paid a heavy bill, and off to the railway. The country green, hilly, with a river running by the side of the line. Small fields, hedgerows, and cattle — like, but not so pretty as, Devonshire. It would be nice if the sun ever shone, but it has been raining for eight months. My wife takes refuge in sleep. I groan and grumble to myself. We arrived at the junction for Villedieu, a capital buffet, and seated ourselves in a dark room with three Frenchmen, a mother, a *bonne*, and a baby ; all ate in a

hurry; all, the baby included, wore a sad and preoccu-
pied air. . . .

May 25.—I think we have seen Avranches. It is a
healthy town, sir, a clean town, sir; it has fine air, sir,
it is so high, and there are many English living here. . . .
Poor things! I pity them, and almost forget my discontent when I think of the perfect quiet of their lives. How
the ladies must dislike each other, and how thoroughly
they must know each other's faults and failings. . . . I
am thankful, and so is my wife, that we are not obliged
to live there. How dull—with no work, but to read and
walk and talk—eat, drink, and sleep.

We found a carriage to take us on to Granville with
difficulty. . . . The horses, poor things! The coachman
a sturdy red-faced Norman. He did not know the way
to —— where the —— live, . . . but Bohren piloted
him. Their cottage is a pretty one. . . . Poor Mrs
—— is, she says, quite tired of apple-blossom, and
there is nothing else. Her husband most anxious to
hear of something to do—anywhere and of any kind.
I never met a man so eager to get away from himself and
his own society. I asked if his wife was coming to England. "I will bring her at once, if I can find anything
in the shape of employment—India, Turkey, anywhere."

How much better it is to have too much to do than too
little. Never give up present employment, however disagreeable it may be, until one has made sure of something
else. Poverty with work is Paradise compared with
either riches or poverty without work. . . . Granville
is a disappointment. There is a church—an old one—
but not interesting. . . . There are several dull streets
without *trottoirs*, many children crying in them, with
women who appear to be scolding each other. . . . Our
hotel—Hôtel du Nord—was comfortable enough. We

were waited upon by a Jersey woman who spoke English, talking incessantly, and always of her own good qualities and the many merits of her family. . . . So I have done and go home, more content than I left home, and certainly the better of my absence.

Meanwhile the development of new methods of parliamentary warfare began to be painfully apparent at this time. Inordinate discussion upon votes in Supply, dilatory motions for adjournment, and questions to Ministers upon subjects of the most trivial parochial, and even personal, subjects, formed part of the plan of campaign adopted by Irish Nationalist members in order, by bringing proceedings to a deadlock, to force attention to their demands. If the legitimacy of their ambition be granted, their strategy and the energy and patience with which it was pursued are deserving of admiration. This new reign of terror began in earnest on Tuesday, July 31. The House met that afternoon at 4 P.M., and the sitting continued till past six on Wednesday evening—more than twenty-six hours. Mr Butt, nominal leader of the Home Rulers, protested against the methods favoured by his colleagues, Messrs Parnell and Biggar, but to no purpose; and henceforward Parnell was *de facto* the director of the policy of his party. The state of matters was so serious as to bring about what has proved to be the first in a long series of

ERRATUM.

Facsimile of Letter from the Earl of Beaconsfield has, by an oversight, been inserted at p. 299 of vol. ii. instead of at this place.

successive alterations in the rules of Procedure, rendered more and more necessary as legislators departed further and further from the reasonable practice of a more decorous age.

After introducing the Navy Estimates, Mr Ward Hunt, First Lord of the Admiralty, fell into such a state of health as to oblige his going to Homburg, where he shortly after died.

There is every reason to believe that the letter referred to in the following one, written to Mrs Smith, who was at Homburg, came to Smith as a complete surprise :—

HOUSE OF COMMONS, *Aug.* 3.

This morning as I was driving down to the Treasury I met Lord Beaconsfield's messenger with this letter. I have accepted the office, if the Queen approves. . . . The responsibility is very great, and nothing would have induced me to seek it, but as I am told I am deemed fit for the work, I do not think I ought to refuse it. . . . It has not been offered to any one else. . . . Do not say one word to any one about the story, until you see it in the papers, or hear from me that you may talk.

The letter is given in facsimile on opposite page.

Two days later he wrote from Greenlands to his wife, who was at Homburg :—

It is a lovely day—such rest and peace around—and yet I am not quite at rest, for I feel the weight of responsibility which I have incurred in accepting the Cabinet and the Admiralty. Until now, in graver matters, I only advised. Now I must act on my own judgment, and the sphere of that action concerns the country's honour and its strength. I shall want all your help— such help as you have ever given me since we were happily made one—in asking that I may have wisdom and strength according to my need. I think I shall, because we shall both ask.

There is a heavy drawback to this new duty. Beach tells me the Cabinet have been warned that none of them must go out of reach of a sudden summons to a meeting, so that while Foreign affairs are in the present critical state, I could not go further from London than this or the coast.

The ladder which brings a Minister from the Financial Secretaryship into the Cabinet has frequently proved to be a short one, but it has not often led to an office the holder of which, representing as he does the Lord High Admiral of old, had up to this time been nearly always occupied by some Peer of high rank, by a territorial magnate, or at least by the scion of a noble house. That a London tradesman should step into such an exalted sphere was an ascent almost as rapid and not less remarkable than Whittington's.

The first thing Smith did on receiving Lord Beaconsfield's letter was to seek the advice of his old ally, Lord Sandon, who urged him warmly to accept the offer.

The announcement of Smith's appointment

to the Admiralty was favourably received by the public. There was, of course, the usual degree of mild surprise at the working of a system which places at the head of the naval and military establishments individuals who by training, habit, and occupation are least likely to have any technical or practical acquaintance with the services; but the press generally indorsed the sagacity of the Prime Minister's choice.[1] Smith's own friends, of course, were enthusiastic in congratulation, and he possessed friends on both sides of politics. Sir William Harcourt wrote —:

I heard your writ moved to-day with great satisfaction, & greeted it with an approving cheer. No one has better earned & deserved the great post which you have reached in a comparatively short Parliamentary career. Your opponents, no less than your friends, sympathise in your well-merited success, and none more amongst them than

Yours sincerely, W. V. HARCOURT.

Mr Rathbone, another sturdy Liberal, gave his approval thus :—

I had no idea when speaking to you last night what

---

[1] The appointment is supposed to have suggested to the irreverent fancy of Mr W. S. Gilbert the character of Sir Joseph Porter in the opera "Pinafore," who, it will be remembered, "stuck to his desk and never went to sea," yet became the "Ruler of the Queen's Navee."

a great dignity I was addressing.   I congratulate you
most heartily, though as an ex-Quaker I would rather
your country had your services for the works of peace
than of war.   As you have no doubt heard, it has been
received not only with pleasure but great approval on
our side, as a very good appointment richly deserved.

The unflinching Radical, Joseph Cowen, member
for Newcastle, was not behindhand :—

You carry with you to your new office the good wishes
& the sympathy of the entire House of Commons. . . . I
have never voted for a Conservative in my life ; but if
there should be a contest in Westminster (where I am an
elector), you can safely calculate on at least one radical
recording his vote for you.

The voice of the Navy found expression in a
characteristic note from Lord Charles Beres-
ford :—

Let me congratulate you & the Navy also at your
appointment.   Don't think me rude if I say I was long
enough Shipmates with you in the House to appreciate
what a real good appointment the Prime Minister has
made.

In a letter from Sir Stafford Northcote to Mrs
Smith there is mingled a strain of regret at
losing his Financial Secretary :—

I must ask leave to send you one line of Congratulation
and sympathy, though, by the way, I can more easily
sympathise with you than you can with me, for you will

not have to contend with the mixed feelings which are distracting me. It is something like what I felt when my daughter chose to go and marry herself off. I am as troubled to know what to do without my right hand now as I was then. . . . Nobody could have succeeded as your husband has done in this office. He has had a very important, laborious, and delicate task to discharge, and I don't think he has made a slip in the whole three years. He carries with him the affection as well as the respect and good wishes of us all.

An old friend of the family wrote to Smith :—

When I first heard of your acceptance of the office of First Lord of the Admiralty, the text came into my mind, "His sons come to honour and he knoweth it not," as I thought of the high gratification the knowledge of this appointment would have afforded to those who have now passed away.

But Smith himself felt none of that confidence which those who knew him best were most ready to repose in him.

I am really almost sad [he wrote to Miss Giberne], for now I am one of the 12 men who are responsible for the Government of the country, and I am at the head of a great department in which it is more easy to fail than to succeed ; but I look for strength and wisdom, and I trust it may be given me. Don't you understand it is not matter for rejoicing with me, except as it might be with a soldier charged with a great work. He may fail and he may fall, but his country's welfare depends in a manner on his performance of duty.

Again, to his sister Augusta :—

I wish my father had been alive. He certainly did not
expect that at 52 I should be a Cabinet Minister, and
now I almost wish I had never entered public life, for it
seems impossible to stop or to refuse work. . . . I hope I
may have strength and judgment to do it well, and at the
same time to preserve the love and affection of my family.

On August 13 he wrote to Mrs Smith :—

I wrote to you this evening under difficulties, as I was
trying to listen to discussions in Cabinet and yet catch the
post. I told you we went down by a special train to Portsmouth with ceremony and honour. Bishop Thorold was
going down to do homage for his see, with Lord Wriothesley
Russell as Clerk of the Closet. They, Mr Cross, Lord
Coventry, Mr Sclater Booth, the Clerk of the Council, and
I, went in one saloon. . . . At Portsmouth the train went
into the dockyard, and drew up at the jetty, where we
were received by the Admiral. The Fire Queen was
waiting, and we all steamed off, taking the Duke of
Richmond, who came from Goodwood, and Lord Hertford, the Lord Chamberlain, with us. On our way we
met the Thunderer, which was going out for big gun
practice, with the Prince of Wales and some ladies on
board. The carriages were not at the pier when we
landed, but they soon overtook us. . . . We had to wait
some time at the house, which reminds me very much of
Denbies. At last Lord Hertford called in Lord Coventry
and myself. The Queen was standing before a table. We
knelt down rather by her side. The oath of allegiance
was read over to us. We kissed the book on our knees,
and then kissed her hand and rose up. Then standing,
the Privy Councillor's oath, which is a very long one, was

read, and we again kissed the book, and then I shook hands with all the Privy Councillors present. The Queen then approved a number of Orders in Council, the titles of which were read over to her; the Privy Councillors, not being members of the Cabinet, withdrew, and then the Speech to be delivered to-morrow was approved. We then withdrew, bowing with our faces to her—the Queen smiling, but not saying a word. . . . A cab to Downing Street for the Cabinet at 5.45. I was most kindly welcomed by all, sitting between Northcote and Salisbury, opposite Lord Derby.

And on August 14 :—

So much kindness brings a sense of sadness with it, of weight and of fear lest failure should follow. My Patent has come to-day, and I have taken my seat at the Board, who address me as " Sir " in every sentence. It is strange, and makes me shy at first; and I have to do what I hardly like—to send for them, not to go to them; but I am told they expect me, as their chief, to require respect.

Mrs Smith went to Homburg during the autumn, and her husband, detained in England by his official duties, wrote as frequently and tenderly as he was wont to do. Here is part of a letter written from Greenlands :—

If I cannot look at you and talk to you, I can write to you, and that is, I think, a very fit use to be made of half an hour on a Sunday afternoon. . . . The swallows, which are flying very low and in great numbers, just skimming the top of the grass, don't seem to miss you, but it is another thing with us.

Before closing the record of Smith's connection with the Treasury as its Financial Secretary, it is important to notice one proposal which he laid before the Chancellor of the Exchequer, which retains more interest at the present day than most of the dusty papers which have to be turned over in pursuing the actions of a public servant. These may have absorbed all the attention and been the subject of much anxiety to men of the day, consisting as they largely do of deliberations on points of departmental administration and the abundant record of grievances, but they are now as the withered leaves of an oak, the branches of which go on growing while these moulder into dust below. But this proposal — contained in the following letter to Sir Stafford Northcote—may yet bear fruit in the future —:

Feb. 11, 1877.

My dear Northcote,—Will you consider whether the moment is opportune for entertaining suggestions for a change in the present system of administering the Post Office ?

It is a department of infinite detail. The gross Revenue of upwards of seven millions sterling is collected by pennies and shillings, at a cost of more than five millions ; but every letter and telegram brings the servant of the Post Office into contact with the Public in some shape or way. There are 40,000 of these servants, and the Government is made responsible for all their errors and shortcomings.

It is a vast Government carrying-trade, protected as a monopoly by Act of Parliament, but requiring the most careful watchfulness in management—more so than either the Customs or Inland Revenue, which collect revenue without giving back anything in return.

The Postmaster-General has been frequently changed. He is regarded as a high political officer, and is expected to give assistance in Parliament to his Government. In the past . . . it is notorious that Postmasters-General have not controlled or directed the policy and really managed the business of the Department. It has been open to able and ambitious officers in the Department to do practically what they pleased in the name of their Chief, whose nominal responsibility completely covered their acts.

The whole of the ——— scandal arose in this way. He was daring and skilful, and not being responsible himself, he had no hesitation in setting the law at defiance behind the back of his Chief, who was absolutely ignorant of his acts. I do not think he would have taken this course if he had been a Commissioner responsible to his Colleagues and to the Chancellor of the Exchequer.

There is reason to believe that there is, for the time, a more general sense of responsibility at the Post Office, but the system which produced these evils remains.

It is beyond the power of a Postmaster-General to obtain, during his short term of office, a sufficient grasp of detail and of principle really to direct and control his department. Is it worth while to examine whether a permanent Board, similar to those of the Customs and Inland Revenue, would not be a desirable substitution for the office of Postmaster?

The relations between the Treasury and the Post Office are anomalous and difficult. The Postmaster cannot

change the organisation of his Department or do any act
tending to increase the cost of the Service without coming
to the Treasury for approval. It is a Revenue Department (which, however, must be managed with a view
to the public convenience) presided over by a Cabinet
Minister, and his recommendations are challenged by
Members of the Government of lower official rank than
himself. The Treasury can, and often does, check the
Postmaster-General in the course he is advised by his
subordinates to pursue, but in the House of Commons he
answers for his Department as if he had no such responsibility. . . . If there were a Board in his place, there
would be continuity of management and of policy : there
would be real subordination of departmental officers, and
the relations between the Treasury and the Post Office
would be as free from strain and difficulty as they are
with the Boards of Customs and Inland Revenue.

This question was suffered to drop when Smith
left the Treasury, but the case for a change has
been so well made out, Smith's arguments thus
set forth are so clear and weighty, that it seems
far from improbable that the matter must come
up for decision at a future day.

Smith's re-election for Westminster on appointment to the Admiralty had not been contested;
but his friends and constituents were not content
to allow the distinction conferred upon him to
pass without special marks of approval and congratulation. On November 29 he was entertained

at a banquet in St James's Hall, where Lord Henry Scott, M.P., presided over a company of more than 500, assembled to do honour to the First Lord. Smith, as every one knows, was not an orator; his speeches were never of the order to *faire rémuer le sang*, but he never spoke unless he had something to say, and always succeeded in making that something intelligible, and in convincing his hearers of his perfect frankness. In a few simple sentences he conveyed on this occasion a clear impression of the circumstances which had brought him into a position of such dignity :—

When I look back upon the past—and it is only twelve years ago when I was invited by some friends whom I now see around me to offer myself as a candidate for the representation of Westminster—when I remember that I failed then (not disastrously and not disgracefully) to obtain the object which they rather more than I had on that occasion—when I remember that again in 1868 you were patient and kind enough to entertain the proposal that was made to you to return me as your member for Westminster—when I think of the period of liberty, of freedom, and of comparative absence from responsibility which I enjoyed as the representative of Westminster for the five years that succeeded the election,—I say that it appears like a dream; and I can hardly understand how it is I am here to-day, not only wearing the blue ribbon of parliamentary representative of the city of Westminster, but also as a servant of the Crown and of

the people.   Frankly, I cannot tell you how it has come
to pass, but it has happened, that your exceeding kindness,
and the sympathy and support of my friends, have pushed
me forward into the position which I should not have been
tempted to seek for myself.   Never once did I entertain
the idea of standing for Westminster until I was asked to
do so, and I did not again entertain the idea of seeking
election till I was pressed to do so.   I did not seek office;
it has come to me in a manner which, when I think of it,
is surprising to myself, and I feel deeply the responsibility which has fallen upon me.

Next morning the ' Times,' in a leading article
on the principal guest at this banquet, correctly
defined the position which Smith had attained
to in the esteem of his countrymen :—

Mr W. H. Smith is eminently representative of that
special order of men whom it is the boast of our political
institutions to possess.   Neither an orator nor a man of
genius, he has risen to the foremost rank among his fellow-
citizens by the excellent way in which he did all the work
before him, and by his sterling manly character.

Another critic remarked :—

One of the chief reasons of the popularity the Ministry
still enjoys, and of the confidence it still commands, is that
it numbers in its list so many men of the Liberal type,
and of the special type to which Mr Smith belongs.   Sir
Stafford Northcote, Mr Cross, and Mr Smith are all men
who, without conspicuous oratorical power, or any claim
to originality, have raised themselves to the front rank
by moderation, honesty, skill in business, conciliatory
manners, and a broad and genial Liberalism.   To Lord

Beaconsfield much credit is due for having recognised the merits of men so totally unlike himself. . . . They import prudence and good sense into every Conservative gathering. They are always, as it were, brightening up the boots of the party, and making it look tidy and respectable when it appears before the public.

Even ' Punch,' Liberal by tradition and practice, had a kindly word for the new ruler of the Queen's Navy:—

Of Mr W. H. Smith all parties may say, as a great opponent said of Lord Palmerston, " We are all proud of him." . . . Never has man or Minister more fairly earned the addition of " Right Honourable."

Some sentences in Smith's speech expressing his horror of war and his earnest hope for the preservation of peace were received with much satisfaction in the country; for all eyes were turning anxiously towards the East, where there might happen any day that which might involve Great Britain in the conflict which throughout the summer and autumn had been raging on the Danube and the Black Sea.

The refusal of the Porte to comply with the recommendations of the Constantinople Conference, and the consequent failure of all attempts to bring Turkey into concert with other European Powers, brought that country and Russia to the brink of war. On April 24, 1877, the

Czar, who looked upon himself as the ordained
champion of Sclavonic nationality, had issued a
declaration of war against the Sultan, without
the customary formula of an ultimatum. Englishmen have never been chary of chivalrous
sympathy for a weaker nation defending itself
against invasion by a stronger; the old feeling
of comradeship, handed down from Crimean
days, began to revive in this country in favour
of our ancient allies, and was fanned into something like fervour by the opening acts of the
campaign. The gallantry and soldierly qualities
displayed by the Turkish troops, their successes
at Batoum on May 4, and at Sukhum Kalé on
the 14th, their stout defence of Kars, and the
raising of the siege of that oft-beleaguered city
by Mukhtar Pasha, proved that far from being
an effete, spiritless race, the Turks were as capable as ever they had been of splendid service
in the field. The Bulgarian atrocities faded into
insignificance before the brilliancy of the double
victory gained by Osman Pasha over the Russians at Plevna in July, and the desperate obstinacy of the defence of the Shipka Pass. But
the tide of victory turned in late autumn. The
bravery of her devoted soldiers could not save
the territory of a State so rotten as that of
Turkey. Russian victories in Asia were followed

by the fall of Kars and Erzeroum, not without
suspicion of treason; blood-boltered Plevna was
at last taken, and the Shipka Pass occupied in
January 1878, and then the Porte sent a Circular Note to the Powers, imploring them to ex-
tricate it from the disasters into which its own
obstinacy and indolence had plunged it.

On January 31 an armistice was signed at
Adrianople, and the preliminaries of peace for-
mulated.

Parliament was summoned to meet a full fortnight or three weeks earlier than usual — on
January 17—amid a feeling of intense uneasiness
and public excitement. The Queen's Speech contained nothing to allay these : on the contrary,
the paragraphs referring to the Eastern situation
were of ominous import. After reciting how,
when all attempts to avert war had proved
futile, her Majesty had resolved to preserve
strict neutrality as between the belligerents,
and the success of Russian arms compelled the
Porte to bring hostilities to a close, the Speech
went on to describe how the Sultan, having appealed to the neutral Powers for their good
offices, and the majority of these Powers not
having been in favour of interfering, had addressed a separate appeal to her Majesty's Government. Then followed sentences of which

every one who had heard or read them felt the solemn significance.

Upon this subject communications have taken place between the Governments of Russia and Turkey, through my good offices, and I earnestly trust that they may lead to a peaceful solution of the points at issue, and to a termination of the war. No efforts on my part will be wanting to promote that result.

Hitherto, so far as the war has proceeded, neither of the belligerents has infringed the conditions on which my neutrality is founded, and I willingly believe that both parties are desirous to respect them, so far as it may be in their power. So long as these conditions are not infringed, my attitude will continue the same. But I cannot conceal from myself that, should hostilities be unfortunately prolonged, some unexpected occurrence may render it incumbent upon me to adopt measures of precaution. Such measures could not be adequately taken without adequate preparation, and I trust to the liberality of my Parliament to supply the means which may be required for that purpose.

Meanwhile the Russians were at the gates of Constantinople: the prize for which they had so long panted was within their grasp; would they relinquish it at the bidding of Great Britain?

That the Cabinet intended to forbid the occupation of the Sultan's capital was made certain by the notice given in the House of Commons that a Vote of Credit for £6,000,000 was to be moved for immediately. Suddenly, on January

23, the startling news went abroad that the British fleet had been ordered to the Dardanelles. The Earl of Carnarvon, Secretary of State for the Colonies, announced in the House of Lords that he had resigned office, and in explaining the reasons which compelled him to do so, stated that he had resisted the proposal, made to the Cabinet on January 12, that the fleet should be sent up the Dardanelles, that he had resigned on the 15th when this course had been decided on, but had consented to retain office when the decision was rescinded. Now, however, that the action to which he objected as dangerous and unnecessary had actually been taken, he had no course but to leave a Cabinet with whom he found himself at direct issue.

It was understood that the Earl of Derby had also resigned, but, as he appeared on the Government bench with his colleagues on this occasion, it was evident that he was still a member of the Cabinet.

Smith had a difficult task to perform on this very day. In the afternoon he and Sir Charles Adderley, President of the Board of Trade, received the freedom of the Ancient Company of Shipwrights, and were entertained at a public banquet in the evening. It must have been no light problem how to speak as a Cabinet Minister

for the Cabinet, conscious as he was that the
Cabinet was rent by dissension on a question so
momentous and beset with peril.   One sentence,
and one only, he permitted himself to utter in reference to the subject uppermost in the minds of
all, and it was one which Englishmen of all parties
could receive with ringing cheers : " No greater
disaster than to be engaged in war could happen
to the country, except the loss of honour."

The view which Smith took at this most critical
juncture is expressed in two letters to Northcote,
illustrating the strain of anxiety which lay upon
Ministers :—

ADMIRALTY, *Jan.* 12, 1878.

DEAR NORTHCOTE,—I wish you would see Lord Derby.
I quite understood yesterday that he agreed to the occupation of Gallipoli in the sense you suggested, and although
I have satisfied myself that the Fleet can anchor there
without serious risk, it would be a more sensible operation
to take possession of the lines.

You will remember, however, that the most formidable
forts are at the entrance to the Black Sea, above Constantinople.   If a foreign Power holds the City, it holds
also the key of the Black Sea.

If we cannot come to an agreement on our policy on
Monday in certain events, it is a question whether it would
not be more patriotic to break up and resign now.   It
will not do to be fighting in the House with the Opposition, and in the Cabinet with each other.—Yours sincerely,

W. H. SMITH.

Then on 15th :—

> I hope the telegram will not be sent to-night if Lord
> Derby objects to it. The delay of a few hours is im-
> portant, but the loss of Lord Derby would be a greater
> evil.

Nevertheless, man of peace as he was by training and inclination, there is the testimony of
more than one of his surviving colleagues in
that Cabinet to prove that Smith showed
much firmness in this crisis. Though slow in
forming a judgment, he had the enviable gift,
once it was formed, of adhering to it without
anxiety.

It was not to be expected that the Vote of
Credit would be granted without animated debate. The opposition to it took the form of a
motion of censure on the Government, moved
by Mr W. E. Forster. The debate is memorable for this, if for nothing else, that it gave
birth to a term which has become the English
equivalent of the French *chauviniste*.[1] Sir
Wilfrid Lawson, who is nothing if not humor-
ous, even when he is most in earnest, quoted a
couplet from a popular music-hall ditty of the

---

[1] Derived from Chauvin, a character in Scribe's 'Soldat Labor-
eur,' one of Napoleon Buonaparte's veterans, and expressive of
boastful and aggressive patriotism.

day, which he said exactly described the aggressive spirit of the Government's policy :—

> " We don't want to fight, but by Jingo ! if we do,
> We've got the ships, we've got the men, we've got the
> money too."

Henceforward the war party in our country, or the party suspected of warlike sentiments, was to be distinguished by the name of Jingoes.

It was Smith's duty in the debate to follow Mr Goschen, who had called on the Government to say exactly how much money they wanted, and how they intended to spend it.

The right hon. gentleman opposite says he desires to strengthen the Government in the Conference in which we expect shortly to take part. He is willing to give the great support of his name in favour of the expression of our views in the Congress, but he thinks it right to say that he refuses, on the grounds of precedent and financial policy, to give the six millions. It appears that the right hon. gentleman refuses to give the Government a cheque for six millions, but he will give us a blank cheque, without money expressed, to be filled up by ourselves at the right time. Now if the Government are not to be trusted with the responsibility of spending so much as they think necessary in making preparations for guarding their interests, in strengthening themselves where they think strength is needed, then I say they ought not to be trusted in going into the Conference to speak for England and to commit her to the decision which will be arrived at. I have taken part in financial questions during the past few years, and I know no higher duties than to require the most exact accounts for the administration of public money. But I think the principles of high finance can be carried too far. It is the most earnest desire and hope of her Majesty's Government that the issue of war may be avoided, and none except those who have occupied positions as Ministers of the Crown can conceive the amount of responsibility which rests upon a Minister when he expresses an opinion on such a question. We believe that the course we are asking the House of Commons to adopt is one which will tend in the most complete and sure manner to save England from the horrors of war. We believe that the making of such preparations as we may deem to be necessary will be a security against war.

Despite these reassuring words, each day seemed to bring nearer to Great Britain the necessity of a rupture with Russia. At last, on February 7, there arrived a telegram from Mr Layard, our Ambassador at Constantinople, to the effect that the Russian army had occupied that city. The effect upon Parliament and the country was electric; the fighting spirit of the nation was afire; Mr Forster withdrew his amendment to the motion for the Vote of Credit, and although the extreme Radicals insisted upon going to a division, the Vote was carried that night by 295 to 96—a majority of 199 for the Government. It turned out that the telegram was untrue: Mr Layard had been deceived by the presence of a number of Russian officers and men on leave in the streets of Stamboul. Nevertheless, nothing could be more threatening or critical than the situation, and on February 8 part of the British fleet was moved up to Constantinople as a precautionary measure.

Next came a message from the Sovereign announcing that it had been deemed expedient to call out a portion of the Reserves, and the Address in reply to this formed the subject of another vote of no confidence in the policy of the Government. But this was easily disposed of : the Opposition, however deep and sincere might be their disapproval of the policy of Ministers, were resolved to adhere to honourable tradition, and to let it be known that in foreign policy there is one England and not two Englands. The Address was agreed to by 310 votes to 64.

By an extract from the diary of one of the First Lord of the Admiralty's daughters, a glimpse is afforded of the anxious and disturbed state of affairs at this time :—

Sunday, Feb. 10.—Very excited and peculiar Sunday owing to telegrams on Eastern Question. Papa roused between 5 & 6 A.M. to decipher telegrams ; not able to go to Ch. Going to see Sir S. Northcote, Ld. Salisbury, also Ld. Beaconsfield at 10.15 P.M. Ld. Tenterden [1] called at 5.30, & again a few minutes after 10. Capt. Codring-

---

[1] Permanent Secretary at the Foreign Office.

ton[1] to lunch and dinner. Six ironclads have been sent to the Straits to protect English life & property at Constantinople, but Turks would not open them passage.

Military preparations in this country went forward amain : arsenals and factories were working double time, and orders were issued from the Admiralty to fit out every available ship. All this time Mr Gladstone kept rather quiet within Parliament; but from time to time he addressed meetings in the country, denouncing the policy of "Jingoism." At length it appeared as if the promptness and vigour displayed by the British Government were beginning to take effect. The Czar, it was known, passionately longed for peace : he could not but be impressed by the prospect of entering upon war with a powerful enemy, wealthy, fresh, and determined, after the terrible losses which his armies had endured in the campaign of 1877. An agreement was come to that the Russians should not occupy Gallipoli, provided the English fleet withdrew from the immediate neighbourhood of Constantinople. Negotiations, however, which had been set on foot for a Congress of the Powers failed, owing to dissensions in the English Cabinet. The Earl of Derby resigned the seals of the Foreign Office,

---

[1] Private Secretary to the First Lord of the Admiralty, who afterwards married Mr Smith's step-daughter, Miss Leach.

and was succeeded by the Marquis of Salisbury.
One of the causes which led to the last-named occurrence, to avert which so many precautions had
been taken, was the ordering of 7000 Indian
troops to Malta, and this formed the subject of
a second motion of censure on the Government
in the House of Commons.

Some idea of the intense anxiety of the situation may be formed from the following despatches
exchanged between the First Lord of the Admiralty and the Admiral commanding the Mediterranean Squadron.   They afford an interesting
illustration of the effect which the means of rapid
communication have had in controlling and directing the actions of armies and navy at great distances, and it suggests some curious reflections
that this duty should have been discharged by
one so pacific in training and character as W. H.
Smith.   Yet it is not always the most warlike
who have resoluteness at command : *suaviter in
modo* is not seldom merely ancillary to *fortiter
in re.*

The First Lord of the Admiralty to the Prime Minister.

Private.

ADMIRALTY,
Sunday Morning, Feb. 10, 1878.

DEAR LORD BEACONSFIELD,—We have had three messages from Admiral Hornby during the night.   The two

first are more or less unintelligible, and efforts are still being made to decypher them. The last, dated 9 P.M., shows, I think, that Mr Layard has not yet been able to communicate with him. Chanak is a very strong fort at the entrance of the Narrows, and it was there that the Admiral received the message on the 24th ordering him back to Besika Bay.—Yours sincerely,   W. H. SMITH.

The Same to the Same.

ADMIRALTY, S.W.,
Feb. 10, 1878, 7.40 P.M.

DEAR LORD BEACONSFIELD,—I have just received the telegram enclosed from Admiral Hornby, dated this morning from Besika Bay.

It is most singular that nothing has been heard from Mr Layard ; . . . but I suppose we must wait for an answer to our telegram of to-day before we give Hornby instructions.

I shall be ready to come over to you at any time you may require this evening ; but I am afraid we can do nothing.—Yours very truly,   W. H. SMITH.

Telegram from Vice-Admiral Hornby.

No. 10.

BESIKA, *Feb.* 10, 9 A.M.

Sent Salamis to Chanak yesterday, and weighed with ships ordered at 6 P.M. When inside Koumkaleh, Salamis returned. No telegraphic communication with Ambassador : no Firman, and Pacha protests against squadron entering. Anchored before Koumkaleh at night. At 1 A.M. Pacha received answer from Constantinople : no request made by British Ambassador to Porte : contrary to treaty for squadron to enter : Pacha to enforce the treaty. Have returned Besika Bay: no telegraphic communication yet from Ambassador.

Am I to proceed by night with ships named, or to force passage by day with whole squadron? Squadron insufficient to begin the——[*unintelligible*]——at once should be to pass the two lower forts and silence Medjideh first, then return and silence the lower ones————if passage is to be kept open. Request instructions.

The First Lord of the Admiralty to the Prime Minister.

Private.

ADMIRALTY,
Feb. 13, 1878, 1.15 P.M.

DEAR LORD BEACONSFIELD.—I have a telegram from Hornby, dated from the Alexandra at 1.30 this morning, stating his intention to sail at daybreak with six ironclads in pursuance of orders.—Yours sincerely,

W. H. SMITH.

The Same to the Same.

Feb. 14, 1878, 9 A.M.

We have a telegram from the Vice-Consul at the Dardanelles that "the six armoured ships passed through yesterday at 3 P.M. into the Sea of Marmora, the Turkish authorities protesting but not resisting."

Telegram from Vice-Admiral Hornby.

No. 18.

GALLIPOLI, 2 P.M., *Feb.* 14, '78·

Capt. Fife informs me the Russians are in force near Karak, twelve miles from Bulair: they may have 50,000 men there to-morrow evening: are believed to have a feasible plan to cross the Gulf of Zeros and land in the rear of Bulair lines, while they attack in front. I recommend all ships at Besika Bay, except one, be moved to Zeros with me to oppose any attack arising on this peninsula, and that Rear-Admiral Commerell assist to defend Bulair lines, and if they are (in) considerable force to destroy heavy guns in evacuating fort of Dardanelles: also that I should return immediately (to) eastward end of Marmora. Rear-Admiral remains at Gallipoli with Agincourt and Swiftsure. I proceed immediately to Prince's Island.

Following sharply on this came an order from the First Lord of the Admiralty to Vice-Admiral Hornby, which seemed to shut out all hopes of the maintenance of peace with Russia.

No. 23.

February 15.

All ships but one are to go from Besika Bay to Gulf of Xeros, with orders to watch Russian troops, and if they observe preparations for embarkation with a view to landing on the peninsula of Gallipoli, they are to warn Russian commander they have orders to prevent such landing, and they are to oppose it by force if persevered in.   W. H. S.

Telegram from Rear-Admiral Commerell to the First Lord of the Admiralty.

GALLIPOLI, *Feb.* 15, 11.55 A.M.

I visited Gallipoli lines to-day with permission of Suleiman Pacha. Was not favourably impressed with

state of defences. Advanced post of Russians at Kadikoi
in sight of Bulair, from which place I am of opinion that
determined attack in force would carry Turkish position.
Am informed positively that large quantity of munitions
are being collected at Kadikoi.

Telegram from Vice-Admiral Hornby to the First Lord
of the Admiralty.

No. 24.

PRINCE'S ISLAND, *Feb.* 17, 8 P.M.

In reference to their lordships' telegraphic communication of yesterday, I beg to report our force at Gallipoli is
insufficient to destroy heavy guns unless the Turks consent. If the Russians capture the peninsula, the Turks
would probably make better terms by leaving it in their
hands. I beg to urge upon their lordships that I consider
the position of Gallipoli to be most critical, and it cannot
be assured without a speedy understanding with the Turkish Government. . . . It seems certain that Suleiman
Pacha cannot be replaced by a trustworthy general, and
the positions held by the united forces of the expedition
under English and Turkish, or English alone. I need
hardly point out that the squadron would render very
small service if Gallipoli peninsula were lost. Your telegraphic communication, No. 23 of 15th, received. Understand it to be answer to mine of 14th, No. 18, and have
moved from Prince's Island to rendezvous, seven miles
S.S.W. of it temporarily, according to Ambassador's
wishes.

Please telegraph to Rear-Admiral Commerell at Gallipoli result of Professor Abel's experiments on bursting
guns.

Letter from Sir Stafford Northcote to the Prime Minister.

12 DOWNING STREET, WHITEHALL,
Feb. 20, 1878.

DEAR LORD BEACONSFIELD,—Will you call a Cabinet at twelve to-morrow? Smith has news which requires immediate attention.—Yours faithfully,   S. H. N.

The news referred to is contained in the following telegrams :—

Telegram from Vice-Admiral Hornby to the First Lord of the Admiralty.

PERA, *Feb.* 20, 6 P.M. (from Dardanelles).

Ambassador has informed me that the Russians have demanded peremptorily Turkish fleet and to enter Constantinople with 30,000 men. Do my orders still hold not to interfere? I have sent this by sea to Dardanelles to avoid Russian telegraph station.

The Same to the Same.

TUZLA BAY, *Feb.* 20, 2.30 P.M.

Telegram number 28 of 19th received. No number 27 received. One telegram of 18th in the vocabulary cipher received, not numbered. Russians reported to be advancing to M. San Stephano, thus turning will get in rear of the last line of defence Moukhtar Pacha was preparing for Constantinople. The city and Bosphorus will be at their mercy.

From Captain of Raleigh to the Same.

KOUMKALEH, *Feb.* 20, 6.30 P.M.

Rear-Admiral reports wire to Constantinople cut both sides.

Vice-Admiral Hornby to the Same.

Rear - Admiral Commerell reports good progress in strengthening Bulair lines, but, the assistance of ships to cover the flanks is indispensable. If he might co-operate he thinks Russia would not pass. This squadron might assist materially in preventing Russians entering Constantinople, as it could command the best road for guns on each flank. I think they could not enter if we assist Turks at once.

The Same to the Same.

ISMID, *March* 10, 4.10 P.M.

Secret.

. . . Bosphorus forts would probably not stop ironclads going into Black Sea, but would stop all supplies. If in Russian hands and strengthened by torpedoes, no squadron could pass without severe loss. If there is any idea of moving in that direction, no time should be lost in opening negotiations with the Turks. Without their help the Straits cannot be saved, and the Turks seem daily succumbing to Russian influence.

N.B.—The group (of cipher) standing for " Black Sea " is still doubtful.

The Same to the Same.

No. 64.

ISMID, *March* 23, 7.30 P.M.

Your telegram No. 48 of 22d received. The Rear-Admiral will decidedly require two powerful steam-vessels as long as he remains on his present duty at Gallipoli. Rear - Admiral has observed two merchant steam - vessels pass towards Dedeagatch under Russian merchant colours. He ordered our cruisers in the Gulf of Zeros, in the event of Russian troops embarking at Dedeagatch or elsewhere aboard any steam-vessel for the purpose of passing Dardanelles, to follow such vessel in an unobtrusive manner as far as Gallipoli; and if any attempt be made to land the troops, the cruiser is to act in pursuance of Admiralty instructions communicated to me in your telegram of Feb. 15. . . . Ambassador, Constantinople, acquaints me that the minister at Athens reports Greek Minister of Foreign Affairs has informed him, on the authority of Italian Vice-Consul at Volo, that Turks have pillaged and destroyed three villages near Mount Olympus; that they have murdered old men, women, and children, and that some families escaped to the mountains, where, unless rescued, they must perish. I have telegraphed to send Ruby to inquire, and if necessary remove fugitives; if not, she returns immediately.

The Same to the Same.

No. 71.

ISMID, *March* 31, 2.55 P.M.

Following telegraphic communication received last night from Ambassador—viz.:

" From British Consul I hear that from more than one source, but give the information under reserve, that Generals Scobeleff and Gourko have received orders to prepare to make a dash on Gallipoli in the event of a war between England and Russia being imminent; and that a *corps d'armée* is to take possession at the same time of Kavak near entrance of the Bosphorus. A Greek merchant who has been a large contractor for provisions for the Russian army has received orders to keep them at Constantinople."

In view of the gravity of the situation the Ambassador would like two small vessels stationed at Constantinople. With Russians collecting torpedoes at Rodosto, Rear-Admiral requires assistance, and Condor is going to Gallipoli to him to-day. This leaves only three small ships for this port and Constantinople, and to keep up communication between them.

I request instructions for guidance in the event of war being imminent, observing that the ships cannot remain with safety in the Bosphorus at night whilst the north shore is in possession of an enemy provided with White-head torpedoes.

The Same to the Same.

Ismid, *March* 31, 3.50 P.M.

Ambassador telegraphs following message, dated to-day, . . . from Captain Fife, dated Gallipoli to-day: " Large bodies of Russians expected at Keshan to-day on the way of Cadi Keni from Adrianople. Keshan ceased to reply by telegraph to-day."

The Same to the Same.

Ismid, *April* 2, 2.30 P.M.

Affairs at Constantinople said to be very critical. Grand Duke obtaining great influence with several military Pachas. Appointment of Ministry favourable to Russia thought probable. General Dickson tells me he thinks Bulair lines could be held by troops now there if ordered to defend them, but recommends assistance of men and officers from the fleet in the event of attack to prove to the troops that we are in alliance with Turkey.

He fears orders would be given from Constantinople not to defend the lines. In that case he thinks we should defend the lines by taking General and troops into our pay.   I concur with him, and submit that the Rear-Admiral should have authority to do so if the Russians prepare to attack.

Russians have lately been increasing their forces at Kadikoi.

Submit in future that ˙ treaty should be made with Turkish Government to join us if we are forced into war with Russia.   Our fleet cannot stay in the Sea of Marmora or Black Sea for more than a very few days unless some ports are open to us. If alliance with Turkey could be formed, I submit that, if war is imminent, this squadron should be withdrawn to Gallipoli or Besika Bay.

I cannot believe Turkey would defend Gallipoli for us, unless we will do something for them as well as for ourselves.   Time seems precious. . . . Have ordered about 1500 tons of Welsh coal from Malta.   I think as precautionary measure equal quantity should follow shortly: submit, therefore, that another steam collier should be sent from England with agreement for delivery.

Telegram from Rear-Admiral Sir J. Commerell to the Same.

BESIKA, *April* 3, 12.5 P.M.

Secret and confidential.

I think First Pacha at Bulair would hail with delight an order from Constantinople to surrender lines.   Second Pacha is different man altogether.

—— ? soldiers would defend them if First Pacha were away.

Of course if lines were given up, Hussein at Dardanelles would not let me destroy guns on European side.   The only way I can see to ensure safety of Gallipoli is to order —— ? be given over : embark the Maltese garrison in the Channel Squadron and Indian troop-ships : cutting the wires and allowing no ships to touch there, and send the ships to *rendezvous* in Gulf Xeros.   They need not land until Russians make movement : excuse suggestion.

The Same to the Same.

Secret and confidential.

BESIKA, *April* 4, 8 P.M.

I am not sure about the money.   If I see my way, what sum may I offer ?   It must be high to succeed.

By this time—the month of April—the war-clouds were beginning to break ; Count Schouva-loff had arrived in England on a special mission from the Russian Court, the Berlin Congress had been agreed on, and a second time the House of Commons ratified the policy of Ministers by a majority of 121—347 votes to 226.

Needless to do more than allude to the result of the Congress, the return of our Plenipoten-tiaries—Lord Beaconsfield and Lord Salisbury— an event marked in public memory by the speech made by the Prime Minister from a window of his house in Downing Street, in which he claimed, before an enthusiastic multitude, to have brought back " Peace with Honour."[1]   Relieved from the

---

[1] Lord Beaconsfield, it is said, piqued himself on his fluency in French, but his idioms were rather intrepid than correct. He had command of a copious vocabulary, but his accent was courageously

apprehension which had weighed so heavily on them for so many months, people were jubilant in their approval of the success gained by English diplomacy. Great Britain was rehabilitated in the eyes of Europe, and at the same time delivered from the imminence of war.

cis-pontine, a survival of that Anglo-Gallic which developed itself among English officers during the Peninsular and Waterloo campaigns. Some consternation, therefore, arose among the English who accompanied him to Berlin, when they learnt that the British Prime Minister intended to deliver his opening speech at the Conference in French, and had already devoted much time to its preparation. It would have been a delicate matter to explain to his lordship that, while it was of the utmost importance that his speech should be understood by the other Plenipotentiaries, that object could not be attained unless he spoke in his native tongue. In this dilemma recourse was had to the good offices of Lord Odo Russell, British Minister at Berlin—could he diplomatically convey to Lord Beaconsfield how necessary it was that he should speak in English?

Lord Odo pondered for some moments, and then said—

"Yes, I think I see my way. Leave it to me."

That afternoon he visited Lord Beaconsfield, and before taking his leave, remarked—

"By the by, I must tell you how much disappointment was felt by the other Plenipotentiaries when it became known that your lordship intended to address the Congress in French."

"Why should they be disappointed?" asked the Prime Minister, putting up his eyeglass. "Is not French the language most generally understood on the Continent?"

"Undoubtedly, my dear lord; but they had been looking forward with the keenest anticipation to the pleasure of hearing English spoken by its greatest living master, and, if I might venture to intercede, I would beg you to give them this gratification. It is of some importance, you know, to predispose them favourably to the consideration of the questions which will arise."

"I think there is a good deal in what you say," observed Beaconsfield; and, in the end, he complied with Lord Odo's suggestion.

Nevertheless, for the third time this session, the Government had to defend themselves against a vote of censure, moved by the Marquis of Hartington, and supported by the impassioned oratory of Gladstone, Lowe, and Forster. It was a false move in tactics, as the division list proved, for the House acquitted the Administration of blame by 338 votes to 195—a crushing majority of 143.

CHAPTER XII.

1878.

JOURNAL OF A TOUR TO CYPRUS.

ONE result of the Berlin Congress had been the cession of Cyprus to England, to be, as Lord Beaconsfield described it, a "place of arms" in the Eastern Mediterranean. The accounts of the capabilities, resources, condition, and popular feeling of this island were so conflicting that the First Lord of the Admiralty and the Secretary of State for War (Colonel the Hon. F. R. Stanley, M.P.[1]) set out in the autumn to inspect it for themselves.

The occasion was one not to be lost by that gentle satirist, Mr Bromley Davenport, M.P., who, *more suo*, celebrated the expedition in verse :—

> "The Chief of the Army and Lord of the Fleet
> Have gone out to visit both Cyprus and Crete;
> The natives, delighted to see such fine stars,
> Christened one of them Neptune, the other one Mars;
> They erected an altar to Stanley forthwith,
> And put up a bookstall to W. H. Smith."

---

[1] Now sixteenth Earl of Derby.

On the eve of his departure for the East, Smith received a letter from H.R.H. the Duke of Cambridge referring to the Royal Marines in terms which, as expressing the confidential opinion of the Commander-in-Chief, cannot fail of being pleasant reading to the members of that distinguished branch of the service.

Private.　　　Gloucester House, Park Lane, W.,
Sunday, October 20, '78.

My dear Mr Smith,—I returned late last night from a general tour of inspections, & hearing that you are to start to-night for Cyprus with Colonel Stanley, I write a line to say that I have had an opportunity of seeing the *four* Divisions of Royal Marines at their respective Stations, and cannot speak in too high terms of their state of efficiency & smartness. They are splendid fellows, in excellent military order, & fit for any work that may be required of them. I am anxious to bear testimony to their excellent condition, as I occasionally see rumours in the public prints that there is some idea of reducing their numbers, and some naval officers go even so far as to say that the Royal Marines are now become a *useless* body. I hope you will *never* be induced to listen to such views. All the old & valuable Officers of the Navy do *not* share their opinions, & I trust they will not find any encouragement on the part of the First Lord, who, after all, is the authority upon whom these matters depend. I am not a Naval Man and know little of Naval matters, but I have been a public servant of the Crown for many years, & have gained some experience in that position, & I feel satisfied that the Royal Marines are a valuable branch of our public services, & as such deserve every encouragement & support, & certainly *not* abolition, or even reduction.—I remain, dear Mr Smith, yours most sincerely,

GEORGE.

To this the First Lord made the following reply :—

H.M.S. HIMALAYA,.
Off CYPRUS, *Oct.* 29, '78·

SIR,—I had the honour to receive your Royal Highness's letter on the subject of the Royal Marines on the day of my departure from London, and as it was only a few minutes before the train started, I was unable to reply.

I am really very much obliged to your Royal Highness for the information contained in the letter. It is most gratifying to us at the Admiralty to have the very high authority of your Royal Highness bearing testimony to the efficiency of the Marines. They have appeared to me, with my very limited knowledge of discipline and drill, to be in a satisfactory state, but I am perfectly assured now as to their condition by the statement of your Royal Highness.

So far as the present Board of Admiralty are concerned, there is certainly no foundation whatever for the rumours to which your Royal Highness has referred. We have no intention of effecting a permanent reduction in the numbers of the corps, still less of abolishing it. For my own part I regard them as a very valuable reserve, capable of being used at sea or on land, and until wars cease such a reserve certainly should be retained.—I have the honour to be, sir, your obedient humble servant,

W. H. SMITH.

As was always the case when duty obliged him to make a prolonged absence from home, Smith felt the pain of parting from wife and children in a degree which, to some people, might appear disproportionate to the length of the separation. But his was a warmly affectionate nature, and he was not ashamed to give expression to his feelings in the journal which he kept during this tour.

Monday, Oct. 21, 1878.—Started from Greenlands for the 10.10 train. Did not "light up" in the brougham as we had been accustomed to do. Neither of us cared for it. The two dear children had our last good-bye as we drove rapidly through the gate, and although we were not sad, we were, as once before, not talkative. The weather cleared up, and we cleared up too, and we began to say to each other, What a blessing it will be not to see a pouch[1] for perhaps a month!

The Admiralty was a rush. I took leave of Admiral Hood, and gave him parting directions. . . .

At the Charing Cross station a saloon was provided, and there we met Sir George Elliot, who had come from Newcastle on Saturday to join us.

Leave-taking again with Lethbridge, and, to my surprise, White, Sandifer, and Taylor, old Strand faces, came to shake hands, and say, God bless you, sir.

We were off, with a box of cigars with which Alpin MacGregor actually ran from the Admiralty to Charing Cross at the last moment, that we might not lack good tobacco on the road.

---

[1] An official "pouch": the leather bags in which papers and despatches are sent from the public departments to Ministers.

At Folkestone :—

. . . There was also Mr Romaine, a past Secretary to the Admiralty, his wife and child, all going back to Egypt.

Codrington also found an officer friend; but the steamer would not stay: the order was given, "Half speed ahead," the paddles turned, and there was a good deal of dirty water, but no motion in the ship, and so it went on for half an hour. At last we got off fairly; the rain had ceased, and we had a good but a slow passage across. On the other side we found a carriage reserved for us, and we travelled comfortably to Paris, now and then saying a very few words to each other, and they were very few, of those we loved. Some thoughts are too precious to be given expression to. There is a sort of sacrilege in allowing the birds of the air to listen to them.

Paris had been *en fête.* There had been a great giving away of prizes in the day, and flags on the houses and illuminations in the streets; but the people were returning home, and the gas-lustres were out and the Chinese lanterns were going out, but still the place looked cheerful and the people happy, lingering to see the last of the show.

Tuesday, 22d.— . . . Called on Stanley at the Hôtel Balmoral. Found Lord and Lady Skelmersdale with them. Promised to dine with them that evening, and start with them. Proceeded to the Embassy. Saw Lord Lyons, who promised his assistance to get us a comfortable journey, and sent Collet off with the Embassy *facteur* to the station to secure a saloon for the trip to Turin. . . . We went on to the Exhibition, and as we entered at the Trocadero, looking down on the fair below us, it was impossible not to admire the energy which had done so much in a short time.

Our object was to see the naval models of ships, and the specimens of iron and steel exhibited by France and England. The Creuzat Exhibition was very interesting, and might almost alarm one for the supremacy of our national industries in iron and steel.

Then we tried to get luncheon, and failed. Every place was crammed, and the rain fell piteously. We found our carriage; *cocher* had left the windows open, and the seats were wet, the back was wet, everything was wet.

We drove to the Hôtel Bristol, and the Prince requested me to see him. He told me he was almost tired of the functions he had to go through. Prize-giving yesterday; deputation to-day; a *fête* at Versailles at night; it was too much. He said that his brother the Duke of Edinburgh had been staying two days with him, and only left the night before for Marseilles to join his ship, and he wished very much I could have seen him. We parted. I returned with Codrington to the hotel to write letters, and at 5 in came Mr Lawson of the 'Daily Telegraph' to ask me what I thought of affairs.

Well, I did not think much; what did Mr Lawson think? He said his wife had not seen Venice, and he was going there to-morrow for three weeks. I was off that night to Cyprus. "Ah! then you don't think anything will happen just at present?"—" I hope not."— "You wouldn't go if you thought anything would happen?"—"Oh, certainly not! and it is just as well to show -confidence." The 'Daily Telegraph' and the First Lord shook hands and parted, with professions of profound esteem and friendship; and then we finished our letters, and went out for a stroll, and to buy Tauchnitz for the journey. Up and down the Rue de la Paix, lingering at the jewellers' windows, admiring Sirandin's baskets, and the nattily dressed girls who presided over the sweetie-shop; wondering whether the electric light really was so wonderful; thinking in between of home, and of all that makes home lovely. The time passed, and it was necessary to go at once to Colonel Stanley's hotel, where we were all to dine together. At dinner, in addition to the travellers, there were Lady Constance Stanley, and Lord and Lady Skelmersdale. Dinner was late, and there was frequent looking at watches; but we got off in good time, and drove to the Lyons Station, where we found a good saloon carriage reserved for us.

So the real journey commenced, and we found ourselves a party of seven, with four servants and a courier, Sir George Elliot, Sir Henry Holland,[1] and Captain Fitzgeorge joining us at the station.

Thursday, 24th.— . . . In Italy on the Adriatic coast —a rich garden-like country, with olive and mulberry trees planted in rows in the fields. The sea is very Italian-like. Fishing-boats with the peculiar Mediterranean sails, half red, half orange-colour, sitting like large birds on the water.

. . . At Ancona we found breakfast prepared for us, ordered by telegraph by the consul at Turin. Still an hour behind time, but we were waited for while we breakfasted nevertheless.

Ancona is a large and ancient town with a considerable trade, and an important port. It evidently possesses great churches and public buildings of antiquity, and it is a little sad that we should have to run through places possessing such historical interest without looking at them. The people are busily at work in the fields; women barelegged and barefooted, with stiff white petticoats, blue bodices, red kerchiefs over head and

---

[1] Created Baron Knutsford in 1888.

neck, and straw hats over all. They look vigorous and
picturesque. On the shore are fishermen pulling their
nets ashore in the hot sun, with very little on but a pair
of thin trousers and a shirt. We passed Loretto, with its
church built round the house in which Joseph lived,
which flew from the Holy Land—first to Albania, and
then, not being appreciated there, to the opposite shore,
alighting on the hill now named Loretto.

On we go in heat, but, thanks to the late rain, not
in dust.

At Foggia we left the sea and struck across a vast plain
to Naples, a five-and-a-half-hours' fast run. To the westward was a range of very grand hills. There were some
dark clouds about them, and as the sun passed through
them they seemed to divide, giving golden fringes to their
edges, and lighting up all below and around with a golden
haze which could be felt but not described. The plain
was mostly uncultivated, and houses few and far between.
Troops of horses here, some hundreds together, being
driven home apparently; cattle in the same way, and now
and then sheep. Darkness settled upon us; the stars
came out brightly. We were all very tired, and those
who did not sleep thought again of home.

At 10.30 we rumbled into the station. Evan Macgregor
and Wilson were there to meet us, and, leaving them to
bring on the servants and the luggage, we drove off
through the town along the sea-front to the Mole. None
of us could speak Italian, and at the point where the
Mole turns off at right angles to the sea, three men
stopped the coachman and said we were to get out there.
We hesitated, as they did not look trustworthy, and two
went down to see if our boat was there. The men said it
had gone off with the three—Codrington, Dalyell, and
Fitzgeorge—who had preceded us in a carriage. We still

mistrusted them, when fortunately Myers, who was in charge of our pinnace, came up with his lantern, and said the boat was lying waiting for us further on. The three men disappeared like evil spirits in the darkness, and Myers got on the box of the carriage with his lantern, seated himself on the coachman's seat, and told him where to drive.

It was very pleasant to find ourselves in the pinnace again, and steaming out, we were soon on board the Himalaya, where we were very heartily welcomed by our friends who had gone before. . . .

Friday, Oct. 25.—A bath—what luxury! On deck, and the whole Bay of Naples in sunshine before us; Vesuvius smoking, but clear to the top, the Observatory standing on a shoulder of the mountain, olive-groves and vineyards clambering up its sides, and white houses, surrounded by gardens, glistening. Description is out of the question; every variety of shape in rock, the sea deep blue, and the curves where land and sea meet moulded by Nature as man could not mould them. The Bay of Naples is very lovely, but, if I dare say it, it wants the bright green of an English landscape. I did not land, and therefore I saw nothing of Naples and of Pompeii, which I could not see from the ship; but I should be glad when holiday-time comes to visit the place again.

. . . Having agreed with Wellesley and the Controller that I ought to visit the Italia, a large ship building by the Italian Government at the Castellamare Dockyard, permission was obtained from the admiral, and we steamed out of Naples Harbour at about 11, coasting past the site of Herculaneum, in full view of the shore, to Castellamare.

We dropped anchor at about 12, and went ashore

in the pinnace. The health officer wanted to stop us, but we told him the Himalaya was a man-of-war, and he was at once dumb. A moment after the captain of the port met us, came into the pinnace, and guided us in.

On landing, we were received by the assistant contractor in charge and shown over the ship, which is larger and will have more powerful engines than any ship in the English ·navy. Her lines are very fine, calculated for speed.

Here follows a technical description of the ship.

I was much interested, as was also Mr T. Brassey,[1] who came with me, and who parted from me here. I had previously visited his yacht the Sunbeam, which was lying close to the Himalaya. Mrs Brassey was spending the day at Pæstum, but we saw the cabins, and they were certainly as unlike a ship's cabins as can well be imagined. Every square inch of wall was covered with ornaments—glass, china, pictures, nick-nacks—all securely fastened, but to the eye only looking fragile and unsafe. The yacht is a very good sea-boat, and Brassey himself a thorough sailor.

The party on board the Himalaya, besides Mr Smith and Colonel Stanley, consisted of Admiral George Wellesley, C.B., First Naval Lord ; Sir Massey Lopes, Bart., M.P., a Lord Commissioner of the Admiralty ; Admiral Sir W. Houston Stewart, K.C.B., Controller of the Navy ; the

---

[1] Created Baron Brassey in 1886.

Hon. Algernon Egerton, M.P., Secretary to the Admiralty; Captain Codrington, R.N., private secretary to the First Lord; Mr R. Dalyell, private secretary to Colonel Stanley; Captain Fitzgeorge, of the Intelligence Department of the War Office; Lord Colville of Culross; Sir Henry Holland, M.P.; and Sir George Elliot, M.P.

. . . Steaming away from Castellamare, we passed slowly out of the Bay of Naples. We left Capri behind us, and gradually drew away from the land, but still near enough to see its beauty. Volcanoes and earthquakes have tossed up the rocks into every conceivable shape and form, but almost always peaked and rugged; and then tempests have scored out the softer particles of the rocks, and left the harder in bold relief. We had just a few clouds to produce shadows, light, and shade, and the deep blue of the sea formed a contrast and pictures impossible to describe. For a long way we could trace a road running terrace-like high up on the mountain-side, dipping from time to time into orange and olive woods and emerging again. . . . A gorgeous sunset followed, and now I can understand pictures which have hitherto appeared exaggerated and untrue.

We have now settled down to sea-life. I take my place at dinner, with Wellesley opposite to me and Stanley on my right, it being understood that others change about from day to day. Everything appears well arranged, and everybody quite certain we are going to have a very pleasant trip. Holland and Elliot do not appear the worse for their long journey, and we all agree there is not a bad fellow in the party.

At dinner I give H.M. the Queen, and our band
strikes up, and we all stand while the first bars of " God
save the Queen " are played.   Before turning in I asked
the captain to call me when we passed Stromboli, if there
was any fire visible.

Saturday, Oct. 26.—Captain White, at 3 A.M., " Stromboli, sir, on the starboard beam."   It was very hot, and I
had not been sleeping very soundly, so I was quite glad
to turn out, and for an hour I watched the mountain,
being rewarded by one flare, like a lurid furnace at night
in the Black Country.

In the morning we found ourselves close in to the
shores of brigand Calabria, the same high mountains,
tossed about, seamed, rugged, convulsed, torn, and looking
often bare, but, with a glass, vines and olives could be discovered, and many villages and even considerable towns
perched up in commanding positions in the rocks.   Sicily
and Mount Etna had been in sight for some time, and we
steered rapidly to the Straits of Messina, passing through
Charybdis and close to the famous Scylla.   Off Messina
we signalled to the Telegraph Station to send word home
that the Himalaya had passed.

Leaving Messina, our course was altered to the eastward, pointing to Cyprus, and we soon left Sicily behind,
keeping, however, nearer to the end of Italy.   Once I
think I saw smoke issuing from Etna, and, if that was so,
I had seen three volcanoes smoking within twenty-four
hours.

Sunday, Oct. 27.—A lovely morning.   I had previously
suggested to Wellesley that the band should play hymn-
tunes, and they appeared with the crew at church-parade
at 11 o'clock.   We had two hymns and a good sermon, in
its way, from the clergyman, a Mr Kavanagh. . . . Sunset
again lovely ; a few clouds in the west to take the golden

light: the sun drops through them; they seem to open to let him go, and with a light too dazzling to look upon, he is gone, and there remain a few light clouds which seem to have absorbed his light, and they seem for a few minutes only to float on the sea in the horizon like the bright burning embers of a furnace. Then succeeds rapidly every hue of which sky and water are capable. In the east what appears to be a cloud of darkness quickly rises; in the west gold melts into deep red, red into orange, orange into bluish green, and that into the colder blue of the zenith; that again disappearing before the darkness rising from the east;—and it is night in a few minutes from daylight.

At 10 P.M. we are off Crete, and at 11 pass Cape Sparta.

Monday, Oct. 28.—Still steaming away in sight of Crete, four to eight miles from the shore. The island, like all the rest, looks barren, and is very mountainous, but trees could be detected by the glass. The outline is grand and beautiful. At 11 we part company with Crete, having on our port bow in the distance Caxos and Scarpento. . . .

I had sundry serious talks to-day with Stanley, Wellesley, and others as to our work at Cyprus; for it is, I hope, to be real work.

. . . When we reach Larnaca we shall be 2½ hours in advance of English time. I have kept my watch to "home" hours; and it is very pleasant to turn to it and know perfectly well what is doing at home. I see the boy [1] running out for a rose, and I almost hear the gong, and I imagine the cold foggy mornings you have had, while we are inclined to be languid from heat. . . . We are now drawing close to Cyprus. Mount Olympus

---

[1] His son, Frederick.

and the western range of hills have been in view for some hours. . . . I am afraid my journal may now be interrupted for a few days, as we shall be busy looking about the island, but I will try to pick up the threads.

Oct. 29.—We saw a good deal of the island as we passed up. There are many trees, and in some places forests; on the side nearest Limasol a gentle slope from the mountains, now looking brown where there are few trees, but evidently green enough in winter. We could make out Paphos, famous in ancient history, and we are coming on to Atium or Shittim, spoken of in Solomon's time, when the island was far more prosperous than it is now. It was 7.30 P.M. before we dropped anchor at Larnaca last night. . . . At 10 P.M. Hornby, Wolseley, and Lord John Hay, with their belongings, came on board, and we had a friendly greeting. They looked well and cheery. We arranged to go ashore for a ride through the town to the salt lakes, to visit a mosque, and the camping-ground of the troops. At daylight this morning, and before the sun rose, Stanley and I started. We landed near Wolseley's place, and for the first time saw a Turkish house. Horses were brought, and we mounted. The horses seemed accustomed to the very broken ground, and to going up and down steps.

Imagine an Italian town—Orta or Lugano—exaggerated, and you have Larnaca, excepting that the houses are lower. Everybody is up and taking coffee, and everybody is very respectful. We ride along dusty paths, and reach the salt lakes, which are a great source of revenue, as the sun dries up the water in summer, and leaves a crust of salt, which is gathered like a harvest.

Then we rode on to a mosque where the Prophet's nurse is buried. We went into the mosque, the sheik, who is a young man, being very civil. While the mollahs took off their shoes, we took off our hats, and examined the temple, the doorway to which has very good carved stone-work.

The place is very old. They gave me some myrtle leaves from the enclosure, which I send with this. Great palms in fruit grew in the courtyard, and camels laden lay down outside.

Wednesday, Oct. 30.—Sir Garnet Wolseley, Stanley, and I, with attendants, started on ponies to make the round of the Government stores, offices, and hospitals. On our way we passed through Printing-house Square, and by the Beaconsfield Chambers, Anglo-Egyptian Street, and hosts of others newly named by the municipality. The Marina, from which we started, is a narrow ledge in front of the houses on the beach here, and it is being widened by a concrete wall built on the gravelly shingle between piles and a cofferdam, the ground inside being made good with stones. A motley group they were at work—Negroes, Arabs, Greeks, Turks. One was reminded of " Parthians, Medes, and Elamites," people of every nation and tongue. Every kind of costume was seen to almost none at all, for the men worked in the water with little more than a shirt, and a waist-belt. It was curious to be saluted by Englishmen and recognised as one passed up and down, the pony threading its way over stones and through dust and dirt up and down steps.

The Commissioner, Colonel White, had always two zaptiehs, or mounted police, in front, who rode on to make way, ordering bullock-carts to stop and make way, —swarthy fellows, all dressed differently, wearing large boots, into which their baggy breeches of blue or brown cotton were thrust; then came a sash or belt, then perhaps a red and white shawl, pattern shirt or waistcoat, and over that a gay tunic of red, green, or yellow; but, always contrasting with other colours, a fez or turban covered the head.   The commissariat stores were very numerous, and it was curious to see camels standing outside and mules picketed waiting for work.

. . . We went at a gallop through six inches of dust to old Larnaca, to visit the hospitals, which are in two really nice old houses, with a capital garden of oranges, citrons, and fig-trees attached.   The people came out to look at us in great numbers.   The Turkish women dressed entirely in white linen or muslin, covering their faces so that only their eyes could peep through, but they were quite as curious as the rest. . . .

As there is no mention here of an incident which made the subject of a messroom story at the time, it may be set down as the malicious invention of some idle subaltern.   It was alleged, however, that during this ride the guard on duty turned smartly out to salute the distinguished party—so smartly that the ponies of the First Lord of the Admiralty and the Secretary of State for War turned sharply round, and these dignitaries were both precipitated into the dust.

Thursday, Oct. 31.—We were on shore at daylight to start by the waggonette for Nicosia.   The carriage was really a good one, holding eight comfortably inside.   We started with two on the box, and one, young Lopes, on the roof.   We had a team of three ponies harnessed abreast, and three mules in front of them.   The air was quite cold before the sun was up, but by the time we reached Dewdrop Inn, a tent pitched by an Englishman at the first change of horses, it became very hot.   The road was undulating and better than I expected, but the country had an arid look from the want of rain; and, as much of the rock is limestone and very white, there is a painful glare in the sun under the deep blue and absolutely unclouded sky. The desolate look too is increased by the fact that any houses or villages you see are built of mud brick baked in the sun, and of the same colour as the ground. The houses in the village are mostly of one storey, with flat roofs, and from a distance they look like an English stable or outhouse, but they are frequently comfortable, and have trees and gardens inside the enclosure. Away we sped from the Dewdrop Inn, rising to the watershed between Nicosia and Larnaca, about 800 feet up, from which we had a good view of the plain which lies to the south of the crater or northern range of mountains. Generally the ground was arid-looking, but there were patches of green in considerable numbers, and it was evident that wherever a stream ran there was great fertility and beauty. Wells were numerous, and they resembled the pictures one has seen of Jacob's well; a hole in the ground and stone basins into which the water is poured when it is raised, from which and the stone troughs around them the sheep and the cattle drink.

We arrived outside the walls of Nicosia at eleven, and were met by the Commissioner, Colonel Biddulph, who ordered the driver to go across some fields to the camp without entering the town, and we passed for nearly a mile outside the walls, which are still in good repair and very thick. At the camp I was put into a hut which was divided in three compartments, first occupied by Stanley, the next by Wellesley, and the last by me. The rest of the party were lodged in the same way, the servants being under canvas.

In the afternoon we were all mounted on ponies and
mules, and went off, escorted by zaptiehs, to Nicosia. I
rode on with Sir Garnet and Colonel Stanley, the rest
following.

Our way lay through the gate, passing the place where
camels and mules camped outside. On arriving inside
the gate we were received by a bodyguard of mounted
zaptiehs. Two led the way, and the rest followed us
through the bazaar, or street of shops. There were
quarters of bootmakers and leather-sellers—a great trade
in Nicosia; greengrocers, butchers, silk-mercers, every
trade keeping very much together. The streets are
paved very badly, and the horses, shod with a round ring
of iron, slid about. The people stared and gaped, frequently bowing and touching their foreheads and chests
as we passed by. The mixture of colours and races,—
Turkish women in white from head to foot; Greeks with
black hair, large eyes, and olive face, always having contrasting colours to light them up; men with turbans and
green jackets, some with a kind of long dressing-gown.
All but ourselves in Eastern as compared with European
dress.

The streets were much shaded from the sun by vines
trained on lattices overhead or by matting with little
openings overhead.

The shops were just as they are painted by J. F. Lewis;
no glass fronts, and the whole front open. We went on
to the Mosque of St Sophia, which is an old Gothic
Christian church of about the thirteenth century. The
doorway and portico are in excellent preservation, and
very rich and beautiful, but the Turks have marred the
windows, and have of course not restored anything. It
is sad to witness the havoc they have made, and their
apparent inability to keep anything alive. . We saw an-

other fine old church, which is now a granary; went on to the Konah or Government office, and a kahn which is turned into zaptieh barracks and prison, the crowd increasing to witness our proceedings.

Returning, we stopped for tea at Colonel Biddulph's house, where I met the Financial Officer of the island, Mr Kelner, and the legal adviser of Sir Garnet, Mr Cookson.

On our way back to camp we rode over a Turkish burial-ground, which is quite unprotected, and past the battle-ground where Richard Cœur-de-Lion fought and conquered just a few years ago, and as darkness came on we returned to camp.

Dinner under canvas with Sir Garnet Wolseley and my colleagues.

Friday, Nov. 1.—Very clear and very fine. Morning a little cold before the sun was fairly up; and we were all in the saddle by 6.30 for a 35-mile ride to visit Mattyani camp and the 71st regiment, and General Payn's camp at Dali. On our way we met many people going in to market at Nicosia. The route lay for some miles over a rich plain, now burnt up except where there happened to be irrigation. We crossed several water-courses, some quite deep and all rough, but our horses seemed rather to like the climbing about. My pony was a capital one, but it was smaller than Brownie, and sometimes when we were cantering on broken ground I felt there was danger of my legs getting mixed up with his legs. The country towards Mattyani was very bare and rocky, and there was no shade. When we arrived at the camp we saw breakfast laid out for us under a tent, and notwithstanding heat, we set to work vigorously. Then we visited the tents and huts, especially the hospital, and were very glad to find the regiment healthy and in good spirits. We then

started for General Payn's camp, and lunched there. It
was a striking sight. The horses tethered under trees as
their stables, and having no other shelter, the bed of the
river below quite dry, and, at the back of the tents,
cotton plantations and trees and wells. As we were
lunching, a Bengal *syce*, used as a postman, passed in
front, and, with his copper-coloured face, black hair, and
white turban and dress, he looked, as he was, a striking
evidence of the variety of form England can bring to bear
to discharge her duties in the world. After lunch I
mounted a fresh horse, and rode home in the cool of the
evening, passing few human habitations, but many evi-
dences of past prosperity. Dinner in tent again and to
bed.

Saturday, Nov. 2.—We were waited upon in camp by
the chief monk of the monastery, with attendant priests,
to pay his respects to the " Ministers." Sir Garnet uses
a portion of the building for his offices, and we are en-
camped on ground belonging to the monks. The chief
was a handsome old man, with a long white beard. He
and his friends appeared exceedingly anxious to express
their delight at being under English rule. After breakfast we rode into Nicosia, and paid another visit to the
bazaar. We made purchases of silk, and then proceeded
to Colonel Biddulph's house, until it was time to start in
the waggonette for Larnaca. We had to wait for a few
minutes for some of our party, and during that time a
respectful but a curious crowd gathered round. Away we
went with our team of six, up the rugged street and out
through the massive gate, on which the winged lion of St
Mark still remains to mark Venetian rule. At the gate
the mounted zaptiehs formed as a guard of honour, and
headed by their captain, followed as an escort up to the

top of the first hill, where they saluted, wheeled, and returned to Nicosia.

Our journey down was as the journey up. We took a
cup of 4 o'clock tea at sixpence apiece all round at the
Dewdrop Inn, and found the landlord cheery in his little
bell-tent. An English friend of his, who had just come
over from Syria to pay him a visit, told us the people
there all thought themselves badly served that we had
not taken the mainland instead of Cyprus. Heat and
dust, and yet it is November 2d. . . .

Sunday, Nov. 3.—Under weigh early. Church as usual
at 10.30, and this time the band played the usual chants
for the psalms as well as the hymns. I think we most of
us enjoyed the service thoroughly.

At 12 we were off Famagusta, where Admiral Hornby
was already anchored in the Helicon. We went inside
the reef which runs from the old harbour parallel with
the land, so as to constitute a breakwater almost as good
as that at Plymouth, within which large ships can lie in
perfect safety.

The town is surrounded by a very thick wall, and it is
only approached from the sea by a water-gate. The ship's
boat drew near the shore, and we saw a crowd of people
on the shore waiting our arrival. On landing, we had to
pass under the domed gateway some hundred feet thick.
Inside there were ponies and mules awaiting to take us to
see the ruins of the town. It was impossible to walk, for
the sun was hotter than we had before felt it. Our first
work was up to the top of the bastion commanding a view
of the port. Such desolation I had never before witnessed. Everything is a ruin, and much of the ruin is as
if it had been accomplished only a few months, or at most
years, ago. There are, they say, remains of forty churches

in the town, and not one perfect one remaining. The cathedral is turned into the one mosque in the town, disfigured and dirty, with tower and pinnacles gone, the pillars outside coated with whitewash and green paint where the stone capitals should be, but still in its mournful decay retaining externally in its doorways, windows, and flying buttresses the most delicate and beautiful tracery, no one window or pinnacle being like another.

We visited another splendid ruin, and on the walls of the roofless apse we could trace perfectly mural paintings of the Agony, Crucifixion, and other scenes in our Lord's Passion, the peculiarity being that the drawing was perfect and the colours strong and good. The place was the most mournful I have ever seen. It was literally a heap of ruins, and from the good preservation in which some parts are found, man and not decay must have created the havoc. We rode between the remains of palaces and churches, and there are now only a few hovels left, which are built out of the *débris* of past greatness. The Commissioner, Captain Inglis, took us to the Konah, and it seemed to give pleasure to the soldier-servants to see our faces. We now returned by the palace, really a vast outline of a fine building, to the port, where we took leave of our friends and re-embarked on the Himalaya.

There are the remains of forty churches, and only 250 living men in the town. Mr Millard, our surveying officer, navigated the ship out of the harbour, and after a lovely sunset, we steamed slowly round the land towards Kyrenia, where we arrived by daylight on

Monday, Nov. 4.—Fancy a range of hills, extending quite to the height of Scottish hills, at the distance of from five to ten miles from the shore, sloping from the last half of the distance gradually towards the sea, with a somewhat thick wood as it appears from the sea; but when we got ashore we found they were fine carob-trees, olives, and pines, thickly planted in fields which, although mostly bare now, are all under cultivation. We landed at Kyrenia, an old Venetian port with castle and walls still standing, and looking very picturesque from the sea as the Union-jack floated from the ramparts. Passing through the small town, we soon came to the camp of the 42d Highlanders, the Black Watch. The poor fellows were in a very depressed state, as they had had a good deal of fever and ague, which made them look washed out, and they had no games or amusements; but if all is well they will soon be moved. There is one lady, a wife of an officer, but there is only one other officer to call on her, so her life cannot be very cheerful.

Some of our party went up to a monastery in the mountains, and brought down beautiful flowers and fruit —oranges, lemons. The country appears to produce everything. In the evening we said good-bye to Admiral Hornby, who returned to Constantinople, and we sailed to Paphos or Baffo.

Tuesday, Nov. 5.—Arrived at Baffo, and landed in a little harbour full of rocks. There was a tower or castle there, in which death was certain, it was so unhealthy. More zaptiehs and more receptions. Negroes and Nubians seem especially to prevail here.

On our way round from Kyrenia, and while we were lying there, we could see clearly the mountains of Asia Minor, and I shall therefore have seen all the quarters of the world by the time I get home.

Landing at Baffo was a serious business. Our boat bumped on rocks, and our poor coxswain trembled for

the Enchantress pinnace.   At one time it appeared likely
we should want the aid of an Arab boat, but we got
on shore safely.

Every description of steed met us—English ponies, Arab
horses, mules, donkeys—with a corresponding variety of
saddles.

I first mounted a pony, which, however, insisted on
showing himself off as Ruby does sometimes, and as the
sun poured down upon me, I begged after a few minutes
to be allowed to exchange it.

Another was found, and the stirrup-leather broke as I
put my foot into it.   Then a beautiful mule was brought
forward with a pad on its back and loose stirrups thrown
across it.   I mounted, balancing myself carefully, and
had a very comfortable ride.

Our road lay through ruins, marble and granite columns
many hundred years old lying by the wayside—remnants
of two separate periods of civilisation, pagan and Christian.   There were rock tombs—and one realises that
Abraham was buried in a trough hewn out of the rock
—and bits of arches and carvings of Christian churches.

So we proceeded, passing near where tradition says
Venus arose out of the sea, and a temple to Aphrodite
was raised on to the ground on which the camp of the 42d
detachment stands.

The men were better and more in fettle than those
at Kyrenia, but some were unwell.   We returned in a
blazing sun and embarked for Limasol, coasting along a
rich country.

At Limasol we landed at a little pier covered with
myrtle, and carpeted in honour of our arrival.   There
was a crowd and a deputation.   The municipality wished
to present an address, which was read to us with great

emphasis by a gentleman in black and a top-hat. When he finished there was " Leto ! " or " Long live the Queen ! " " Long live the Commissioner and the Ministers ! " in good round cheers, and these were followed by " God save the Queen " in Greek, sung by the schoolboys of the town. We hurried through the town, for time was precious, to the castle, the kahn, and the jail; and coming out of that, we were met by another crowd and another address in Greek, to which we listened gravely, not understanding a word, and all agreeing that Mr Gladstone ought to be there to translate it.

We went on board, transferred Sir Garnet Wolseley and Lord Gifford to the Humber, which was waiting, and started for Port Said. Poor Sir Garnet felt our parting, but he said our visit had been a real comfort to him. Fine weather again favoured us, and on Wednesday, November 6, we arrived at Port Said, the mouth of the Suez Canal. There were ceremonies to be gone through—a French admiral with his flag-ship, the Governor of Port Said, the Admiralty agent, were all come on board. We got through all this, and started for a short run up the canal. It is much to the credit of France that M. de Lesseps, persevering, accomplished the greatest work of the century in making a navigable canal through the sands of the desert. We returned to Port Said, and took a stroll in the town. There is an Arab lake (dwelling) village just outside on piles over the Lake Menzaleh, which might have been one of the Swiss lake villages of some hundred years ago, now being discovered or uncovered. The town of Port Said is most uninteresting, but it seems to embrace every kind of people and language under the sun. The Arab boys were troublesome in their attention to us, but a school we saw amused us much.   All the children made as much noise as they could. They, master and all, sat as Arabs sit together, squatting on a mat, and as they said or learned their lessons their bodies swayed to and fro like seesaws, the master, in turban, using a bamboo stick for the heads of the most distant, if they failed to jabber and to sway.   We went on board, and sailed at 5 P.M. for Alexandria.

END OF THE FIRST VOLUME.

PRINTED BY WILLIAM BLACKWOOD AND SONS

Catalogue

of

Messrs Blackwood & Sons'

Publications

PHILOSOPHICAL CLASSICS FOR ENGLISH READERS.

EDITED BY WILLIAM KNIGHT, LL.D.,

Professor of Moral Philosophy in the University of St Andrews.

In crown 8vo Volumes, with Portraits, price 3s. 6d.

Contents of the Series.

DESCARTES, by Professor Mahaffy, Dublin.—BUTLER, by Rev. W. Lucas Collins, M.A.—BERKELEY, by Professor Campbell Fraser.—FICHTE, by Professor Adamson, Owens College, Manchester. — KANT, by Professor Wallace, Oxford.—HAMILTON, by Professor Veitch, Glasgow. — HEGEL, by Professor Edward Caird, Glasgow.—LEIB- NIZ, by J. Theodore Merz.—VICO, by Professor Flint, Edinburgh.—HOBBES, by Professor Croom Robertson.—HUME, by the Editor.—SPINOZA, by the Very Rev. Principal Caird, Glasgow. — BACON: Part I. The Life, by Professor Nichol.—BACON: Part II. Philosophy, by the same Author. LOCKE, by Professor Campbell Fraser.

FOREIGN CLASSICS FOR ENGLISH READERS.

EDITED BY MRS OLIPHANT.

In crown 8vo, 2s. 6d.

Contents of the Series.

DANTE, by the Editor. — VOLTAIRE, by General Sir E. B. Hamley, K.C.B. —PASCAL, by Principal Tulloch. — PETRARCH, by Henry Reeve, C.B.—GOETHE, by A. Hayward, Q.C.—MOLIÈRE, by the Editor and F. Tarver, M.A.—MONTAIGNE, by Rev. W. L. Collins, M.A.—RABELAIS, by Walter Besant, M.A. — CALDERON, by E. J. Hasell. — SAINT SIMON, by Clifton W. Collins, M.A. — CERVANTES, by the Editor. — CORNEILLE AND RACINE, by Henry M. Trollope. — MADAME DE SÉVIGNÉ, by Miss Thackeray.—LA FONTAINE, AND OTHER FRENCH FABULISTS, by Rev. W. Lucas Collins, M.A.—SCHILLER, by James Sime, M.A., Author of 'Lessing, his Life and Writings.'—TASSO, by E. J. Hasell. — ROUSSEAU, by Henry Grey Graham. — ALFRED DE MUSSET, by C. F. Oliphant.

ANCIENT CLASSICS FOR ENGLISH READERS.

EDITED BY THE REV. W. LUCAS COLLINS, M.A.

Complete in 28 Vols. crown 8vo, cloth, price 2s. 6d. each. And may also be had in 14 Volumes, strongly and neatly bound, with calf or vellum back, £3, 10s.

Contents of the Series.

HOMER: THE ILIAD, by the Editor.— HOMER: THE ODYSSEY, by the Editor.— HERODOTUS, by George C. Swayne, M.A.— XENOPHON, by Sir Alexander Grant, Bart., LL.D. — EURIPIDES, by W. B. Donne.— ARISTOPHANES, by the Editor.—PLATO, by Clifton W. Collins, M.A.—LUCIAN, by the Editor. — ÆSCHYLUS, by the Right Rev. the Bishop of Colombo.—SOPHOCLES, by Clifton W. Collins, M.A. —.HESIOD AND THEOGNIS, by the Rev. J. Davies, M.A.— GREEK ANTHOLOGY, by Lord Neaves. — VIRGIL, by the Editor.—HORACE, by Sir Theodore Martin, K.C.B. — JUVENAL, by Edward Walford, M.A. — PLAUTUS AND TERENCE, by the Editor — THE COMMENTARIES OF CÆSAR, by Anthony Trollope. —TACITUS, by W. B. Donne.—CICERO, by the Editor. — PLINY'S LETTERS, by the Rev. Alfred Church, M.A., and the Rev. W. J. Brodribb, M.A. — LIVY, by the Editor.—OVID, by the Rev. A. Church, M.A. — CATULLUS, TIBULLUS, AND PROPERTIUS, by the Rev. Jas. Davies, M.A. — DEMOSTHENES, by the Rev. W. J. Brodribb, M.A.—ARISTOTLE, by Sir Alexander Grant, Bart., LL.D.—THUCYDIDES, by the Editor. — LUCRETIUS, by W. H. Mallock, M.A.—PINDAR; by the Rev. F. D. Morice, M.A.

Saturday Review.—"It is difficult to estimate too highly the value of such a series as this in giving ' English readers ' an insight, exact as far as it goes, into those olden times which are so remote, and yet to many of us so close."

CATALOGUE

OF

MESSRS BLACKWOOD & SONS'

PUBLICATIONS.

ALISON.

History of Europe. By Sir ARCHIBALD ALISON, Bart., D.C.L.

1. From the Commencement of the French Revolution to the Battle of Waterloo.
   LIBRARY EDITION, 14 vols., with Portraits. Demy 8vo, £10, 10s.
   ANOTHER EDITION, in 20 vols. crown 8vo, £6.
   PEOPLE'S EDITION, 13 vols. crown 8vo, £2, 11s.

2. Continuation to the Accession of Louis Napoleon.
   LIBRARY EDITION, 8 vols. 8vo, £6, 7s. 6d.
   PEOPLE'S EDITION, 8 vols. crown 8vo, 34s.

Epitome of Alison's History of Europe. Thirtieth Thousand, 7s. 6d.

Atlas to Alison's History of Europe. By A. Keith Johnston.
   LIBRARY EDITION, demy 4to, £3, 3s.
   PEOPLE'S EDITION, 31s. 6d.

Life of John Duke of Marlborough. With some Account of his Contemporaries, and of the War of the Succession. Third Edition. 2 vols. 8vo. Portraits and Maps, 30s.

Essays: Historical, Political, and Miscellaneous. 3 vols. demy 8vo, 45s.

ACROSS FRANCE IN A CARAVAN: BEING SOME ACCOUNT OF A JOURNEY FROM BORDEAUX TO GENOA IN THE "ESCARGOT," taken in the Winter 1889-90. By the Author of 'A Day of my Life at Eton.' With fifty Illustrations by John Wallace, after Sketches by the Author, and a Map. Cheaper Edition, demy 8vo, 7s. 6d.

ACTA SANCTORUM HIBERNIÆ; Ex Codice Salmanticensi. Nunc primum integre edita opera CAROLI DE SMEDT et JOSEPHI DE BACKER, e Soc. Jesu, Hagiographorum Bollandianorum; Auctore et Sumptus Largiente JOANNE PATRICIO MARCHIONE BOTHAE. In One handsome 4to Volume, bound in half roxburghe, £2, 2s.; in paper cover, 31s. 6d.

AGRICULTURAL HOLDINGS ACT, 1883. With Notes by a MEMBER OF THE HIGHLAND AND AGRICULTURAL SOCIETY. 8vo, 3s. 6d.

AIKMAN.

Manures and the Principles of Manuring. By C. M. AIKMAN, B.Sc., F.R.S.E., &c., Lecturer on Agricultural Chemistry, West of Scotland Technical College; Examiner in Chemistry, University of Glasgow. Crown 8vo.
[Shortly.]

AIKMAN.

Farmyard Manure : Its Nature, Composition, and Treatment. Crown 8vo, 1s. 6d.

AIRD. Poetical Works of Thomas Aird. Fifth Edition, with Memoir of the Author by the Rev. JARDINE WALLACE, and Portrait. Crown 8vo, 7s. 6d.

ALLARDYCE.

Balmoral : A Romance of the Queen's Country. By ALEXANDER ALLARDYCE, Author of 'The City of Sunshine.' 3 vols. crown 8vo, 25s. 6d.

Memoir of the Honourable George Keith Elphinstone, K.B., Viscount Keith of Stonehaven, Marischal, Admiral of the Red. 8vo, with Portrait, Illustrations, and Maps, 21s.

ALMOND. Sermons by a Lay Head-master. By HELY HUTCHINSON ALMOND, M.A. Oxon., Head-master of Loretto School. Crown 8vo, 5s.

ANCIENT CLASSICS FOR ENGLISH READERS. Edited by Rev. W. LUCAS COLLINS, M.A. Price 2s. 6d. each. *For List of Vols., see p. 2.*

ANNALS OF A FISHING VILLAGE. By "A SON OF THE MARSHES." *See page 28.*

AYTOUN.

Lays of the Scottish Cavaliers, and other Poems. By W. EDMONDSTOUNE AYTOUN, D.C.L., Professor of Rhetoric and Belles-Lettres in the University of Edinburgh. New Edition. Fcap. 8vo, 3s. 6d.
    ANOTHER EDITION. Fcap. 8vo, 7s. 6d.
    CHEAP EDITION. 1s. Cloth, 1s. 3d.

An Illustrated Edition of the Lays of the Scottish Cavaliers. From designs by Sir NOEL PATON. Small 4to, in gilt cloth, 21s.

Bothwell : a Poem. Third Edition. Fcap., 7s. 6d.

Poems and Ballads of Goethe. Translated by Professor AYTOUN and Sir THEODORE MARTIN, K.C.B. Third Edition. Fcap., 6s.

Bon Gaultier's Book of Ballads. By the SAME. Fifteenth Edition. With Illustrations by Doyle, Leech, and Crowquill. Fcap. 8vo, 5s.

The Ballads of Scotland. Edited by Professor AYTOUN. Fourth Edition. 2 vols. fcap. 8vo, 12s.

Memoir of William E. Aytoun, D.C.L. By Sir THEODORE MARTIN, K.C.B. With Portrait. Post 8vo, 12s.

BACH.

On Musical Education and Vocal Culture. By ALBERT B. BACH. Fourth Edition. 8vo, 7s. 6d.

The Principles of Singing. A Practical Guide for Vocalists and Teachers. With Course of Vocal Exercises. Crown 8vo, 6s.

The Art of Singing. With Musical Exercises for Young People. Crown 8vo 3s.

The Art Ballad : Loewe and Schubert. With Musical Illustrations. With a Portrait of LOEWE. Third Edition. Small 4to, 5s.

BAIRD LECTURES.

Theism. By Rev. Professor FLINT, D.D., Edinburgh. Eighth Edition. Crown 8vo, 7s. 6d.

Anti-Theistic Theories. By Rev. Professor FLINT, D.D., Edinburgh. Fourth Edition. Crown 8vo, 10s. 6d.

BAIRD LECTURES.

The Early Religion of Israel. As set forth by Biblical Writers and modern Critical Historians. By Rev. Professor ROBERTSON, D.D., Glasgow. Fourth Edition. Crown 8vo, 10s. 6d.

The Inspiration of the Holy Scriptures. By Rev. ROBERT JAMIESON, D.D. Crown 8vo, 7s. 6d.

The Mysteries of Christianity. By Rev. Professor CRAWFORD, D.D. Crown 8vo, 7s. 6d.

Endowed Territorial Work : Its Supreme Importance to the Church and Country. By Rev. WILLIAM SMITH, D.D. Crown 8vo, 6s.

BALLADS AND POEMS. By MEMBERS OF THE GLASGOW BALLAD CLUB. Crown 8vo, 7s. 6d.

BANNATYNE. Handbook of Republican Institutions in the
United States of America. Based upon Federal and State Laws, and other reliable sources of information. By DUGALD J. BANNATYNE, Scotch Solicitor, New York; Member of the Faculty of Procurators, Glasgow. Crown 8vo, 7s. 6d.

BELLAIRS.

The Transvaal War, 1880-81. Edited by Lady BELLAIRS. With a Frontispiece and Map. 8vo, 15s.

Gossips with Girls and Maidens, Betrothed and Free. New Edition. Crown 8vo, 3s. 6d. Cloth, extra gilt edges, 5s.

BELLESHEIM. History of the Catholic Church of Scotland.
From the Introduction of Christianity to the Present Day. By ALPHONS BELLESHEIM, D.D., Canon of Aix-la-Chapelle. Translated, with Notes and Additions, by D. OSWALD HUNTER BLAIR, O.S.B., Monk of Fort Augustus. Complete in 4 vols. demy 8vo, with Maps. Price 12s. 6d. each.

BENTINCK. Racing Life of Lord George Cavendish Bentinck,
M.P., and other Reminiscences. By JOHN KENT, Private Trainer to the Goodwood Stable. Edited by the Hon. FRANCIS LAWLEY. With Twenty-three full-page Plates, and Facsimile Letter. Third Edition. Demy 8vo, 25s.

BESANT.

The Revolt of Man. By WALTER BESANT. Tenth Edition. Crown 8vo, 3s. 6d.

Readings in Rabelais. Crown 8vo, 7s. 6d.

BEVERIDGE.

Culross and Tulliallan ; or Perthshire on Forth. Its History and Antiquities. With Elucidations of Scottish Life and Character from the Burgh and Kirk-Session Records of that District. By DAVID BEVERIDGE. 2 vols. 8vo, with Illustrations, 42s.

Between the Ochils and the Forth ; or, From Stirling Bridge to Aberdour. Crown 8vo, 6s.

BIRCH.

Examples of Stables, Hunting-Boxes, Kennels, Racing Estab- lishments, &c. By JOHN BIRCH, Architect, Author of 'Country Architecture,' &c. With 30 Plates. Royal 8vo, 7s.

Examples of Labourers' Cottages, &c. With Plans for Improving the Dwellings of the Poor in Large Towns. With 34 Plates. Royal 8vo, 7s.

Picturesque Lodges. A Series of Designs for Gate Lodges, Park Entrances, Keepers', Gardeners', Bailiffs', Grooms', Upper and Under Servants' Lodges, and other Rural Residences. With 16 Plates. 4to, 12s. 6d.

BLACK. Heligoland and the Islands of the North Sea. By
WILLIAM GEORGE BLACK. Crown 8vo, 4s.

BLACKIE.

Lays and Legends of Ancient Greece. By JOHN STUART BLACKIE, Emeritus Professor of Greek in the University of Edinburgh. Second Edition. Fcap. 8vo, 5s.

The Wisdom of Goethe. Fcap. 8vo. Cloth, extra gilt, 6s.

Scottish Song: Its Wealth, Wisdom, and Social Significance. Crown 8vo. With Music. 7s. 6d.

A Song of Heroes. Crown 8vo, 6s.

BLACKMORE. The Maid of Sker. By R. D. BLACKMORE, Author of 'Lorna Doone,' &c. New Edition. Crown 8vo, 6s.

BLACKWOOD.

Blackwood's Magazine, from Commencement in 1817 to November 1893. Nos. 1 to 937, forming 153 Volumes.

Index to Blackwood's Magazine. Vols. 1 to 50. 8vo, 15s.

Tales from Blackwood. First Series. Price One Shilling each, in Paper Cover. Sold separately at all Railway Bookstalls. They may also be had bound in 12 vols., cloth, 18s. Half calf, richly gilt, 30s. Or the 12 vols. in 6, roxburghe, 21s. Half red morocco, 28s.

Tales from Blackwood. Second Series. Complete in Twenty-four Shilling Parts. Handsomely bound in 12 vols., cloth, 30s. In leather back, roxburghe style, 37s. 6d. Half calf, gilt, 52s. 6d. Half morocco, 55s.

Tales from Blackwood. Third Series. Complete in Twelve Shilling Parts. Handsomely bound in 6 vols., cloth, 15s.; and in 12 vols., cloth, 18s. The 6 vols. in roxburghe, 21s. Half calf, 25s. Half morocco, 28s.

Travel, Adventure, and Sport. From 'Blackwood's Magazine.' Uniform with 'Tales from Blackwood.' In Twelve Parts, each price 1s. Handsomely bound in 6 vols., cloth, 15s. And in half calf, 25s.

New Educational Series. *See separate Catalogue.*

New Uniform Series of Novels (Copyright). Crown 8vo, cloth. Price 3s. 6d. each. Now ready:—

LADY LEE'S WIDOWHOOD. By General Sir E. B. Hamley.	HURRISH. By the Hon. Emily Lawless.
KATIE STEWART, and other Stories. By Mrs Oliphant.	ALTIORA PETO. By Laurence Oliphant.
	PICCADILLY. By the Same. With Illustrations.
VALENTINE, AND HIS BROTHER. By the Same.	THE REVOLT OF MAN. By Walter Besant.
SONS AND DAUGHTERS. By the Same.	LADY BABY. By D. Gerard.
MARMORNE. By P. G. Hamerton.	THE BLACKSMITH OF VOE. By Paul Cushing.
REATA. By E. D. Gerard.	
BEGGAR MY NEIGHBOUR. By the Same.	THE DILEMMA. By the Author of 'The Battle of Dorking.'
THE WATERS OF HERCULES. By the Same.	
FAIR TO SEE. By L. W. M. Lockhart.	MY TRIVIAL LIFE AND MISFORTUNE. By A Plain Woman.
MINE IS THINE. By the Same.	
DOUBLES AND QUITS. By the Same.	POOR NELLIE. By the Same.

Others in preparation.

Standard Novels. Uniform in size and binding. Each complete in one Volume.

FLORIN SERIES, Illustrated Boards. Bound in Cloth, 2s. 6d.

TOM CRINGLE'S LOG. By Michael Scott.	PEN OWEN. By Dean Hook.
THE CRUISE OF THE MIDGE. By the Same.	ADAM BLAIR. By J. G. Lockhart.
CYRIL THORNTON. By Captain Hamilton.	LADY LEE'S WIDOWHOOD. By General Sir E. B. Hamley.
ANNALS OF THE PARISH. By John Galt.	
THE PROVOST, &c. By the Same.	SALEM CHAPEL. By Mrs Oliphant.
SIR ANDREW WYLIE. By the Same.	THE PERPETUAL CURATE. By the Same.
THE ENTAIL. By the Same.	MISS MARJORIBANKS. By the Same.
MISS MOLLY. By Beatrice May Butt.	JOHN: A Love Story. By the Same.
REGINALD DALTON. By J. G. Lockhart.	

BLACKWOOD.
Standard Novels.

SHILLING SERIES, Illustrated Cover. Bound in Cloth, 1s. 6d.

THE RECTOR, and THE DOCTOR'S FAMILY. By Mrs Oliphant.

THE LIFE OF MANSIE WAUCH. By D. M. Moir.

PENINSULAR SCENES AND SKETCHES. By F. Hardman.

SIR FRIZZLE PUMPKIN, NIGHTS AT MESS, &c.

THE SUBALTERN.

LIFE IN THE FAR WEST. By G. F. Ruxton.

VALERIUS: A Roman Story. By J. G. Lockhart.

BON GAULTIER'S BOOK OF BALLADS. Fifteenth Edition. With Illustrations by Doyle, Leech, and Crowquill. Fcap. 8vo, 5s.

BONNAR. Biographical Sketch of George Meikle Kemp, Architect of the Scott Monument, Edinburgh. By THOMAS BONNAR, F.S.A. Scot., Author of 'The Present Art Revival,' &c. With Three Portraits and numerous Illustrations. Post 8vo, 7s. 6d.

BOSCOBEL TRACTS. Relating to the Escape of Charles the Second after the Battle of Worcester, and his subsequent Adventures. Edited by J. HUGHES, Esq., A.M. A New Edition, with additional Notes and Illustrations, including Communications from the Rev. R. H. BARHAM, Author of the 'Ingoldsby Legends.' 8vo, with Engravings, 16s.

BROUGHAM. Memoirs of the Life and Times of Henry Lord Brougham. Written by HIMSELF. 3 vols. 8vo, £2, 8s. The Volumes are sold separately, price 16s. each.

BROWN. A Manual of Botany, Anatomical and Physiological. For the Use of Students. By ROBERT BROWN, M.A., Ph.D. Crown 8vo, with numerous Illustrations, 12s. 6d.

BROWN. The Book of the Landed Estate. Containing Directions for the Management and Development of the Resources of Landed Property. By ROBERT E. BROWN, Factor and Estate Agent. Royal 8vo, with Illustrations, 21s.

BROWN. The Forester: A Practical Treatise on the Planting, Rearing, and General Management of Forest-trees. By JAMES BROWN, LL.D. New Edition, Revised by JOHN NISBET, Author of 'British Forest Trees,' &c.
[*In active preparation.*

BROWN. Stray Sport. By J. MORAY BROWN, Author of 'Shikar Sketches,' 'Powder, Spur, and Spear,' 'The Days when we went Hog-Hunting.' 2 vols. post 8vo, with Fifty Illustrations, 21s.

BRUCE.
In Clover and Heather. Poems by WALLACE BRUCE. New and Enlarged Edition. Crown 8vo, 4s. 6d.
A limited number of Copies of the First Edition, on large hand-made paper, 12s. 6d.
Here's a Hand. Addresses and Poems. Crown 8vo, 5s.
Large Paper Edition, limited to 100 copies, price 21s.

BRYDALL. Art in Scotland; its Origin and Progress. By ROBERT BRYDALL, Master of St George's Art School of Glasgow. 8vo, 12s. 6d.

BUCHAN. Introductory Text-Book of Meteorology. By ALEXANDER BUCHAN, LL.D., F.R.S.E., Secretary of the Scottish Meteorological Society, &c. Crown 8vo, with 8 Coloured Charts and Engravings, 4s. 6d.

BUCHANAN. The Shire Highlands (East Central Africa). By JOHN BUCHANAN, Planter at Zomba. Crown 8vo, 5s.

BURBIDGE.
Domestic Floriculture, Window Gardening, and Floral Decorations. Being practical directions for the Propagation, Culture, and Arrangement of Plants and Flowers as Domestic Ornaments. By F. W. BURBIDGE. Second Edition. Crown 8vo, with numerous Illustrations, 7s. 6d.
Cultivated Plants: Their Propagation and Improvement. Including Natural and Artificial Hybridisation, Raising from Seed, Cuttings, and Layers, Grafting and Budding, as applied to the Families and Genera in Cultivation. Crown 8vo, with numerous Illustrations, 12s. 6d.

BURROWS. Commentaries on the History of England, from the Earliest Times to 1865. By MONTAGU BURROWS, Chichele Professor of Modern History in the University of Oxford; Captain R.N.; F.S.A., &c.; "Officier de l'Instruction Publique," France. Crown 8vo, 7s. 6d.

BURTON.

The History of Scotland: From Agricola's Invasion to the Extinction of the last Jacobite Insurrection. By JOHN HILL BURTON, D.C.L., Historiographer-Royal for Scotland. New and Enlarged Edition, 8 vols., and Index. Crown 8vo, £3, 3s.

History of the British Empire during the Reign of Queen Anne. In 3 vols. 8vo. 36s.

The Scot Abroad. Third Edition. Crown 8vo, 10s. 6d.

The Book-Hunter. New Edition. With Portrait. Crown 8vo, 7s. 6d.

BUTE.

The Roman Breviary: Reformed by Order of the Holy Œcumenical Council of Trent; Published by Order of Pope St Pius V.; and Revised by Clement VIII. and Urban VIII.; together with the Offices since granted. Translated out of Latin into English by JOHN, Marquess of Bute, K.T. In 2 vols. crown 8vo, cloth boards, edges uncut. £2, 2s.

The Altus of St Columba. With a Prose Paraphrase and Notes. In paper cover, 2s. 6d.

BUTT.

Miss Molly. By BEATRICE MAY BUTT. Cheap Edition, 2s.

Eugenie. Crown 8vo, 6s. 6d.

Elizabeth, and other Sketches. Crown 8vo, 6s.

Delicia. New Edition. Crown 8vo, 2s. 6d.

CAIRD.

Sermons. By JOHN CAIRD, D.D., Principal of the University of Glasgow. Seventeenth Thousand. Fcap. 8vo, 5s.

Religion in Common Life. A Sermon preached in Crathie Church, October 14, 1855, before Her Majesty the Queen and Prince Albert. Published by Her Majesty's Command. Cheap Edition, 3d.

CALDER. Chaucer's Canterbury Pilgrimage. Epitomised by WILLIAM CALDER. With Photogravure of the Pilgrimage Company, and other Illustrations, Glossary, &c. Crown 8vo, gilt edges, 4s.

CAMPBELL. Critical Studies in St Luke's Gospel: Its Demonology and Ebionitism. By COLIN CAMPBELL, D.D., Minister of the Parish of Dundee, formerly Scholar and Fellow of Glasgow University. Author of the 'Three First Gospels in Greek, arranged in parallel columns.' Post 8vo, 7s. 6d.

CAMPBELL. Sermons Preached before the Queen at Balmoral. By the Rev. A. A. CAMPBELL, Minister of Crathie. Published by Command of Her Majesty. Crown 8vo, 4s. 6d.

CAMPBELL. Records of Argyll. Legends, Traditions, and Recollections of Argyllshire Highlanders, collected chiefly from the Gaelic. With Notes on the Antiquity of the Dress, Clan Colours, or Tartans of the Highlanders. By Lord ARCHIBALD CAMPBELL. Illustrated with Nineteen full-page Etchings. 4to, printed on hand-made paper, £3, 3s.

CAMPBELL, W. D., AND V. K. ERSKINE. The Bailie M'Phee: A Curling Song. With Illustrations, and the Music to which it may be sung. Small 4to, 1s. 6d.

CANTON. A Lost Epic, and other Poems. By WILLIAM CANTON. Crown 8vo, 5s.

CARRICK. Koumiss; or, Fermented Mare's Milk: and its uses in the Treatment and Cure of Pulmonary Consumption, and other Wasting Diseases. With an Appendix on the best Methods of Fermenting Cow's Milk. By GEORGE L. CARRICK, M.D., L.R.C.S.E. and L.R.C.P.E., Physician to the British Embassy, St Petersburg, &c. Crown 8vo, 10s. 6d.

CARSTAIRS. British Work in India. By R. CARSTAIRS. Crown 8vo, 6s.

CAUVIN. A Treasury of the English and German Languages. Compiled from the best Authors and Lexicographers in both Languages. By JOSEPH CAUVIN, LL.D. and Ph.D., of the University of Göttingen, &c. Crown 8vo, 7s. 6d.

CAVE-BROWNE. Lambeth Palace and its Associations. By J. CAVE-BROWNE, M.A., Vicar of Detling, Kent, and for many years Curate of Lambeth Parish Church. With an Introduction by the Archbishop of Canterbury. Second Edition, containing an additional Chapter on Medieval Life in the Old Palaces. 8vo, with Illustrations, 21s.

CHARTERIS. Canonicity; or, Early Testimonies to the Existence and Use of the Books of the New Testament. Based on Kirchhoffer's 'Quellensammlung.' Edited by A. H. CHARTERIS, D.D., Professor of Biblical Criticism in the University of Edinburgh. 8vo, 18s.

CHENNELLS. Recollections of an Egyptian Princess. By her English Governess (Miss E. CHENNELLS). Being a Record of Five Years' Residence at the Court of Ismael Pasha, Khédive. Second Edition. With Three Portraits. Post 8vo, 7s. 6d.

CHRISTISON. Life of Sir Robert Christison, Bart., M.D., D.C.L. Oxon., Professor of Medical Jurisprudence in the University of E burgh. Edited by his SONS. In 2 vols. 8vo. Vol. I.—Autobiography. 16s. Vol. II.—Memoirs. 16s.

CHRONICLES OF WESTERLY: A Provincial Sketch. By the Author of 'Culmshire Folk,' 'John Orlebar,' &c. 3 vols. crown 8vo, 25s. 6d.

CHURCH SERVICE SOCIETY.
A Book of Common Order: being Forms of Worship issued by the Church Service Society. Sixth Edition. Crown 8vo, 6s. Also in 2 vols. crown 8vo, 6s. 6d.
Daily Offices for Morning and Evening Prayer throughout the Week. Crown 8vo, 3s. 6d.
Order of Divine Service for Children. Issued by the Church Service Society. With Scottish Hymnal. Cloth, 3d.

CLOUSTON. Popular Tales and Fictions: their Migrations and Transformations. By W. A. CLOUSTON, Editor of 'Arabian Poetry for English Readers,' &c. 2 vols. post 8vo, roxburghe binding, 25s.

COCHRAN. A Handy Text-Book of Military Law. Compiled chiefly to assist Officers preparing for Examination; also for all Officers of the Regular and Auxiliary Forces. Comprising also a Synopsis of part of the Army Act. By Major F. COCHRAN, Hampshire Regiment Garrison Instructor, North British District. Crown 8vo, 7s. 6d.

COLQUHOUN. The Moor and the Loch. Containing Minute Instructions in all Highland Sports, with Wanderings over Crag and Corrie, Flood and Fell. By JOHN COLQUHOUN. Cheap Edition. With Illustrations. Demy 8vo, 10s. 6d.

COLVILE. Round the Black Man's Garden. By ZÉLIE COLVILE, F.R.G.S. With 2 Maps and 50 Illustrations from Drawings by the Author and from Photographs. Demy 8vo, 16s.

CONSTITUTION AND LAW OF THE CHURCH OF SCOTLAND. With an Introductory Note by the late Principal Tulloch. New Edition, Revised and Enlarged. Crown 8vo, 3s. 6d.

COTTERILL. Suggested Reforms in Public Schools. By C. C. COTTERILL, M.A. Crown 8vo, 3s. 6d.

CRANSTOUN.

The Elegies of Albius Tibullus. Translated into English Verse, with Life of the Poet, and Illustrative Notes. By JAMES CRANSTOUN, LL.D., Author of a Translation of 'Catullus.' Crown 8vo, 6s. 6d.

The Elegies of Sextus Propertius. Translated into English Verse, with Life of the Poet, and Illustrative Notes. Crown 8vo, 7s. 6d.

CRAWFORD. An Atonement of East London, and other Poems. By HOWARD CRAWFORD, M.A. Crown 8vo, 5s.

CRAWFORD. Saracinesca. By F. MARION CRAWFORD, Author of 'Mr Isaacs,' &c. &c. Sixth Edition. Crown 8vo, 6s.

CRAWFORD.

The Doctrine of Holy Scripture respecting the Atonement. By the late THOMAS J. CRAWFORD, D.D., Professor of Divinity in the University of Edinburgh. Fifth Edition. 8vo, 12s.

The Fatherhood of God, Considered in its General and Special Aspects. Third Edition, Revised and Enlarged. 8vo, 9s.

The Preaching of the Cross, and other Sermons. 8vo, 7s. 6d.

The Mysteries of Christianity. Crown 8vo, 7s. 6d.

CROSS. Impressions of Dante, and of the New World ; with a Few Words on Bimetallism. By J. W. CROSS, Editor of 'George Eliot's Life, as related in her Letters and Journals.' Post 8vo, 6s.

CUSHING.

The Blacksmith of Voe. By PAUL CUSHING, Author of 'The Bull i' th' Thorn,' 'Cut with his own Diamond.' Cheap Edition. Crown 8vo, 3s. 6d.

DAVIES.

Norfolk Broads and Rivers ; or, The Waterways, Lagoons, and Decoys of East Anglia. By G. CHRISTOPHER DAVIES. Illustrated with Seven full-page Plates. New and Cheaper Edition. Crown 8vo, 6s.

Our Home in Aveyron. Sketches of Peasant Life in Aveyron and the Lot. By G. CHRISTOPHER DAVIES and Mrs BROUGHALL. Illustrated with full-page Illustrations. 8vo, 15s. Cheap Edition, 7s. 6d.

DE LA WARR. An Eastern Cruise in the 'Edeline.' By the Countess DE LA WARR. In Illustrated Cover. 2s.

DESCARTES. The Method, Meditations, and Principles of Philosophy of Descartes. Translated from the Original French and Latin. With a New Introductory Essay, Historical and Critical, on the Cartesian Philosophy. By Professor VEITCH, LL.D., Glasgow University. Tenth Edition. 6s. 6d.

DEWAR. Voyage of the "Nyanza," R.N.Y.C. Being the Record of a Three Years' Cruise in a Schooner Yacht in the Atlantic and Pacific, and her subsequent Shipwreck. By J. CUMMING DEWAR, late Captain King's Dragoon Guards and 11th Prince Albert's Hussars. With Two Autogravures, numerous Illustrations, and a Map. Demy 8vo, 21s.

DICKSON. Gleanings from Japan. By W. G. DICKSON, Author of 'Japan: Being a Sketch of its History, Government, and Officers of the Empire.' With Illustrations. 8vo, 16s.

DILEMMA, The. By the Author of 'The Battle of Dorking.' New Edition. Crown 8vo, 3s. 6d.

DOGS, OUR DOMESTICATED : Their Treatment in reference to Food, Diseases, Habits, Punishment, Accomplishments. By 'MAGENTA.' Crown 8vo, 2s. 6d.

DOMESTIC EXPERIMENT, A. By the Author of 'Ideala: A Study from Life.' Crown 8vo, 6s.

DOUGLAS. Chinese Stories. By ROBERT K. DOUGLAS. With numerous Illustrations by Parkinson, Forestier, and others. Small demy 8vo, 12s. 6d.

DU CANE. The Odyssey of Homer, Books I.-XII. Translated into English Verse. By Sir CHARLES DU CANE, K.C.M.G. 8vo, 10s. 6d.

DUDGEON. History of the Edinburgh or Queen's Regiment Light Infantry Militia, now 3rd Battalion The Royal Scots; with an Account of the Origin and Progress of the Militia, and a Brief Sketch of the Old Royal Scots. By Major R. C. DUDGEON, Adjutant 3rd Battalion the Royal Scots. Post 8vo, with Illustrations, 10s. 6d.

DUNCAN. Manual of the General Acts of Parliament relating to the Salmon Fisheries of Scotland from 1828 to 1882. By J. BARKER DUNCAN. Crown 8vo, 5s.

DUNSMORE. Manual of the Law of Scotland as to the Relations between Agricultural Tenants and the Landlords, Servants, Merchants, and Bowers. By W. DUNSMORE. 8vo, 7s. 6d.

DUPRÉ. Thoughts on Art, and Autobiographical Memoirs of Giovanni Duprè. Translated from the Italian by E. M. PERUZZI, with the permission of the Author. New Edition. With an Introduction by W. W. STORY. Crown 8vo, 10s. 6d.

ELIOT.

George Eliot's Life, Related in Her Letters and Journals. Arranged and Edited by her husband, J. W. CROSS. With Portrait and other Illustrations. Third Edition. 3 vols. post 8vo, 42s.

George Eliot's Life. (Cabinet Edition.) With Portrait and other Illustrations. 3 vols. crown 8vo, 15s.

George Eliot's Life. With Portrait and other Illustrations. New Edition, in one volume. Crown 8vo, 7s. 6d.

Works of George Eliot (Cabinet Edition). 21 volumes, crown 8vo, price £5, 5s. Also to be had handsomely bound in half and full calf. The Volumes are sold separately, bound in cloth, price 5s. each—viz.: Romola. 2 vols.—Silas Marner, The Lifted Veil, Brother Jacob. 1 vol.— Adam Bede. 2 vols.—Scenes of Clerical Life. 2 vols.—The Mill on the Floss. 2 vols.—Felix Holt. 2 vols.—Middlemarch. 3 vols.—Daniel Deronda. 3 vols.—The Spanish Gypsy. 1 vol.—Jubal, and other Poems, Old and New. 1 vol.—Theophrastus Such. 1 vol.—Essays. 1 vol.

Novels by George Eliot. Cheap Edition. Adam Bede. Illustrated. 3s. 6d., cloth.—The Mill on the Floss. Illustrated. 3s. 6d., cloth.—Scenes of Clerical Life. Illustrated. 3s., cloth.— Silas Marner: the Weaver of Raveloe. Illustrated. 2s. 6d., cloth.—Felix Holt, the Radical. Illustrated. 3s. 6d., cloth.—Romola. With Vignette. 3s. 6d., cloth.

Middlemarch. Crown 8vo, 7s. 6d.

Daniel Deronda. Crown 8vo, 7s. 6d.

Essays. New Edition. Crown 8vo, 5s.

Impressions of Theophrastus Such. New Edition. Crown 8vo, 5s.

The Spanish Gypsy. New Edition. Crown 8vo, 5s.

The Legend of Jubal, and other Poems, Old and New. New Edition. Crown 8vo, 5s.

Wise, Witty, and Tender Sayings, in Prose and Verse. Selected from the Works of GEORGE ELIOT. New Edition. Fcap. 8vo, 3s. 6d.

ELIOT.
The George Eliot Birthday Book. Printed on fine paper, with red border, and handsomely bound in cloth, gilt. Fcap. 8vo, 3s. 6d. And in French morocco or Russia, 5s.

ESSAYS ON SOCIAL SUBJECTS. Originally published in the 'Saturday Review.' New Edition. First and Second Series. 2 vols. crown 8vo, 6s. each.

FAITHS OF THE WORLD, The. A Concise History of the Great Religious Systems of the World. By various Authors. Crown 8vo, 5s.

FARRER. A Tour in Greece in 1880. By RICHARD RIDLEY FARRER. With Twenty-seven full-page Illustrations by Lord WINDSOR. Royal 8vo, with a Map, 21s.

FERRIER.
Philosophical Works of the late James F. Ferrier, B.A. Oxon., Professor of Moral Philosophy and Political Economy, St Andrews. New Edition. Edited by Sir ALEXANDER GRANT, Bart., D.C.L., and Professor LUSHINGTON. 3 vols. crown 8vo, 34s. 6d.
Institutes of Metaphysic. Third Edition. 10s. 6d.
Lectures on the Early Greek Philosophy. 4th Edition. 10s. 6d.
Philosophical Remains, including the Lectures on Early Greek Philosophy. New Edition. 2 vols., 24s.

FITZROY. Dogma and the Church of England. By A. I. FITZROY. Post 8vo, 7s. 6d.

FLINT.
The Philosophy of History in Europe. By ROBERT FLINT, D.D., LL.D., Professor of Divinity, University of Edinburgh. 3 vols. 8vo.
Vol. I.—FRANCE. 21s.   [*Just ready.*
Agnosticism. Being the Croall Lecture for 1887-88.
                    [*In the press.*
Theism. Being the Baird Lecture for 1876. Eighth Edition, Revised. Crown 8vo, 7s. 6d.
Anti-Theistic Theories. Being the Baird Lecture for 1877. Fourth Edition. Crown 8vo, 10s. 6d.

FORBES. Insulinde : Experiences of a Naturalist's Wife in the Eastern Archipelago. By Mrs H. O. FORBES. Crown 8vo, with a Map. 4s. 6d.

FOREIGN CLASSICS FOR ENGLISH READERS. Edited by Mrs OLIPHANT. Price 2s. 6d. *For List of Volumes, see page 2.*

FOSTER. The Fallen City, and other Poems. By WILL FOSTER. Crown 8vo, 6s.

FRANCILLON. Gods and Heroes ; or, The Kingdom of Jupiter. By R. E. FRANCILLON. With 8 Illustrations. Crown 8vo, 5s.

FULLARTON. Merlin : A Dramatic Poem. By RALPH MACLEOD FULLARTON. Crown 8vo, 5s.

GALT. Novels by JOHN GALT. Fcap. 8vo, boards, each 2s. ; cloth, 2s. 6d.
ANNALS OF THE PARISH.—THE PROVOST.—SIR ANDREW WYLIE.—THE ENTAIL.

GENERAL ASSEMBLY OF THE CHURCH OF SCOTLAND.

Scottish Hymnal, With Appendix Incorporated. Published for use in Churches by Authority of the General Assembly. 1. Large type, cloth, red edges, 2s. 6d.; French morocco, 4s. 2. Bourgeois type, limp cloth, 1s.; French morocco, 2s. 3. Nonpareil type, cloth, red edges, 6d.; French morocco, 1s. 4d. 4. Paper covers, 3d. 5. Sunday-School Edition, paper covers, 1d., cloth, 2d. No. 1, bound with the Psalms and Paraphrases, French morocco, 8s. No. 2, bound with the Psalms and Paraphrases, cloth, 2s.; French morocco, 3s.

Prayers for Social and Family Worship. Prepared by a Special Committee of the General Assembly of the Church of Scotland. Entirely New Edition, Revised and Enlarged. Fcap. 8vo, red edges, 2s.

Prayers for Family Worship. A Selection of Four Weeks' Prayers. New Edition. Authorised by the General Assembly of the Church of Scotland. Fcap. 8vo, red edges, 1s. 6d.

GERARD.

Reata : What's in a Name. By E. D. GERARD. Cheap Edition. Crown 8vo, 3s. 6d.

Beggar my Neighbour. Cheap Edition. Crown 8vo, 3s. 6d.

The Waters of Hercules. Cheap Edition. Crown 8vo, 3s. 6d.

GERARD.

The Land beyond the Forest. Facts, Figures, and Fancies from Transylvania. By E. GERARD. With Maps and Illustrations. 2 vols. post 8vo, 25s.

Bis : Some Tales Retold. Crown 8vo, 6s.

A Secret Mission. 2 vols. crown 8vo, 17s.

GERARD.

Lady Baby. By DOROTHEA GERARD. Cheap Edition. Crown 8vo, 3s. 6d.

Recha. Second Edition. Crown 8vo, 6s.

GERARD. Stonyhurst Latin Grammar. By Rev. JOHN GERARD.
Second Edition. Fcap. 8vo, 3s.

GILL.

Free Trade : an Inquiry into the Nature of its Operation. By RICHARD GILL. Crown 8vo, 7s. 6d.

Free Trade under Protection. Crown 8vo, 7s. 6d.

GOETHE. Poems and Ballads of Goethe. Translated by Professor AYTOUN and Sir THEODORE MARTIN, K.C.B. Third Edition. Fcap. 8vo, 6s.

GOETHE'S FAUST. Translated into English Verse by Sir
THEODORE MARTIN, K.C.B. Part I. Second Edition, post 8vo, 6s. Ninth Edition, fcap., 3s. 6d. Part II. Second Edition, Revised. Fcap. 8vo, 6s.

GORDON CUMMING.

At Home in Fiji. By C. F. GORDON CUMMING. Fourth Edition, post 8vo. With Illustrations and Map. 7s. 6d.

A Lady's Cruise in a French Man-of-War. New and Cheaper Edition. 8vo. With Illustrations and Map. 12s. 6d.

Fire-Fountains. The Kingdom of Hawaii : Its Volcanoes, and the History of its Missions. With Map and Illustrations. 2 vols. 8vo, 25s.

Wanderings in China. New and Cheaper Edition. 8vo, with Illustrations, 10s.

Granite Crags : The Yo-semité Region of California. Illustrated with 8 Engravings. New and Cheaper Edition. 8vo, 8s. 6d.

GRAHAM. The Life and Work of Syed Ahmed Khan, C.S.I.
By Lieut.-Colonel G. F. I. GRAHAM, B.S.C. 8vo, 14s.

GRAHAM. Manual of the Elections (Scot.) (Corrupt and Illegal Practices) Act, 1890. With Analysis, Relative Act of Sederunt, Appendix containing the Corrupt Practices Acts of 1883 and 1885, and Copious Index. By J. EDWARD GRAHAM, Advocate. 8vo, 4s. 6d.

GRANT. Bush-Life in Queensland. By A. C. GRANT. New Edition. Crown 8vo, 6s.

GRANT. Extracts from the Journals of the late Sir Hope Grant, 1841-75, with Selections from his Correspondence. Edited by Lieut.-Colonel HENRY KNOLLYS, Royal Artillery, his former A.D.C., Editor of 'Incidents in the Sepoy War;' Author of 'Sketches of Life in Japan,' &c. With Portrait of Sir Hope Grant, Map and Plans. In 2 vols. demy 8vo.

[*Shortly.*]

GUTHRIE-SMITH. Crispus: A Drama. By H. GUTHRIE-SMITH. Fcap. 4to, 5s.

HAINES. Unless! A Romance. By RANDOLPH HAINES. Crown 8vo, 6s.

HALDANE. Subtropical Cultivations and Climates. A Handy Book for Planters, Colonists, and Settlers. By R. C. HALDANE. Post 8vo, 9s.

HAMERTON.

Wenderholme: A Story of Lancashire and Yorkshire Life. By P. G. HAMERTON, Author of 'A Painter's Camp.' Crown 8vo, 6s.

Marmorne. New Edition. Crown 8vo, 3s. 6d.

HAMILTON.

Lectures on Metaphysics. By Sir WILLIAM HAMILTON, Bart., Professor of Logic and Metaphysics in the University of Edinburgh. Edited by the Rev. H. L. MANSEL, B.D., LL.D., Dean of St Paul's; and JOHN VEITCH, M.A., LL.D., Professor of Logic and Rhetoric, Glasgow. Seventh Edition. 2 vols. 8vo, 24s.

Lectures on Logic. Edited by the SAME. Third Edition, Revised. 2 vols., 24s.

Discussions on Philosophy and Literature, Education and University Reform. Third Edition. 8vo, 21s.

Memoir of Sir William Hamilton, Bart., Professor of Logic and Metaphysics in the University of Edinburgh. By Professor VEITCH, of the University of Glasgow. 8vo, with Portrait, 18s.

Sir William Hamilton: The Man and his Philosophy. Two Lectures delivered before the Edinburgh Philosophical Institution, January and February 1883. By Professor VEITCH. Crown 8vo, 2s.

HAMLEY.

The Operations of War Explained and Illustrated. By General Sir EDWARD BRUCE HAMLEY, K.C.B., K.C.M.G. Fifth Edition, Revised throughout. 4to, with numerous Illustrations, 30s.

National Defence; Articles and Speeches. Post 8vo, 6s.

Shakespeare's Funeral, and other Papers. Post 8vo, 7s. 6d.

Thomas Carlyle: An Essay. Second Edition. Crown 8vo, 2s. 6d.

On Outposts. Second Edition. 8vo, 2s.

Wellington's Career; A Military and Political Summary. Crown 8vo, 2s.

Lady Lee's Widowhood. New Edition. Crown 8vo, 3s. 6d. Cheaper Edition, 2s. 6d.

Our Poor Relations. A Philozoic Essay. With Illustrations, chiefly by Ernest Griset. Crown 8vo, cloth gilt, 3s. 6d.

HAMLEY. Guilty, or Not Guilty? A Tale. By Major-General W. G. HAMLEY, late of the Royal Engineers. New Edition. Crown 8vo, 3s. 6d.

HARRIS. A Journey through the Yemen, and some General Remarks upon that Country. By WALTER B. HARRIS, F.R.G.S., Author of 'The Land of an African Sultan; Travels in Morocco,' &c. With 3 Maps and numerous Illustrations by Forestier and Wallace from Sketches and Photographs taken by the Author. Demy 8vo, 16s.

HARRISON. The Scot in Ulster. The Story of the Scottish Settlement in Ulster. By JOHN HARRISON, Author of 'Oure Tounis Colledge.' Crown 8vo, 2s. 6d.

HASELL.

Bible Partings. By E. J. HASELL. Crown 8vo, 6s.

Short Family Prayers. Cloth, 1s.

HAWKER. The Prose Works of Rev. R. S. HAWKER, Vicar of Morwenstow. Including 'Footprints of Former Men in Far Cornwall.' Re-edited, with Sketches never before published. With a Frontispiece. Crown 8vo, 3s. 6d.

HAY. The Works of the Right Rev. Dr George Hay, Bishop of Edinburgh. Edited under the Supervision of the Right Rev. Bishop STRAIN. With Memoir and Portrait of the Author. 5 vols. crown 8vo, bound in extra cloth, £1, 1s. The following Volumes may be had separately—viz.: The Devout Christian Instructed in the Law of Christ from the Written Word. 2 vols., 8s.—The Pious Christian Instructed in the Nature and Practice of the Principal Exercises of Piety. 1 vol., 3s.

HEATLEY.

The Horse-Owner's Safeguard. A Handy Medical Guide for every Man who owns a Horse. By G. S. HEATLEY, M.R.C.V.S. Crown 8vo, 5s.

The Stock-Owner's Guide. A Handy Medical Treatise for every Man who owns an Ox or a Cow. Crown 8vo, 4s. 6d.

HEDDERWICK.

Lays of Middle Age; and other Poems. By JAMES HEDDERWICK, LL.D. Price 3s. 6d.

Backward Glances; or, Some Personal Recollections. With a Portrait. Post 8vo, 7s. 6d.

HEMANS.

The Poetical Works of Mrs Hemans. Copyright Ed Royal 8vo, 5s. The Same with Engravings, cloth, gilt edges, 7s. 6d.

Select Poems of Mrs Hemans. Fcap., cloth, gilt edges, 3s.

HERKLESS. Cardinal Beaton: Priest and Politician. By JOHN HERKLESS, Minister of Tannadice. With a Portrait. Post 8vo, 7s. 6d.

HOME PRAYERS. By Ministers of the Church of Scotland and Members of the Church Service Society. Second Edition. Fcap. 8vo, 3s.

HOMER.

The Odyssey. Translated into English Verse in the Spenserian Stanza. By PHILIP STANHOPE WORSLEY. 3d Edition. 2 vols. fcap., 12s.

The Iliad. Translated by P. S. WORSLEY and Professor CINGTON. 2 vols. crown 8vo, 21s.

HUTCHINSON. Hints on the Game of Golf. By HORACE G. HUTCHINSON. Seventh Edition, Enlarged. Fcap. 8vo, cloth, 1s.

IDDESLEIGH.

Lectures and Essays. By the late EARL of IDDESLEIGH, G.C.B., D.C.L., &c. 8vo, 16s.

Life, Letters, and Diaries of Sir Stafford Northcote, First Earl of Iddesleigh. By ANDREW LANG. With Three Portraits and a View of Pynes. Third Edition. 2 vols. post 8vo, 31s. 6d.

POPULAR EDITION. With Portrait and View of Pynes. Post 8vo, 7s. 6d.

INDEX GEOGRAPHICUS: Being a List, alphabetically arranged, of the Principal Places on the Globe, with the Countries and Subdivisions of the Countries in which they are situated, and their Latitudes and Longitudes. Imperial 8vo, pp. 676, 21s.

JEAN JAMBON. Our Trip to Blunderland ; or, Grand Excursion to Blundertown and Back. By JEAN JAMBON. With Sixty Illustrations designed by CHARLES DOYLE, engraved by DALZIEL. Fourth Thousand. Cloth, gilt edges, 6s. 6d. Cheap Edition, cloth, 3s. 6d. Boards, 2s. 6d.

JENNINGS. Mr Gladstone : A Study. By LOUIS J. JENNINGS, M.P., Author of 'Republican Government in the United States,' 'The Croker Memoirs,' &c. Popular Edition. Crown 8vo, 1s.

JERNINGHAM.
Reminiscences of an Attaché. By HUBERT E. H. JERNINGHAM. Second Edition. Crown 8vo, 5s.

Diane de Breteuille. A Love Story. Crown 8vo, 2s. 6d.

JOHNSTON.
The Chemistry of Common Life. By Professor J. F. W. JOHNSTON. New Edition, Revised. By ARTHUR HERBERT CHURCH, M.A. Oxon.; Author of 'Food: its Sources, Constituents, and Uses,' &c. With Maps and 102 Engravings. Crown 8vo, 7s. 6d.

Elements of Agricultural Chemistry. An entirely New Edition from the Edition by Sir CHARLES A. CAMERON, M.D., F.R.C.S.I., &c. Revised and brought down to date by C. M. AIKMAN, M.A., B.Sc., F.R.S.E., Lecturer on Agricultural Chemistry, West of Scotland Technical College. Fcap. 8vo. [*In preparation.*]

Catechism of Agricultural Chemistry. An entirely New Edition from the Edition by Sir CHARLES A. CAMERON. Revised and Enlarged by C. M. AIKMAN, M.A., &c. 92d Thousand. With numerous Illustrations. Crown 8vo, 1s.

JOHNSTON. Patrick Hamilton : a Tragedy of the Reformation in Scotland, 1528. By T. P. JOHNSTON. Crown 8vo, with Two Etchings. 5s.

JOHNSTON. Agricultural Holdings (Scotland) Acts, 1883 and 1889 ; and the Ground Game Act, 1880. With Notes, and Summary of Procedure, &c. By CHRISTOPHER N. JOHNSTON, M.A., Advocate. Demy 8vo, 5s.

KEBBEL. The Old and the New : English Country Life. By T. E. KEBBEL, M.A., Author of 'The Agricultural Labourers,' 'Essays in History and Politics,' 'Life of Lord Beaconsfield.' Crown 8vo, 5s.

KENNEDY. Sport, Travel, and Adventure in Newfoundland and the West Indies. By Captain W. R. KENNEDY, R.N. With Illustrations by the Author. Post 8vo, 14s.

KING. The Metamorphoses of Ovid. Translated in English Blank Verse. By HENRY KING, M.A., Fellow of Wadham College, Oxford, and of the Inner Temple, Barrister-at-Law. Crown 8vo, 10s. 6d.

KINGLAKE.
History of the Invasion of the Crimea. By A. W. KINGLAKE. Cabinet Edition, Revised. With an Index to the Complete Work. Illustrated with Maps and Plans. Complete in 9 vols., crown 8vo, at 6s. each.

History of the Invasion of the Crimea. Demy 8vo. Vol. VI. Winter Troubles. With a Map, 16s. Vols. VII. and VIII. From the Morrow of Inkerman to the Death of Lord Raglan. With an Index to the Whole Work. With Maps and Plans. 28s.

Eothen. A New Edition, uniform with the Cabinet Edition of the 'History of the Invasion of the Crimea.' 6s.

KNEIPP. My Water-Cure. As Tested through more than
Thirty Years, and Described for the Healing of Diseases and the Preservation of
Health. By SEBASTIAN KNEIPP, Parish Priest of Wörishofen (Bavaria). With a
Portrait and other Illustrations. Authorised English Translation from the
Thirtieth German Edition, by A. de F. Cheap Edition. With an Appendix, con.
taining the Latest Developments of Pfarrer Kneipp's System, and a Preface by
E. Gerard. Crown 8vo, 3s. 6d.

KNOLLYS. The Elements of Field-Artillery. Designed for
the Use of Infantry and Cavalry Officers. By HENRY KNOLLYS, Colonel Royal
Artillery; Author of, 'From Sedan to Saarbrück,' Editor of 'Incidents in the
Sepoy War,' &c. With Engravings. Crown 8vo, 7s. 6d.

LAMINGTON. In the Days of the Dandies. By the late Lord
LAMINGTON. Crown 8vo. Illustrated cover, 1s.; cloth, 1s. 6d.

LANG. Life, Letters, and Diaries of Sir Stafford Northcote,
First Earl of Iddesleigh. By ANDREW LANG. With Three Portraits and a View
of Pynes. Third Edition. 2 vols. post 8vo, 31s. 6d.
POPULAR EDITION. With Portrait and View of Pynes. Post 8vo, 7s. 6d.

LAWLESS. Hurrish : A Study. By the Hon. EMILY LAWLESS,
Author of 'A Chelsea Householder,' &c. Fourth Edition. Crown 8vo, 3s. 6d.

LEES. A Handbook of the Sheriff and Justice of Peace Small
Debt Courts. With Notes, References, and Forms. By J. M. LEES, Advocate,
Sheriff of Stirling, Dumbarton, and Clackmannan. 8vo, 7s. 6d.

LINDSAY. The Progressiveness of Modern Christian Thought.
By the Rev. JAMES LINDSAY, M.A., B.D., B.Sc., F.R.S.E., F.G.S., Minister of
the Parish of St Andrew's, Kilmarnock. Crown 8vo, 6s.

LLOYD. Ireland under the Land League. A Narrative of
Personal Experiences. By CLIFFORD LLOYD, Special Resident Magistrate.
Post 8vo, 6s.

LOCKHART.
Doubles and Quits. By LAURENCE W. M. LOCKHART. New
Edition. Crown 8vo, 3s. 6d.
Fair to See. New Edition. Crown 8vo, 3s. 6d.
Mine is Thine. New Edition. Crown 8vo, 3s. 6d.

LOCKHART.
The Church of Scotland in the Thirteenth Century. The
Life and Times of David de Bernham of St Andrews (Bishop), A.D. 1239 to 1253.
With List of Churches dedicated by him, and Dates. By WILLIAM LOCKHART,
A.M., D.D., F.S.A. Scot., Minister of Colinton Parish. 2d Edition. 8vo, 6s.
Dies Tristes : Sermons for Seasons of Sorrow. Crown 8vo, 6s.

LORIMER.
The Institutes of Law : A Treatise of the Principles of Juris-
prudence as determined by Nature. By the late JAMES LORIMER, Professor of
Public Law and of the Law of Nature and Nations in the University of Edin-
burgh. New Edition, Revised and much Enlarged. 8vo, 18s.
The Institutes of the Law of Nations. A Treatise of the
Jural Relation of Separate Political Communities. In 2 vols. 8vo. Volume I.,
price 16s. Volume II., price 20s.

LOVE. Scottish Church Music. Its Composers and Sources.
With Musical Illustrations. By JAMES LOVE. Post 8vo, 7s. 6d.

LUGARD. The Rise of our East African Empire : Early Efforts
in Uganda and Nyasaland. By F. D. LUGARD, Captain Norfolk Regiment.
With 140 Illustrations from Drawings and Photographs under the personal
superintendence of the Author, and 7 specially prepared Maps. In 2 vols. large
demy 8vo, 42s.

M'COMBIE. Cattle and Cattle-Breeders. By WILLIAM M'COMBIE,
Tillyfour. New Edition, Enlarged, with Memoir of the Author by JAMES
MACDONALD, of the 'Farming World.' Crown 8vo, 3s. 6d.

M'CRIE.
Works of the Rev. Thomas M'Crie, D.D.   Uniform Edition.
4 vols. crown 8vo, 24s.
Life of John Knox.   Crown 8vo, 6s.   Another Edition, 3s. 6d.
Life of Andrew Melville.   Crown 8vo, 6s.
History of the Progress and Suppression of the Reformation
in Italy in the Sixteenth Century.   Crown 8vo, 4s.
History of the Progress and Suppression of the Reformation
in Spain in the Sixteenth Century.   Crown 8vo, 3s. 6d.
Lectures on the Book of Esther.   Fcap. 8vo, 5s.

M'CRIE.   The Public Worship of Presbyterian Scotland.   Histori-
cally treated.   With copious Notes, Appendices, and Index.   The Fourteenth
Series of the Cunningham Lectures.   By the Rev. CHARLES G. M'CRIE, D.D.
Demy 8vo, 10s. 6d.

MACDONALD.   A Manual of the Criminal Law (Scotland) Procedure Act, 1887.   By NORMAN DORAN MACDONALD.   Revised by the LORD
JUSTICE-CLERK.   8vo, 10s. 6d.

MACDONALD.
Stephens' Book of the Farm.   Fourth Edition.   Revised and
in great part Rewritten by JAMES MACDONALD, Secretary, Highland and Agri-
cultural Society of Scotland.   Complete in 3 vols., bound with leather back, gilt
top, £3, 3s.   In Six Divisional Vols., bound in cloth, each 10s. 6d.
Pringle's Live Stock of the Farm.   Third Edition.   Revised
and Edited by JAMES MACDONALD.   Crown 8vo, 7s. 6d.
M'Combie's Cattle and Cattle - Breeders.   New Edition,
Enlarged, with Memoir of the Author by JAMES MACDONALD.   Crown 8vo, 3s. 6d.
History of Polled Aberdeen and Angus Cattle.   Giving an
Account of the Origin, Improvement, and Characteristics of the Breed.   By JAMES
MACDONALD and JAMES SINCLAIR.   Illustrated with numerous Animal Portraits.
Post 8vo, 12s. 6d.

MACGREGOR.   Life and Opinions of Major-General Sir Charles
MacGregor, K.C.B., C.S.I., C.I.E., Quartermaster-General of India.   From his
Letters and Diaries.   Edited by Lady MACGREGOR.   With Portraits and Maps to
illustrate Campaigns in which he was engaged.   2 vols. 8vo, 35s.

M'INTOSH.   The Book of the Garden.   By CHARLES M'INTOSH,
formerly Curator of the Royal Gardens of his Majesty the King of the Belgians,
and lately of those of his Grace the Duke of Buccleuch, K.G., at Dalkeith Palace.
2 vols. royal 8vo, with 1350 Engravings.   £4, 7s. 6d.   Vol. I.   On the Formation
of Gardens and Construction of Garden Edifices, £2, 10s.   Vol. II.   Practical
Gardening, £1, 17s. 6d.

MACINTYRE.   Hindu - Koh : Wanderings and Wild Sports on
and beyond the Himalayas.   By Major-General DONALD MACINTYRE, V.C., late
Prince of Wales' Own Goorkhas, F.R.G.S.   *Dedicated to H.R.H. The Prince of
Wales.*   New and Cheaper Edition, Revised, with numerous Illustrations.   Post
8vo, 7s. 6d.

MACKAY.   A Sketch of the History of Fife and Kinross.   A
Study of Scottish History and Character.   By Æ. J. G. MACKAY, Sheriff of these
Counties.   Crown 8vo, 6s.

MACKAY.
A Manual of Modern Geography ; Mathematical, Physical,
and Political.   By the Rev. ALEXANDER MACKAY, LL.D., F.R.G.S.   11th
Thousand, Revised to the present time.   Crown 8vo, pp. 688, 7s. 6d.
Elements of Modern Geography.   55th Thousand, Revised to
the present time.   Crown 8vo, pp. 300, 3s.
The Intermediate Geography.   Intended as an Intermediate
Book between the Author's 'Outlines of Geography' and 'Elements of Geo-
graphy.'   Seventeenth Edition, Revised.   Crown 8vo, pp. 238, 2s.

MACKAY.
Outlines of Modern Geography. 191st Thousand, Revised to the present time. 18mo, pp. 128, 1s.

First Steps in Geography. 105th Thousand. 18mo, pp. 56. Sewed, 4d.; cloth, 6d.

Elements of Physiography and Physical Geography. With Express Reference to the Instructions issued by the Science and Art Department. 30th Thousand, Revised. Crown 8vo, 1s. 6d.

Facts and Dates; or, The Leading Events in Sacred and Profane History, and the Principal Facts in the various Physical Sciences. For Schools and Private Reference. New Edition. Crown 8vo, 3s. 6d.

MACKAY. An Old Scots Brigade. Being the History of Mackay's Regiment, now incorporated with the Royal Scots. With an Appendix containing many Original Documents connected with the History of the Regiment. By JOHN MACKAY (late) of Herriesdale. Crown 8vo, 5s.

MACKENZIE. Studies in Roman Law. With Comparative Views of the Laws of France, England, and Scotland. By Lord MACKENZIE, one of the Judges of the Court of Session in Scotland. Sixth Edition, Edited by JOHN KIRKPATRICK, M.A., LL.B., Advocate, Professor of History in the University of Edinburgh. 8vo, 12s.

MACPHERSON. Glimpses of Church and Social Life in the Highlands in Olden Times. By ALEXANDER MACPHERSON, F.S.A. Scot. With 6 Photogravure Portraits and other full-page Illustrations. Small 4to, 25s.

M'PHERSON.
Summer Sundays in a Strathmore Parish. By J. GORDON M'PHERSON, Ph.D., F.R.S.E., Minister of Ruthven. Crown 8vo, 5s.

Golf and Golfers. Past and Present. With an Introduction by the Right Hon. A. J. BALFOUR, and a Portrait of the Author. Fcap. 8vo, 1s. 6d.

MACRAE. A Handbook of Deer-Stalking. By ALEXANDER MACRAE, late Forester to Lord Henry Bentinck. With Introduction by Horatio Ross, Esq. Fcap. 8vo, with two Photographs from Life. 3s. 6d.

MAIN. Three Hundred English Sonnets. Chosen and Edited by DAVID M. MAIN. Fcap. 8vo, 6s.

MAIR. A Digest of Laws and Decisions, Ecclesiastical and Civil, relating to the Constitution, Practice, and Affairs of the Church of Scotland. With Notes and Forms of Procedure. By the Rev. WILLIAM MAIR, D.D., Minister of the Parish of Earlston. Crown 8vo. With Supplements. 8s.

MARCHMONT AND THE HUMES OF POLWARTH. By One of their Descendants. In One Volume, crown 4to. With numerous Portraits and other Illustrations. [In preparation.

MARSHALL.
French Home Life. By FREDERICK MARSHALL, Author of 'Claire Brandon.' Second Edition. 5s.

It Happened Yesterday. A Novel. Crown 8vo, 6s.

MARSHMAN, History of India. From the Earliest Period to the present time. By JOHN CLARK MARSHMAN, C.S.I. Third and Cheaper Edition. Post 8vo, with Map, 6s.

MARTIN.
Goethe's Faust. Part I. Translated by Sir THEODORE MARTIN, K.C.B. Second Edition, crown 8vo, 6s. Ninth Edition, fcap. 8vo, 3s. 6d.

Goethe's Faust. Part II. Translated into English Verse. Second Edition, Revised. Fcap. 8vo, 6s.

The Works of Horace. Translated into English Verse, with Life and Notes. 2 vols. New Edition. Crown 8vo, 21s.

Poems and Ballads of Heinrich Heine. Done into English Verse. Third Edition. Small crown 8vo. [Shortly.

The Song of the Bell, and other Translations from Schiller, Goethe, Uhland, and Others. Crown 8vo, 7s. 6d.

MARTIN.

Madonna Pia ; King René's Daughter ; The Camp of Wallenstein ; and other Translations. Crown 8vo.   [*Immediately.*

Catullus. With Life and Notes. Second Edition, Revised and Corrected. Post 8vo, 7s. 6d.

The 'Vita Nuova' of Dante. Translated, with an Introduction and Notes. Third Edition. Small crown 8vo, 5s.

Aladdin : A Dramatic Poem. By ADAM OEHLENSCHLAEGER. Fcap. 8vo, 5s.

Correggio : A Tragedy. By OEHLENSCHLAEGER. With Notes. Fcap. 8vo, 3s.

MARTIN. On some of Shakespeare's Female Characters. In a Series of Letters. By HELENA FAUCIT, Lady MARTIN. Dedicated by permission to Her Most Gracious Majesty the Queen. Fifth Edition. With a Portrait by Lehmann. Demy 8vo, 7s. 6d.

MARWICK. Observations on the Law and Practice in regard to Municipal Elections and the Conduct of the Business of Town Councils and Commissioners of Police in Scotland. By Sir JAMES D. MARWICK, LL.D., Town-Clerk of Glasgow. Royal 8vo, 30s.

MATHESON.

Can the Old Faith Live with the New ? or, The Problem of Evolution and Revelation. By the Rev. GEORGE MATHESON, D.D. Third Edition. Crown 8vo, 7s. 6d.

The Psalmist and the Scientist ; or, Modern Value of the Religious Sentiment. New and Cheaper Edition. Crown 8vo, 5s.

Spiritual Development of St Paul. Third Edition. Cr. 8vo, 5s.

The Distinctive Messages of the Old Religions. Second Edition. Crown 8vo, 5s.

Sacred Songs. New and Cheaper Edition. Crown 8vo, 2s. 6d.

MAURICE. The Balance of Military Power in Europe. An Examination of the War Resources of Great Britain and the Continental States. By Colonel MAURICE, R.A., Professor of Military Art and History at the Royal Staff College. Crown 8vo, with a Map, 6s.

MAXWELL.

Meridiana : Noontide Essays. By Sir HERBERT MAXWELL, Bart., M.P., F.S.A., &c., Author of ' Passages in the Life of Sir Lucian Elphin,' &c. Post 8vo, 7s. 6d.

Life and Times of the Rt. Hon. William Henry Smith, M.P. With 3 Photogravure Portraits and 3 Etchings from Drawings by Herbert Railton, and other Illustrations by Railton, Seymour, and Others. 2 vols. demy 8vo, 25s.

MICHEL. A Critical Inquiry into the Scottish Language. With the view of Illustrating the Rise and Progress of Civilisation in Scotland. By FRANCISQUE-MICHEL, F.S.A. Lond. and Scot., Correspondant de l'Institut de France, &c. 4to, printed on hand-made paper, and bound in roxburghe, 66s.

MICHIE.

The Larch : Being a Practical Treatise on its Culture and General Management. By CHRISTOPHER Y. MICHIE, Forester, Cullen House. Crown 8vo, with Illustrations. New and Cheaper Edition, Enlarged, 5s.

The Practice of Forestry. Crown 8vo, with Illustrations. 6s.

MIDDLETON. The Story of Alastair Bhan Comyn ; or, The Tragedy of Dunphail. A Tale of Tradition and Romance. By the Lady MIDDLETON. Square 8vo, 10s. Cheaper Edition, 5s.

MILLER. Landscape Geology. A Plea for the Study of Geology by Landscape Painters. By HUGH MILLER, of H.M. Geological Survey. Crown 8vo, 3s. Cheap Edition, paper cover, 1s.

MILNE-HOME. Mamma's Black Nurse Stories. West Indian Folk-lore. By MARY PAMELA MILNE-HOME. With six full-page tinted Illustra. tions. Small 4to, 5s.

MINTO.
A Manual of English Prose Literature, Biographical and Critical: designed mainly to show Characteristics of Style. By W. MINTO, M.A., Hon. LL.D. of St Andrews ; Professor of Logic in the University of Aberdeen. Third Edition, Revised. Crown 8vo, 7s. 6d.
Characteristics of English Poets, from Chaucer to Shirley. New Edition, Revised. Crown 8vo, 7s. 6d.
Plain Principles of Prose Composition. Crown 8vo, 1s. 6d.

MOIR. Life of Mansie Wauch, Tailor in Dalkeith. By D. M. MOIR. With 8 Illustrations on Steel, by the late GEORGE CRUIKSHANK. Crown 8vo, 3s. 6d. Another Edition, fcap. 8vo, 1s. 6d.

MOMERIE.
Defects of Modern Christianity, and other Sermons. By ALFRED WILLIAMS MOMERIE, M.A., D.Sc., LL.D. Fourth Edition. Crown 8vo, 5s.
The Basis of Religion. Being an Examination of Natural Religion. Third Edition. Crown 8vo, 2s. 6d.
The Origin of Evil, and other Sermons. Seventh Edition, Enlarged. Crown 8vo, 5s.
Personality. The Beginning and End of Metaphysics, and a Necessary Assumption in all Positive Philosophy. Fourth Edition, Revised. Crown 8vo, 3s.
Agnosticism. Fourth Edition, Revised. Crown 8vo, 5s.
Preaching and Hearing ; and other Sermons. Third Edition, Enlarged. Crown 8vo, 5s.
Belief in God. Third Edition. Crown 8vo, 3s.
Inspiration ; and other Sermons. Second Edition, Enlarged. Crown 8vo, 5s. .
Church and Creed. Third Edition. Crown 8vo, 4s. 6d.
The Future of Religion, and other Essays. Crown 8vo, 3s. 6d.

MONTAGUE. Military Topography. Illustrated by Practical Examples of a Practical Subject. By Major-General W. E. MONTAGUE, C.B., P.S.C., late Garrison Instructor Intelligence Department, Author of 'Campaigning in South Africa.' With Forty-one Diagrams. Crown 8vo, 5s.

MONTALEMBERT. Memoir of Count de Montalembert. A Chapter of Recent French History. By Mrs OLIPHANT, Author of the 'Life of Edward Irving,' &c. 2 vols. crown 8vo, £1, 4s.

MORISON.
Æolus. A Romance in Lyrics. By JEANIE MORISON. Crown 8vo, 3s.
There as Here. Crown 8vo, 3s.
₊ *A limited impression on hand-made paper, bound in vellum, 7s. 6d.*
Selections from Poems. Crown 8vo, 4s. 6d.
Sordello. An Outline Analysis of Mr Browning's Poem. Crown 8vo, 3s.
Of "Fifine at the Fair," "Christmas Eve and Easter Day," and other of Mr Browning's Poems. Crown 8vo, 3s.
The Purpose of the Ages. Crown 8vo, 9s.
Gordon : An Our-day Idyll. Crown 8vo, 3s.
Saint Isadora, and other Poems. Crown 8vo, 1s. 6d.

MORISON.
Snatches of Song. Paper, 1s. 6d. ; Cloth, 3s.
Pontius Pilate. Paper, 1s. 6d. ; Cloth, 3s.
Mill o' Forres. Crown 8vo, 1s.
Ane Booke of Ballades. Fcap. 4to, 1s.

MOZLEY. Essays from 'Blackwood.' By the late ANNE
MOZLEY, Author of 'Essays on Social Subjects'; Editor of 'The Letters and
Correspondence of Cardinal Newman,' 'Letters of the Rev. J. B. Mozley,' &c.
With a Memoir by her Sister, FANNY MOZLEY. Post 8vo, 7s. 6d.

MUNRO. On Valuation of Property. By WILLIAM MUNRO,
M.A., Her Majesty's Assessor of Railways and Canals for Scotland. Second
Edition, Revised and Enlarged. 8vo, 3s. 6d.

MURDOCH. Manual of the Law of Insolvency and Bankruptcy:
Comprehending a Summary of the Law of Insolvency, Notour Bankruptcy,
Composition-contracts, Trust-deeds, Cessios, and Sequestrations; and the
Winding-up of Joint-Stock Companies in Scotland; with Annotations on the
various Insolvency and Bankruptcy Statutes; and with Forms of Procedure
applicable to these Subjects. By JAMES MURDOCH, Member of the Faculty of
Procurators in Glasgow. Fifth Edition, Revised and Enlarged. 8vo, £1, 10s.

MY TRIVIAL LIFE AND MISFORTUNE: A Gossip with
no Plot in Particular. By A PLAIN WOMAN. Cheap Edition. Crown 8vo, 3s. 6d.

By the SAME AUTHOR.
POOR NELLIE. Cheap Edition. Crown 8vo, 3s. 6d.

NAPIER. The Construction of the Wonderful Canon of Loga-
rithms. By JOHN NAPIER of Merchiston. Translated, with Notes, and a
Catalogue of Napier's Works, by WILLIAM RAE MACDONALD. Small 4to, 15s.
A few large-paper copies on Whatman paper, 30s.

NEAVES.
Songs and Verses, Social and Scientific. By An Old Con-
tributor to 'Maga.' By the Hon. Lord NEAVES. Fifth Edition. Fcap. 8vo, 4s.
The Greek Anthology. Being Vol. XX. of 'Ancient Classics
for English Readers.' Crown 8vo, 2s. 6d.

NICHOLSON.
A Manual of Zoology, for the use of Students. With a
General Introduction on the Principles of Zoology. By HENRY ALLEYNE
NICHOLSON, M.D., D.Sc., F.L.S., F.G.S., Regius Professor of Natural History in
the University of Aberdeen. Seventh Edition, Rewritten and Enlarged. Post
8vo, pp. 956, with 555 Engravings on Wood, 18s.
Text-Book of Zoology, for the use of Schools. Fourth Edi-
tion, Enlarged. Crown 8vo, with 188 Engravings on Wood, 7s. 6d.
Introductory Text-Book of Zoology, for the use of Junior
Classes. Sixth Edition, Revised and Enlarged, with 166 Engravings, 3s.
Outlines of Natural History, for Beginners : being Descrip-
tions of a Progressive Series of Zoological Types. Third Edition, with
Engravings, 1s. 6d.
A Manual of Palæontology, for the use of Students. With a
General Introduction on the Principles of Palæontology. By Professor H.
ALLEYNE NICHOLSON and RICHARD LYDEKKER, B.A. Third Edition, entirely
Rewritten and greatly Enlarged. 2 vols. 8vo, £3, 3s.
The Ancient Life-History of the Earth. An Outline of the
Principles and Leading Facts of Palæontological Science. Crown 8vo, with 276
Engravings, 10s. 6d.
On the "Tabulate Corals" of the Palæozoic Period, with
Critical Descriptions of Illustrative Species. Illustrated with 15 Lithographed
Plates and numerous Engravings. Super-royal 8vo, 21s.

NICHOLSON.
Synopsis of the Classification of the Animal Kingdom. 8vo, with 106 Illustrations, 6s.

On the Structure and Affinities of the Genus Monticulipora and its Sub-Genera, with Critical Descriptions of Illustrative Species. Illustrated with numerous Engravings on Wood and Lithographed Plates. Super-royal 8vo, 18s.

NICHOLSON. ·
Communion with Heaven, and other Sermons. By the late MAXWELL NICHOLSON, D.D., St Stephen's, Edinburgh. Crown 8vo, 5s. 6d.

Rest in Jesus. Sixth Edition. Fcap. 8vo, 4s. 6d.

NICHOLSON.
Thoth. A Romance. By JOSEPH SHIELD NICHOLSON, M.A., D.Sc., Professor of Commercial and Political Economy and Mercantile Law in the University of Edinburgh. Third Edition. Crown 8vo, 4s. 6d.

A Dreamer of Dreams. A Modern Romance. Second Edition. Crown 8vo, 6s.

NICOLSON AND MURE. A Handbook to the Local Government (Scotland) Act, 1889. With Introduction, Explanatory Notes, and Index. By J. BADENACH NICOLSON, Advocate, Counsel to the Scotch Education Department, and W. J. MURE, Advocate, Legal Secretary to the Lord Advocate for Scotland. Ninth Reprint. 8vo, 5s.

OLIPHANT.
Masollam : A Problem of the Period. A Novel. By LAURENCE OLIPHANT. 3 vols. post 8vo, 25s. 6d.

Scientific Religion ; or, Higher Possibilities of Life and Practice through the Operation of Natural Forces. Second Edition. 8vo, 16s.

Altiora Peto. Cheap Edition. Crown 8vo, boards, 2s. 6d. ; cloth, 3s. 6d. Illustrated Edition. Crown 8vo, cloth, 6s.

Piccadilly. With Illustrations by Richard Doyle. New Edition, 3s. 6d. Cheap Edition, boards, 2s. 6d.

Traits and Travesties ; Social and Political. Post 8vo, 10s. 6d.

Episodes in a Life of Adventure ; or, Moss from a Rolling Stone. Fifth Edition. Post 8vo, 6s.

Haifa : Life in Modern Palestine. Second Edition. 8vo, 7s. 6d.

The Land of Gilead. With Excursions in the Lebanon. With Illustrations and Maps. Demy 8vo, 21s.

Memoir of the Life of Laurence Oliphant, and of Alice Oliphant, his Wife. By Mrs M. O. W. OLIPHANT. Seventh Edition. 2 vols. post 8vo, with Portraits. 21s.
   POPULAR EDITION. With a New Preface. Post 8vo, with Portraits. 7s. 6d.

OLIPHANT.
Katie Stewart. By Mrs OLIPHANT. Illustrated boards, 2s. 6d.

Katie Stewart, and other Stories. New Edition. Crown 8vo, cloth, 3s. 6d.

Valentine and his Brother. New Edition. Crown 8vo, 3s. 6d.

Sons and Daughters. Crown 8vo, 3s. 6d.

Diana Trelawny : The History of a Great Mistake. 2 vols. crown 8vo, 17s.

OLIPHANT.
Two Stories of the Seen and the Unseen. The Open Door
—Old Lady Mary. Paper covers, 1s.

OLIPHANT. Notes of a Pilgrimage to Jerusalem and the Holy
Land. By F. R. OLIPHANT. Crown 8vo, 3s. 6d.

ON SURREY HILLS. By "A SON OF THE MARSHES."
See page 28.

OSSIAN. The Poems of Ossian in the Original Gaelic. With
a Literal Translation into English, and a Dissertation on the Authenticity of the
Poems. By the Rev. ARCHIBALD CLERK. 2 vols. imperial 8vo, £1, 11s. 6d.

OSWALD. By Fell and Fjord ; or, Scenes and Studies in Iceland By E. J. OSWALD. Post 8vo, with Illustrations. 7s. 6d.

PAGE.
Introductory Text-Book of Geology. By DAVID PAGE, LL.D.,
Professor of Geology in the Durham University of Physical Science, Newcastle,
and Professor LAPWORTH of Mason Science College, Birmingham. With Engrav-
ings and Glossarial Index. Twelfth Edition, Revised and Enlarged. 3s. 6d.
Advanced Text-Book of Geology, Descriptive and Industrial.
With Engravings, and Glossary of Scientific Terms. Sixth Edition, Revised and
Enlarged. 7s. 6d.
Introductory Text-Book of Physical Geography. With Sketch-
Maps and Illustrations. Edited by Professor LAPWORTH, LL.D., F.G.S., &c.,
Mason Science College, Birmingham. Twelfth Edition, Revised. 2s. 6d.
Advanced Text-Book of Physical Geography. Third Edition,
Revised and Enlarged by Professor LAPWORTH. With Engravings. 5s.

PATON.
Spindrift. By Sir J. NOEL PATON. Fcap., cloth, 5s.
Poems by a Painter. Fcap., cloth, 5s.

PATON. Body and Soul. A Romance in Transcendental Path-
ology. By FREDERICK NOEL PATON. Third Edition. Crown 8vo, 1s.

PATRICK. The Apology of Origen in Reply to Celsus. A
Chapter in the History of Apologetics. By the Rev. J. PATRICK, B.D. Post 8vo,
7s. 6d.

PATTERSON.
Essays in History and Art. By R. HOGARTH PATTERSON.
8vo, 12s.
The New Golden Age, and Influence of the Precious Metals
upon the World. 2 vols. 8vo, 31s. 6d.

PAUL. History of the Royal Company of Archers, the Queen's
Body-Guard for Scotland. By JAMES BALFOUR PAUL, Advocate of the Scottish
Bar. Crown 4to, with Portraits and other Illustrations. £2, 2s.

PEILE. Lawn Tennis as a Game of Skill. With latest revised
Laws as played by the Best Clubs. By Captain S. C. F. PEILE, B.S.C. Cheaper
Edition. Fcap., cloth, 1s.

PETTIGREW. The Handy Book of Bees, and their Profitable
Management. By A. PETTIGREW. Fifth Edition, Enlarged, with Engravings.
Crown 8vo, 3s. 6d.

PHILIP. The Function of Labour in the Production of Wealth.
By ALEXANDER PHILIP, LL.B., Edinburgh. Crown 8vo, 3s. 6d.

PHILOSOPHICAL CLASSICS FOR ENGLISH READERS.
Edited by WILLIAM KNIGHT, LL.D., Professor of Moral Philosophy, University
of St Andrews. In crown 8vo volumes, with Portraits, price 3s. 6d.
[For list of Volumes, see page 2.

POLLOK. The Course of Time : A Poem. By ROBERT POLLOK,
A.M. Cottage Edition, 32mo, 8d. The Same, cloth, gilt edges, 1s. 6d. Another
Edition, with Illustrations by Birket Foster and others, fcap., cloth, 3s. 6d., or
with edges gilt, 4s.

PORT ROYAL LOGIC. Translated from the French; with
Introduction, Notes, and Appendix. By THOMAS SPENCER BAYNES, LL.D., Professor in the University of St Andrews. Tenth Edition, 12mo, 4s.

POTTS AND DARNELL.
Aditus Faciliores : An Easy Latin Construing Book, with
Complete Vocabulary. By A. W. POTTS, M.A., LL.D., and the Rev. C. DARNELL,
M.A., Head-Master of Cargilfield Preparatory School, Edinburgh.· Tenth Edition,
fcap. 8vo, 3s. 6d.

Aditus Faciliores Græci. An Easy Greek Construing Book,
with Complete Vocabulary. Fifth Edition, Revised. Fcap. 8vo, 3s.

POTTS. School Sermons. By the late ALEXANDER WM. POTTS,
LL.D., First Head-Master of Fettes College. With a Memoir and Portrait.
Crown 8vo, 7s. 6d.

PRINGLE. The Live-Stock of the Farm. By ROBERT O.
PRINGLE. Third Edition. Revised and Edited by JAMES MACDONALD. Crown
8vo, 7s. 6d.

PRYDE. Pleasant Memories of a Busy Life. By DAVID PRYDE,
M.A., LL.D., Author of 'Highways of Literature,' 'Great Men in European History,' 'Biographical Outlines of English Literature,' &c. With a Mezzotint Portrait. Post 8vo, 6s.

PUBLIC GENERAL STATUTES AFFECTING SCOTLAND
from 1707 to 1847, with Chronological Table and Index. 3 vols. large 8vo, £3, 3s.

PUBLIC GENERAL STATUTES AFFECTING SCOTLAND,
COLLECTION OF. Published Annually, with General Index.

RADICAL CURE FOR IRELAND, The. A Letter to the
People of England and Scotland concerning a new Plantation. With 2 Maps.
8vo, 7s. 6d.

RAE. The Syrian Church in India. By GEORGE MILNE RAE,
M.A., D.D, Fellow of the University of Madras ; late Professor in the Madras
Christian College. With 6 full-page Illustrations. Post 8vo, 10s. 6d.

RAMSAY. Scotland and Scotsmen in the Eighteenth Century.
Edited from the MSS. of JOHN RAMSAY, Esq. of Ochtertyre, by ALEXANDER
ALLARDYCE, Author of 'Memoir of Admiral Lord Keith, K.B.,' &c. 2 vols.
8vo, 31s. 6d.

RANKIN. The Zambesi Basin and Nyassaland. By DANIEL J.
RANKIN, F.R S.G.S., M.R.A.S. With 3 Maps and 10 full-page Illustrations.
Post 8vo, 10s. 6d.

RANKIN.
A Handbook of the Church of Scotland. By JAMES RANKIN,
D.D., Minister of Muthill; Author of 'Character Studies in the Old Testament,'
&c. An entirely New and much Enlarged Edition. Crown 8vo, with 2 Maps,
7s. 6d.

The First Saints. Post 8vo, 7s. 6d.

The Creed in Scotland. An Exposition of the Apostles'
Creed. With Extracts from Archbishop Hamilton's Catechism of 1552, John
Calvin's Catechism of 1556, and a Catena of Ancient Latin and other Hymns.
Post 8vo, 7s. 6d.

The Worthy Communicant. A Guide to the Devout Observance of the Lord's Supper. Limp cloth, 1s. 3d.

The Young Churchman. Lessons on the Creed, the Com-
mandments, the Means of Grace, and the Church. Limp cloth, 1s. 3d.

First Communion Lessons. 24th Edition. Paper Cover, 2d.

RECORDS OF THE TERCENTENARY FESTIVAL OF THE UNIVERSITY OF EDINBURGH. Celebrated in April 1884. Published under the Sanction of the Senatus Academicus. Large 4to, £2, 12s. 6d.

ROBERTSON. The Early Religion of Israel. As set forth by Biblical Writers and Modern Critical Historians. Being the Baird Lecture for 1888-89. By JAMES ROBERTSON, D.D., Professor of Oriental Languages in the University of Glasgow. Fourth Edition. Crown 8vo, 10s. 6d.

ROBERTSON. Orellana, and other Poems. By J. LOGIE ROBERTSON, M.A. Fcap. 8vo. Printed on hand-made paper. 6s.

ROBERTSON. Our Holiday among the Hills. By JAMES and JANET LOGIE ROBERTSON. Fcap. 8vo, 3s. 6d.

ROBERTSON. Essays and Sermons. By the late W. ROBERTson, B.D., Minister of the Parish of Sprouston. With a Memoir and Portrait. Crown 8vo, 5s. 6d.

RODGER. Aberdeen Doctors at Home and Abroad. The Story of a Medical School. By ELLA HILL BURTON RODGER. Demy 8vo, 10s. 6d.

ROSCOE. Rambles with a Fishing-Rod. By E. S. ROSCOE. Crown 8vo, 4s. 6d.

ROSS. Old Scottish Regimental Colours. By ANDREW ROSS, S.S.C., Hon. Secretary Old Scottish Regimental Colours Committee. Dedicated by Special Permission to Her Majesty the Queen. Folio. £2, 12s. 6d.

RUSSELL. The Haigs of Bemersyde. A Family History. By JOHN RUSSELL. Large 8vo, with Illustrations. 21s.

RUTLAND.
Notes of an Irish Tour in 1846. By the DUKE OF RUTLAND, G.C.B. (Lord JOHN MANNERS). New Edition. Crown 8vo, 2s. 6d.

Correspondence between the Right Honble. William Pitt and Charles Duke of Rutland, Lord-Lieutenant of Ireland, 1781-1787. With Introductory Note by JOHN DUKE OF RUTLAND. 8vo, 7s. 6d.

RUTLAND.
Gems of German Poetry. Translated by the DUCHESS OF RUTLAND (Lady JOHN MANNERS). [*New Edition in preparation.*]

Impressions of Bad-Homburg. Comprising a Short Account of the Women's Associations of Germany under the Red Cross. Crown 8vo, 1s. 6d.

Some Personal Recollections of the Later Years of the Earl of Beaconsfield, K.G. Sixth Edition. 6d.

Employment of Women in the Public Service. 6d.

Some of the Advantages of Easily Accessible Reading and Recreation Rooms and Free Libraries. With Remarks on Starting and Maintaining them. Second Edition. Crown 8vo, 1s.

A Sequel to Rich Men's Dwellings, and other Occasional Papers. Crown 8vo, 2s. 6d.

Encouraging Experiences of Reading and Recreation Rooms, Aims of Guilds, Nottingham Social Guide, Existing Institutions, &c., &c. Crown 8vo, 1s.

SCHEFFEL. The Trumpeter. A Romance of the Rhine. By JOSEPH VICTOR VON SCHEFFEL. Translated from the Two Hundredth German Edition by JESSIE BECK and LOUISA LORIMER. With an Introduction by Sir THEODORE MARTIN, K.C.B. Long 8vo, 3s. 6d.

SCHILLER. Wallenstein. A Dramatic Poem. By FRIEDRICH VON SCHILLER. Translated by C. G. N. LOCKHART. Fcap. 8vo, 7s. 6d.

SCOTCH LOCH FISHING. By "BLACK PALMER." Crown 8vo, interleaved with blank pages, 4s.

SCOUGAL. Prisons and their Inmates; or, Scenes from a Silent World. By FRANCIS SCOUGAL. Crown 8vo, boards, 2s.

SELLAR. Manual of the Education Acts for Scotland. By the late ALEXANDER CRAIG SELLAR, M.P. Eighth Edition. Revised and in great part rewritten by J. EDWARD GRAHAM, B.A. Oxon., Advocate. With Rules for the conduct of Elections, with Notes and Cases. 8vo.
[*New Edition in preparation.*
[SUPPLEMENT TO SELLAR'S MANUAL. Being the Acts of 1889 in so far as affecting the Education Acts. 8vo, 2s.]

SETH.
Scottish Philosophy. A Comparison of the Scottish and German Answers to Hume. Balfour Philosophical Lectures, University of Edinburgh. By ANDREW SETH, LL.D., Professor of Logic and Metaphysics in Edinburgh University. Second Edition. Crown 8vo, 5s.

Hegelianism and Personality. Balfour Philosophical Lectures. Second Series. Second Edition. Crown 8vo, 5s.

SHADWELL. The Life of Colin Campbell, Lord Clyde. Illustrated by Extracts from his Diary and Correspondence. By Lieutenant-General SHADWELL, C.B. With Portrait, Maps, and Plans. 2 vols. 8vo, 36s.

SHAND.
Half a Century; or, Changes in Men and Manners. By ALEX. INNES SHAND, Author of 'Against Time,' &c. Second Edition. 8vo, 12s. 6d.

Letters from the West of Ireland. Reprinted from the 'Times.' Crown 8vo, 5s.

Kilcarra. A Novel. 3 vols. crown 8vo, 25s. 6d.'

SHARPE. Letters from and to Charles Kirkpatrick Sharpe. Edited by ALEXANDER ALLARDYCE, Author of 'Memoir of Admiral Lord Keith, K.B.,' &c. With a Memoir by the Rev. W. K. R. BEDFORD. In 2 vols. 8vo. Illustrated with Etchings and other Engravings. £2, 12s. 6d.

SIM. Margaret Sim's Cookery. With an Introduction by L. B. WALFORD, Author of 'Mr Smith: A Part of his Life,' &c. Crown 8vo, 5s.

SIMPSON. The Wild Rabbit in a New Aspect; or, Rabbit-Warrens that Pay. A book for Landowners, Sportsmen, Land Agents, Farmers, Gamekeepers, and Allotment Holders. A Record of Recent Experiments conducted on the Estate of the Right Hon. the Earl of Wharncliffe at Wortley Hall. By J. SIMPSON. Small crown 8vo, 5s.

SKELTON.
Maitland of Lethington; and the Scotland of Mary Stuart. A History. By JOHN SKELTON, C.B., LL.D., Author of 'The Essays of Shirley.' Demy 8vo, 2 vols., 28s.

The Handbook of Public Health. A Complete Edition of the Public Health and other Sanitary Acts relating to Scotland. Annotated, and with the Rules, Instructions, and Decisions of the Board of Supervision brought up to date with relative forms. Second Edition. With Introduction, containing the Administration of the Public Health Act in Counties. 8vo, 8s. 6d.

The Local Government (Scotland) Act in Relation to Public Health. A Handy Guide for County and District Councillors, Medical Officers, Sanitary Inspectors, and Members of Parochial Boards. Second Edition. With a new Preface on appointment of Sanitary Officers. Crown 8vo, 2s.

SKRINE. Columba: A Drama. By JOHN HUNTLEY SKRINE, Warden of Glenalmond; Author of 'A Memory of Edward Thring.' Fcap. 4to, 6s.

SMITH. For God and Humanity. A Romance of Mount Carmel.
By HASKETT SMITH, Author of 'The Divine Epiphany,' &c. 3 vols. post 8vo
25s. 6d.

SMITH.

Thorndale; or, The Conflict of Opinions. By WILLIAM SMITH,
Author of 'A Discourse on Ethics,' &c. New Edition. Crown 8vo, 10s. 6d.

Gravenhurst; or, Thoughts on Good and Evil. Second Edition. With Memoir and Portrait of the Author. Crown 8vo, 8s.

The Story of William and Lucy Smith. Edited by GEORGE
MERRIAM. Large post 8vo, 12s. 6d.

SMITH. Memoir of the Families of M'Combie and Thoms,
originally M'Intosh and M'Thomas. Compiled from History and Tradition. By
WILLIAM M'COMBIE SMITH. With Illustrations. 8vo, 7s. 6d.

SMITH. Greek Testament Lessons for Colleges, Schools, and
Private Students, consisting chiefly of the Sermon on the Mount and the Parables
of our Lord. With Notes and Essays. By the Rev. J. HUNTER SMITH, M.A.,
King Edward's School, Birmingham. Crown 8vo, 6s.

SMITH. The Secretary for Scotland. Being a Statement of the
Powers and Duties of the new Scottish Office. With a Short Historical Intro-
duction, and numerous references to important Administrative Documents. By
W. C. SMITH, LL.B., Advocate. 8vo, 6s.

"SON OF THE MARSHES, A."

Within an Hour of London Town: Among Wild Birds and
their Haunts. By "A SON OF THE MARSHES." Edited by J. A. OWEN. Second
Edition. Crown 8vo, 6s.

With the Woodlanders, and By the Tide. Crown 8vo, 6s.

On Surrey Hills. Fourth Edition. Crown 8vo, 6s.

Annals of a Fishing Village. New and Cheaper Edition.
Crown 8vo, 5s. Illustrated Edition. Crown 8vo, 7s. 6d.

SORLEY. The Ethics of Naturalism. Being the Shaw Fellow-
ship Lectures, 1884. By W. R. SORLEY, M.A., Fellow of Trinity College, Cambridge, Professor of Logic and Philosophy in University College of South Wales.
Crown 8vo, 6s.

SPEEDY. Sport in the Highlands and Lowlands of Scotland
with Rod and Gun. By TOM SPEEDY. Second Edition, Revised and Enlarged.
With Illustrations by Lieut.-General Hope Crealocke, C.B., C.M.G., and others.
8vo, 15s.

SPROTT. The Worship and Offices of the Church of Scotland.
By GEORGE W. SPROTT, D.D., Minister of North Berwick. Crown 8vo, 6s.

STARFORTH. Villa Residences and Farm Architecture: A
Series of Designs. By JOHN STARFORTH, Architect. 102 Engravings. Second
Edition. Medium 4to, £2, 17s. 6d.

STATISTICAL ACCOUNT OF SCOTLAND. Complete, with
Index. 15 vols. 8vo, £16, 16s.

STEPHENS.

The Book of the Farm; detailing the Labours of the Farmer,
Farm-Steward, Ploughman, Shepherd, Hedger, Farm-Labourer, Field-Worker,
and Cattle-man. Illustrated with numerous Portraits of Animals and Engravings
of Implements, and Plans of Farm Buildings. Fourth Edition. Revised, and
in great part Rewritten by JAMES MACDONALD, Secretary, Highland and Agricultural Society of Scotland. Complete in Six Divisional Volumes, bound in
cloth, each 10s. 6d., or handsomely bound, in 3 volumes, with leather back and
gilt top, £3, 3s.

The Book of Farm Implements and Machines. By J. SLIGHT
and R. SCOTT BURN, Engineers. Edited by HENRY STEPHENS. Large 8vo, £2, 2s.

Catechism of Agriculture. *[New Edition in preparation.*

STEVENSON. British Fungi. (Hymenomycetes). By Rev.
JOHN STEVENSON, Author of 'Mycologia Scotia,' Hon. Sec. Cryptogamic Society
of Scotland. Vols. I. and II., post 8vo, with Illustrations, price 12s. 6d. net each.

STEWART.
Advice to Purchasers of Horses. By JOHN STEWART, V.S.
New Edition. 2s. 6d.
Stable Economy. A Treatise on the Management of Horses
in relation to Stabling, Grooming, Peeding, Watering, and Working. Seventh
Edition. Fcap. 8vo, 6s. 6d.

STEWART. A Hebrew Grammar, with the Pronunciation, Syl-
labic Division and Tone of the Words, and Quantity of the Vowels. By Rev.
DUNCAN STEWART, D.D. Fourth Edition. 8vo, 3s. 6d.

STEWART. Boethius: An Essay. By HUGH FRASER STEWART,
M.A., Trinity College, Cambridge. Crown 8vo, 7s. 6d.

STODDART. Angling Songs. By THOMAS TOD STODDART.
New Edition, with a Memoir by ANNA M. STODDART. Crown 8vo, 7s. 6d.

STORMONTH.
Etymological and Pronouncing Dictionary of the English
Language. Including a very Copious Selection of Scientific Terms. For use in
Schools and Colleges, and as a Book of General Reference. By the Rev. JAMES
STORMONTH. The Pronunciation carefully revised by the Rev. P. H. PHELP, M.A.
Cantab. Eleventh Edition, with Supplement. Crown 8vo, pp. 800. 7s. 6d.
Dictionary of the English Language, Pronouncing, Etymo-
logical, and Explanatory. Revised by the Rev. P. H. PHELP. Library Edition.
Imperial 8vo, handsomely bound in half morocco, 31s. 6d.
The School Etymological Dictionary and Word-Book. Fourth
Edition. Fcap. 8vo, pp. 254. 2s.

STORY.
Nero; A Historical Play. By W. W. STORY, Author of
'Roba di Roma.' Fcap. 8vo, 6s.
Vallombrosa. Post 8vo, 5s.
Poems. 2 vols., 7s. 6d.
Fiammetta. A Summer Idyl. Crown 8vo, 7s. 6d.
Conversations in a Studio. 2 vols. crown 8vo, 12s. 6d.
Excursions in Art and Letters. Crown 8vo, 7s. 6d.
A Poet's Portfolio: Later Readings. 18mo.   [*Immediately.*

STRICKLAND. Life of Agnes Strickland. By her SISTER.
Post 8vo, with Portrait engraved on Steel, 12s. 6d.

STURGIS.
John-a-Dreams. A Tale. By JULIAN STURGIS. New Edi-
tion. Crown 8vo, 3s. 6d.
Little Comedies, Old and New. Crown 8vo, 7s. 6d.

SUTHERLAND (DUCHESS OF). How I Spent my Twentieth
Year. Being a Record of a Tour Round the World, 1886-87. By the DUCHESS
OF SUTHERLAND (MARCHIONESS OF STAFFORD). With Illustrations. Crown 8vo,
7s. 6d.

SUTHERLAND. Handbook of Hardy Herbaceous and Alpine
Flowers, for General Garden Decoration. Containing Descriptions of upwards
of 1000 Species of Ornamental Hardy Perennial and Alpine Plants; along with
Concise and Plain Instructions for their Propagation and Culture. By WILLIAM
SUTHERLAND, Landscape Gardener; formerly Manager of the Herbaceous Depart-
ment at Kew. Crown 8vo, 7s. 6d.

TAYLOR. The Story of my Life. By the late Colonel
MEADOWS TAYLOR, Author of 'The Confessions of a Thug,' &c., &c. Edited by
his Daughter. New and Cheaper Edition, being the Fourth. Crown 8vo, 6s.

THOLUCK. Hours of Christian Devotion. Translated from
the German of A. Tholuck, D.D., Professor of Theology in the University of
Halle. By the Rev. ROBERT MENZIES, D.D. With a Preface written for this
Translation by the Author. Second Edition. Crown 8vo, 7s. 6d.

THOMSON. South Sea Yarns. By Basil Thomson. With Illustrations. Crown 8vo.   [*In preparation.*

THOMSON. A History of the Fife Light Horse. By Colonel
ANSTRUTHER THOMSON. With numerous Portraits. Small 4to, 21s.

THOMSON.
Handy Book of the Flower-Garden : being Practical Direc-
tions for the Propagation, Culture, and Arrangement of Plants in Flower-
Gardens all the year round. With Engraved Plans. By DAVID THOMSON,
Gardener to his Grace the Duke of Buccleuch, K.T., at Drumlanrig. Fourth
and Cheaper Edition. Crown 8vo, 5s.

The Handy Book of Fruit-Culture under Glass : being a
series of Elaborate Practical Treatises on the Cultivation and Forcing of Pines,
Vines, Peaches, Figs, Melons, Strawberries, and Cucumbers. With Engravings
of Hothouses, &c. Second Edition, Revised and Enlarged. Crown 8vo, 7s. 6d.

THOMSON. A Practical Treatise on the Cultivation of the
Grape Vine. By WILLIAM THOMSON, Tweed Vineyards. Tenth Edition. 8vo, 5s.

THOMSON. Cookery for the Sick and Convalescent. With
Directions for the Preparation of Poultices, Fomentations, &c. By BARBARA
THOMSON. Fcap. 8vo, 1s. 6d.

THORNTON. Opposites. A Series of Essays on the Unpopular
Sides of Popular Questions. By LEWIS THORNTON. 8vo, 12s. 6d.

TOM CRINGLE'S LOG. A New Edition, with Illustrations.
Crown 8vo, cloth gilt, 5s. Cheap Edition, 2s.

**TRANSACTIONS OF THE HIGHLAND AND AGRICUL-
TURAL** SOCIETY OF SCOTLAND. Published annually, price 5s.

TRAVEL, ADVENTURE, AND SPORT. From 'Blackwood's
Magazine.' Uniform with 'Tales from Blackwood.' In 12 Parts, each price 1s.
Handsomely bound in 6 vols., cloth, 15s. ; half calf, 25s.

TRAVERS. Mona Maclean, Medical Student. A Novel. By
GRAHAM TRAVERS. Sixth Edition. Crown 8vo, 6s.

TULLOCH.
Rational Theology and Christian Philosophy in England in
the Seventeenth Century. By JOHN TULLOCH, D.D., Principal of St Mary's College in the University of St Andrews ; and one of her Majesty's Chaplains in
Ordinary in Scotland. Second Edition. 2 vols. 8vo, 16s.

Modern Theories in Philosophy and Religion. 8vo, 15s.

Luther, and other Leaders of the Reformation. Third Edition, Enlarged. Crown 8vo, 3s. 6d.

Memoir of Principal Tulloch, D.D., LL.D. By Mrs OLIPHANT,
Author of 'Life of Edward Irving.' Third and Cheaper Edition. 8vo, with
Portrait, 7s. 6d.

TURNBULL. Othello : A Critical Study. By W. R. TURNBULL.
Demy 8vo, 15s.

TWEEDIE. The Arabian Horse : his Country and People.
With Portraits of Typical or Famous Arabians, and numerous other Illustrations ;
also a Map of the Country of the Arabian Horse, and a descriptive Glossary of
Arabic words and proper names. By Major-General W. TWEEDIE, C.S.I., Bengal
Staff Corps ; for many years H.B.M.'s Consul-General, Baghdad, and Political
Resident for the Government of India in Turkish Arabia. In one vol., royal 4to.
Price £3, 3s.

VEITCH.

The History and Poetry of the Scottish Border : their Main Features and Relations. By John Veitch, LL.D., Professor of Logic and Rhetoric in the University of Glasgow. New and Enlarged Edition. 2 vols. demy 8vo, 16s.

Institutes of Logic. Post 8vo, 12s. 6d.

The Feeling for Nature in Scottish Poetry. From the Earliest Times to the Present Day. 2 vols. fcap. 8vo, in roxburghe binding, 15s.

Merlin and other Poems. Fcap. 8vo. 4s. 6d.

Knowing and Being. Essays in Philosophy. First Series. Crown 8vo, 5s.

VIRGIL. The Æneid of Virgil. Translated in English Blank Verse by G. K. Rickards, M.A., and Lord Ravensworth. 2 vols. fcap. 8vo, 10s.

WACE. The Christian Faith and Recent Agnostic Attacks. By the Rev. Henry Wace, D.D., Principal of King's College, London ; Preacher of Lincoln's Inn ; Chaplain to the Queen. In one vol. post 8vo. [*In preparation.*

WALFORD. Four Biographies from 'Blackwood' : Jane Taylor, Hannah More, Elizabeth Fry, Mary Somerville. By L. B. Walford. Crown 8vo, 5s.

WALKER. The Teaching of Jesus in His Own Words. By the Rev. John C. Walker. Crown 8vo, 3s. 6d.

WARREN'S (SAMUEL) WORKS :—

Diary of a Late Physician. Cloth, 2s. 6d. ; boards, 2s.

Ten Thousand A-Year. Cloth, 3s. 6d. ; boards, 2s. 6d.

Now and Then. The Lily and the Bee. Intellectual and Moral Development of the Present Age. 4s. 6d.

Essays : Critical, Imaginative, and Juridical. 5s.

WEBSTER. The Angler and the Loop - Rod. By David Webster. Crown 8vo, with Illustrations, 7s. 6d.

WELLINGTON. Wellington Prize Essays on "the System of Field Manœuvres best adapted for enabling our Troops to meet a Continental Army." Edited by General Sir Edward Bruce Hamley, K.C.B., K.C.M.G. 8vo, 12s. 6d.

WENLEY. Socrates and Christ : A Study in the Philosophy of Religion. By R. M. Wenley, M.A., Lecturer on Mental and Moral Philosophy in Queen Margaret College, Glasgow ; Examiner in Philosophy in the University of Glasgow. Crown 8vo, 6s.

WERNER. A Visit to Stanley's Rear-Guard at Major Barttelot's Camp on the Aruhwimi. With an Account of River-Life on the Congo. By J. R. Werner, F.R.G.S., Engineer, late in the Service of the Etat Indépendant du Congo. With Maps, Portraits, and other Illustrations. 8vo, 16s.

WESTMINSTER ASSEMBLY. Minutes of the Westminster Assembly, while engaged in preparing their Directory for Church Government, Confession of Faith, and Catechisms (November 1644 to March 1649). Edited by the Rev. Professor Alex. T. Mitchell, of St Andrews, and the Rev. John Struthers, LL.D. With a Historical and Critical Introduction by Professor Mitchell. 8vo, 15s.

WHITE.

The Eighteen Christian Centuries. By the Rev. James White. Seventh Edition, post 8vo, with Index, 6s.

History of France, from the Earliest Times. Sixth Thousand. Post 8vo, with Index, 6s.

WHITE.
Archæological Sketches in Scotland—Kintyre and Knapdale.
By Colonel T. P. WHITE, R.E., of the Ordnance Survey. With numerous Illustrations, 2 vols. folio, £4, 4s. Vol. I., Kintyre, sold separately, £2, 2s.

The Ordnance Survey of the United Kingdom. A Popular
Account. Crown 8vo, 5s.

WILLIAMSON. The Horticultural Exhibitor's Handbook. A
Treatise on Cultivating, Exhibiting, and Judging Plants, Flowers, Fruits, and
Vegetables. By W. WILLIAMSON, Gardener. Revised by MALCOLM DUNN, Gardener to his Grace the Duke of Buccleuch and Queensberry, Dalkeith Park.
Crown 8vo, 3s. 6d.

WILLIAMSON. Poems of Nature and Life. By DAVID R.
WILLIAMSON, Minister of Kirkmaiden. Fcap. 8vo, 3s.

WILLIAMSON. Light from Eastern Lands on the Lives of
Abraham, Joseph, and Moses. By the Rev. ALEX. WILLIAMSON, Author of 'The
Missionary Heroes of the Pacific,' 'Sure and Comfortable Words,' 'Ask and
Receive,' &c. Crown 8vo, 3s. 6d.

WILLS AND GREENE. Drawing-Room Dramas for Children.
By W. G. WILLS and the Hon. Mrs GREENE. Crown 8vo, 6s.

WILSON.
Works of Professor Wilson. Edited by his Son-in-Law,
Professor FERRIER. 12 vols. crown 8vo, £2, 8s.
Christopher in his Sporting-Jacket. 2 vols., 8s.
Isle of Palms, City of the Plague, and other Poems. 4s.
Lights and Shadows of Scottish Life, and other Tales. 4s.
Essays, Critical and Imaginative. 4 vols., 16s.
The Noctes Ambrosianæ. 4 vols., 16s.
Homer and his Translators, and the Greek Drama. Crown
8vo, 4s.

WITHIN AN HOUR OF LONDON TOWN. Among Wild
Birds and their Haunts. By "A SON OF THE MARSHES," *See page* 28.

WITH THE WOODLANDERS, AND BY THE TIDE. By
"A SON OF THE MARSHES." *See page* 28.

WORSLEY.
Poems and Translations. By PHILIP STANHOPE WORSLEY,
M.A. Edited by EDWARD WORSLEY. Second Edition, Enlarged. Fcap. 8vo, 6s.
Homer's Odyssey. Translated into English Verse in Spenserian Stanza. By P. S. Worsley. Third Edition. 2 vols. fcap., 12s.
Homer's Iliad. Translated by P. S. Worsley and Prof. Conington. 2 vols. Crown 8vo, 21s.

YATE. England and Russia Face to Face in Asia. A Record of
Travel with the Afghan Boundary Commission. By Captain A. C. YATE, Bombay
Staff Corps. 8vo, with Maps and Illustrations, 21s.

YATE. Northern Afghanistan; or, Letters from the Afghan
Boundary Commission. By Major C. E. YATE, C.S.I., C.M.G. Bombay Staff
Corps, F.R.G.S. 8vo, with Maps, 18s.

YOUNG. A Story of Active Service in Foreign Lands. Compiled from Letters sent home from South Africa, India, and China, 1856-1882. By
Surgeon-General A. GRAHAM YOUNG, Author of 'Crimean Cracks.' Crown 8vo,
Illustrated, 7s. 6d.

YULE. Fortification: For the use of Officers in the Army, and
Readers of Military History. By Colonel YULE, Bengal Engineers. 8vo, with
Numerous Illustrations, 10s.

10/93.